# Applied Theatre: D    ．ｐment

The **Applied Theatre** series is a major innovation in applied theatre scholarship, bringing together leading international scholars that engage with and advance the field of applied theatre. Each book presents new ways of seeing and critically reflecting on this dynamic and vibrant field. Volumes offer a theoretical framework and introductory survey of the field addressed, combined with a range of case studies illustrating and critically engaging with practice.

Series Editors:
Michael Balfour (Griffith University, Australia)
Sheila Preston (University of East London, UK)

*Applied Theatre: Aesthetics*
Gareth White
ISBN 978-1-4725-1355-7

*Applied Theatre: Resettlement*
*Drama, Refugees and Resilience*
Michael Balfour, Bruce Burton, Penny Bundy,
Julie Dunn and Nina Woodrow
ISBN 978-1-4725-3379-1

*Applied Theatre: Research*
*Radical Departures*
Peter O'Connor and Michael Anderson
ISBN 978-1-4725-0961-1

**Related titles from Bloomsbury Methuen Drama**

*Performance and Community: Commentary and Case Studies*
Edited by Caoimhe McAvinchey
ISBN 978-1-4081-4642-2

*Affective Performance and Cognitive Science: Body, Brain and Being*
Edited by Nicola Shaughnessy
ISBN 978-1-4081-8577-3

# Applied Theatre: Development

Tim Prentki

Series Editors
Michael Balfour and Sheila Preston

Bloomsbury Methuen Drama
An imprint of Bloomsbury Publishing Plc

B L O O M S B U R Y
LONDON • NEW DELHI • NEW YORK • SYDNEY

**Bloomsbury Methuen Drama**

An imprint of Bloomsbury Publishing Plc

| | |
|---|---|
| 50 Bedford Square | 1385 Broadway |
| London | New York |
| WC1B 3DP | NY 10018 |
| UK | USA |

**www.bloomsbury.com**

**BLOOMSBURY, METHUEN DRAMA and the Diana logo are trademarks of Bloomsbury Publishing Plc**

First published 2015

© Tim Prentki, 2015

Tim Prentki has asserted his right under the Copyright, Designs and Patents Act, 1988, to be identified as author of this work.

**British Library Cataloguing-in-Publication Data**

A catalogue record for this book is available from the British Library.

ISBN: HB: 978-1-4725-1195-9
PB: 978-1-4725-0986-4
ePDF: 978-1-4725-0518-7
ePub: 978-1-4725-0828-7

**Library of Congress Cataloging-in-Publication Data**

A catalog record for this book is available from the Library of Congress.

Typeset by Deanta Global Publishing Services, Chennai, India
Printed and bound in India

# Contents

# List of Figures

# Notes on Contributors

**Dr Andrea Baldwin** is a Brisbane-based applied theatre researcher and creative writer. Her recent publications include two chapters on drama and mental health, in the forthcoming *Creative Arts in Recovery from Mental Illness*, edited by Neilsen, Baker and King (2014).

**Veronica Baxter**, University of Cape Town, South Africa. Her recent publications include 'Postcards on the aesthetics of applied theatre', Hazel Barnes (ed); *Arts Activism, Education, and Therapies: Transforming Communities Across Africa* (2013); 'Senzeni na (what have we done?) – educational theatre in southern Africa', Chapter 12, Anthony Jackson and Chris Vine (eds); *Learning Through Theatre: The Changing Face of Theatre in Education* (3rd edition, 2013); and 'Practice as Research in South Africa', Chapter 10, Robin Nelson (ed); *Practice as Research in the Arts: Principles, Protocols, Pedagogies, Resistances* (2013).

**Doryan Bedoya** is a literary artist and cultural organizer who started his work with Barrio Comparsa in Medellín, Colombia, before moving to Guatemala. There he became one of the co-founders of Caja Lúdica, a leading community-based arts collective which is also intricately linked with 'La Red', a pan-Latin American network of progressive arts organizations.

**Rodrigo Benza** has a master's degree in theatre from the Universidade do Estado de Santa Catarina, Brazil. His artistic work in community contexts and on the artistic circuit is focused in intercultural creation processes and in the utilization of theatre as a means to generate knowledge and dialogue among people from different realities. In 2009, he won the dramaturgical creation category award of the IBERESCENA fund with the documentary theatre piece 'Proyecto EMPLEADAS' that reflected Peruvian society from the perspective of domestic workers. He has written articles mainly on intercultural and documentary theatre for journals and books in Peru, Brazil and Cuba. www.rodrigobenza. blogspot.com

**Helen Cahill** is an associate professor in the Youth Research Centre at the University of Melbourne, Australia. Her recent publications include a chapter on 'Drama for Health and Human Relationships Education: aligning purpose and design' in *How Drama Activates Learning: Contemporary Research and Practice,* edited by Anderson and Dunn (Bloomsbury, 2013), and she is a regular contributor to international journals of drama education and applied theatre.

**Dimitri Camorlinga** is a research student at the State University of Santa Catarina (UDESC), Brazil.

**Kennedy Chinyowa** is full-time professor in the Department of Drama and Film Studies at Tshwane University of Technology in Pretoria, South Africa. He publishes regularly in international journals such as *Research in Drama Education, Applied Theatre Research* and *Studies in Theatre and Performance.*

**Marcia Pompeo Nogueira** is an associate professor at the State University of Santa Catarina (UDESC), Brazil. Books published in Brazil include the following: *Teatro com Meninas e Meninos de Rua: nos caminhos do Ventoforte* (2008), *Teatro na Comunidade: Interações, Dilemas e Possibilidades.* Florianópolis (2009), *Teatro na Comunidade: Conexões através do Atlântico.* Florianópolis (2013). Chapters published include the following: Prentki, T.; Nogueira, M. Odhiambo, C. 'Aesthetics and Theatre for Development: the Search for Poetical Correctness' in The IDEA – dialogues by Hannu Heikkinen *Special Interest Fields of Drama, Theatre and Education* (2003). Coutinho, M.; Nogueira, M. 'The use of dialogical approach for community theatre by the group Nós do Morro, in the Vidigal Favela of Rio de Janeiro' in Prentki, T.; Preston, S. *The Applied Theatre Reader* (2009), Nogueira, M. 'Taught only by Reality, can Reality be changed?' in Balfour, M.; Somers, J. *Drama as Social Intervention* (2006), and 'Reflections on the impact of a long term theatre for community development project in Southern Brazil'. *Ride v. 11 N2, 2006.*

**Peter O'Connor** is an associate professor and director of the Critical Research Unit in Applied Theatre, Faculty of Education at the University of Auckland, New Zealand. He is a co-author of *Applied Theatre: Research: radical departures* with Michael Anderson. (Bloomsbury Methuen Drama, 2015)

**John O'Toole** was Foundation Chair of Arts Education at the University of Melbourne, Australia, and formerly professor of Drama at Griffith University, Queensland. His numerous textbook and research publications include *The Process of Drama* (1992) and *Drama and Curriculum: A Giant at the Door* (2010).

**Eugene van Erven** is a senior lecturer in Theatre at Utrecht University, the Netherlands, where he teaches community art and coordinates the Creative Cities Minor. He holds a PhD in comparative literature from Vanderbilt University in the United States (1985). Besides his academic work he is also professionally active in the cultural field as artistic director of the International Community Arts Festival (ICAF) in Rotterdam. He is the author of the following books: *Radical People's Theatre* (1988), *The Playful Revolution: Theatre and Liberation in Asia* (1992), *Community Theatre: Global Perspectives* (2001), and *Community Arts Dialogues* (2013).

**Alison Lloyd Williams** works in the field of theatre, education and development, running projects with school and community groups in the United Kingdom and various African countries. She currently holds an honorary research fellow position in the School of Arts, Languages & Cultures at the University of Manchester, United Kingdom, contributing to research on the university's *In Place of War* project.

**Au Yi-Man** is a freelance applied theatre worker in China, based in Hong Kong; she is currently completing her PhD at the University of Melbourne, Australia.

# Introduction

This book is structured in two parts. The first part is conceived as a monograph which explores the origins, theories and practices of the applied theatre sub-genre which has come to be labelled Theatre for Development (TfD). It considers core concepts which underpin its processes as well as differences arising from the varying contexts in which it occurs. From this examination it becomes clear that there is no clear demarcation around the term and that among practitioners it is frequently used interchangeably alongside labels such as popular or community theatre, or simply as applied theatre; subsumed under the umbrella which covers all aspects of theatre that arise outside its formal, commercial spaces and processes.

The book is intended for a wide readership, ranging from students and potential practitioners about to embark upon an engagement with TfD to seasoned academics and theatre and development professionals wishing to maintain their involvement with the ever-shifting discourses swirling around the discipline. Therefore, it offers both history and provocation; achievement and possibility; celebration and critique; past and future. Out of this examination emerges an attempt to define a distinct, albeit unstable, identity for TfD forged from its truculent relationship with development studies and a radical politics inspired by Brecht and Freire. Such an identity guarantees an unresolved tension between addressing developmental goals in the world beyond the theatre and applying the theatrical process itself to the quest for an improved quality of life. In other words TfD encompasses both theatre *for* development and theatre *as* development. The material of this book offers instances of both activities and, while the tension remains inevitably unresolved, there are implications that, to be effective, any TfD process needs elements of both.

The case studies were commissioned to reflect the criteria of a mix of both genders among the authors who represent a range of experience and youth, a broad geographical spread of fieldwork, and a cosmopolitan mix of nationalities. In addition there is an intentional bias towards examples of work from Latin America. This is intended to counter the typical, if understandable, preference among English-speaking authors for drawing upon practice from the erstwhile colonial territories of the British Empire, resulting in a leaning towards fieldwork examples from sub-Saharan Africa and the Indian subcontinent.

For Chapter 3 John O'Toole has curated four mini case studies around the concept of capacity building. The chapter takes up the relationship between NGOs and theatre facilitators as part of the exploration of the archetypal tension between education and theatre. The studies reveal a key theme of the collection: that whatever the overt capacity being built by the project in question, the fundamental capacity addressed by theatre's engagement with the whole person is the capacity for living. Helen Cahill's work, built on the concept of rights, reveals her commitment to women's potential: 'our focus will be on becoming' and to exploiting the theatrical possibilities of play, 'hoping to tease the child out of the woman'. Andrea Baldwin's fieldwork in Papua New Guinea supplies the essential reminder that 'contextual factors are generally more powerful than individual knowledge, attitudes and behavioural intentions'. Kennedy Chinyowa's experience highlights the potential and limitations of trying to match fieldwork in communities with the demands of university curricula. Given that much of the TfD work, particularly in Africa, is conducted out of universities, the academic interface with communities is an important aspect of the continuing development of the discipline. Au Yi-Man offers us a rare insight into the operation of an NGO in China, a country certain to figure more prominently in the landscape of TfD in the years ahead. Marcia Pompeo discusses her practice in the community of Ratones where she has been involved for many years. The long perspective enables her to ponder the consequences for TfD of the changing patterns of community relations, increasingly disrupted by insecure working lives, unstable domestic arrangements and the ubiquitous reach of the virtual. Though long establishment in one community is a feature of Latin American TfD, Pompeo's experience forces a reconsideration of our practices in contemporary, neo-liberal cultures. Rodrigo Benza's chapter centres on the often neglected question of how the TfD process can change the facilitator. His experience of exploring identity with 'the exotic, indigenous other' offers an instance of Freire's notion of the teacher becoming the learner, as well as reminding readers of the ever-growing importance of maintaining cultural diversity in the face of the remorseless monoculture.

Veronica Baxter takes up the theme of problems that can arise from the gaps in understanding between university students as facilitators and community members as learners. She highlights the centrality of stories in the quest to engage alienated participants. Most significantly, she connects the project to the search for beauty in a world acutely impoverished in its material resources: 'a fragment of beauty in stark contrast to their surroundings'. Who has most need of and right to beauty? This question goes to the heart of Peter O'Connor's work with young victims of Christchurch's earthquake, repairing the tears (the pun is intentional) in a cloth of dreams. He dexterously inverts the usual power relations of formal education to enable the children to become 'experts in repairing damaged dream cloths'. The spirit of a youthful W.B. Yeats hovers over the holding metaphor:

> But, I, being poor, have only my dreams;
> I have spread my dreams under your feet;
> Tread softly because you tread on my dreams.[1]

O'Connor writes of the 'wonderment of feeling alive', echoing Brecht's assertion of a practice which contributes to 'the art of living'.

Alison Williams challenges the orthodoxy of Drama in Education by suggesting that her school-based project is better described as 'a pedagogy of Theatre for Development in education' to reflect the way in which she sought to create space for a radical, active citizenship for young people. The TfD process was adopted to support the notion that belonging constitutes a key element of citizenship. By establishing a dialogue between a school in Uganda and one in the United Kingdom, she was able to create the conditions in which the empire could talk back to the erstwhile colonial centre while, at the same time, dispelling the notion that development is only the business of 'developing' nations. This theme is carried on in the final case study chapter where Doryan Bedoya and Eugene van Erven explore a collaborative project between Guatemala and the Netherlands. The project draws heavily on the Latin American traditions of popular theatre, in particular the street carnivals as sites of peaceful resistance. Creating art for the street carries a specific political charge related to a different understanding of post-colonialism from the Anglo-Saxon experience. The project, a theatrical co-production, offers a vivid illustration of theatre *as* development as well as an example of making globalization serve people-centred, as opposed to corporate, ends.

Whatever the arguments that will, doubtless, continue around definitions of applied theatre and its related genres, it is my hope that this book offers a clear and vital demonstration of the function of TfD as an art form that is concerned primarily with the art of living: supporting participants and audiences in the quest to realize what it means to be human and exploring through theatre ways of making the best of it.

Part One

# A Conceptual Framework for Theatre for Development

# History and Origins of
# Theatre for Development

## Applying theatre

As the name implies Theatre for Development (TfD) involves an application of theatre, in this case for the purpose of encouraging development. The question of what is meant by development will occupy many of the following pages. Before approaching it, however, there is a preliminary question concerning what is meant by applied theatre. Although the term is now commonly accepted to describe many areas of theatrical activity, usually happening outside theatres,[1] it begs the question of what unapplied theatre might be. Presumably, taking our cue from the sciences, it must be 'pure' theatre: that is, theatre unsullied by contact with the vagaries and ambiguities of the world beyond the controlled environment of the formal theatre space. Yet, considering that theatre has attempted to engage with these external realities ever since there have been records of performances, it may be more fruitful to conceive of the difference as being between transformative or developmental theatre and theatre which endorses the *status quo* of a given social order whether explicitly in the manner of mainstream propaganda or implicitly by inviting its audiences to escape from the stresses of their lives for a brief interlude of fantasy served up by the magic of the medium. This binary, however, is itself treacherous as the example of many tragedies demonstrates. Although the typical form of tragedy in the European tradition is one where we view the ultimate defeat of antisocial elements, enabling the restoration of societal norms (*Macbeth* for instance), it is frequently the case that the story performed reveals serious contradictions, paradoxes and ironies in the social fabric with, at the least, an implication that some things need to change if the health of a given order is to be maintained. Following Umberto Eco's fictional account, *The Name of the Rose*,[2] we might be inclined to locate the radical, socially transformative muse in comedy but, again, we are faced with the question of intent. Comedy can be both reactionary and progressive. It may seek to resolve differences in the harmony of happy endings, traditionally marriages, or it may defy resolution and throw responsibility for its contradictions back into the laps of the audience in the manner of *Accidental Death of an Anarchist*.[3]

When Euripides wrote *The Trojan Women* in 415 BC, he was using his position as an established playwright to make an intervention into the body politic of Athens. The suffering depicted in his play offered a direct parallel with the real events of the previous year when the Athenian army slaughtered the adult male population of the island of Melos and sold the women and children into slavery because the islanders had attempted to maintain their neutrality in Athens' war with Sparta. Euripides did not flinch from fierce moral condemnation of Athenian politicians and for his pains was not awarded the prize at the Festival of Dionysus. He had applied his art to a burning sociopolitical issue. In a similar vein *King Lear* can be thought of as an applied tragedy where the playwright uses his art to explore the contemporary themes of monarchical rule and the crisis of transition from feudalism to absolutism and on into early capitalism. The violent contrast between the politicians scheming for personal power and material riches at the expense of the 'poor naked wretches' and the dispossessed cast out into the storm, provides a salutary warning for our own neoliberal times. In short, some theatre has been prepared to apply itself to the business of living ever since there has been theatre. There are, however, specific factors which have given rise to those practices labelled applied theatre in recent years and even more precise reasons for the emergence of a subgenre called Theatre for Development. Most of the contributors of the case studies that form Part Two of this volume have opted to use the term applied theatre to describe their activity even though these contain developmental aspirations. My own preference, given the overextended and frequently bland use of the label of applied theatre, is to opt for TfD to describe projects and workshops that exhibit elements of the radical roots of the subgenre in Marxism and popular theatre. Alison Williams makes a similar distinction when opting to make a point of describing her project as TfD, even though contextually it conforms to the designation of Drama in Education.

## The rise of development

A concept as nebulous and fluid as development can no more be assigned a starting date than can the first appearance of our species. However, Development with a capital 'D' might have been launched onto the world through the words of President Harry Truman in his Inaugural Address of 20 January 1949:

> we must embark on a bold new program for making the benefits of our scientific advances and industrial progress available for the improvement and growth of underdeveloped areas. More than half the people of the world are living in conditions approaching misery. Their food is inadequate. They are victims of disease. Their economic life is primitive and stagnant. Their poverty is a handicap and a threat both to them and to more prosperous areas.[4]

By effectively dividing the world into the 'developed' and the 'underdeveloped' (in today's nomenclature 'developing'), Truman set the paradigm with which we are still living. Those who do not live as 'we' do are lacking the benefits of our economic and political systems. It went without saying, since they were not consulted, that they would welcome these systems if given the opportunity. Truman announced a moral obligation on the West to promote its values to the rest and, as a politician, hinted at the self-interest implicated in such an obligation:

> I believe that we should make available to peace-loving peoples [barely disguised code for non-communist nations] the benefits of our store of

technical knowledge in order to help them realize their aspirations for a better life. And, in cooperation with other nations, we should foster capital investment in areas needing development.[5]

So the model of dependency was established and material and economic development according to Western principles was to go global. Provided they were prepared to serve our geopolitical interests, we would provide the finance and expertise by which 'a better life' could be obtained. Lest listeners might worry that the United States were repeating past colonial follies, Truman drew a firm distinction between imperialism and development:

> The old imperialism – exploitation for foreign profit – has no place in our plans. What we envisage is a program of development based on the concepts of democratic fair-dealing.[6]

The gunboats of yesteryear were to be replaced with government, UN and non-governmental organizations (NGOs), democracy exported around the world, and the development industry was born. These early decades in the history of development were marked by a concentration on large-scale infrastructure projects – dams, roads, bridges, etc. – intended to signal the power and influence of the sponsoring government, usually the United States and the Soviet Union vying for supremacy of influence with the 'underdeveloped'. It may not have been 'the old imperialism' but it was certainly the new one and those regimes which played the non-aligned card skilfully were able to extract considerable developmental benefits from one or both of the two superpowers. In the main these government to government projects took no account of the expressed needs of the so-called beneficiaries whose voice went either unsought or ignored. The actual beneficiaries frequently turned out to be the political class together with their cronies in the financial sector. Due to factors such as lack of participation and outright corruption much of the well-intentioned work of development agencies was viewed with cynicism. Writing in his introduction to *The Development Dictionary*

Wolfgang Sachs encapsulates one response to the global reach of the new imperialism:

> The mental space in which people dream and act is largely occupied today by Western imagery. The vast furrows of cultural monoculture left behind are, as in all monocultures, both barren and dangerous. They have eliminated the innumerable varieties of being human and have turned the world into a place deprived of adventure and surprise; the 'Other' has vanished with development. Moreover, the spreading monoculture has eroded viable alternatives to the industrial, growth-oriented society and dangerously crippled humankind's capacity to meet an increasingly different future with creative responses. The last 40 years have considerably impoverished the potential for cultural evolution. It is only a slight exaggeration to say that whatever potential for cultural evolution remains is there in spite of development.[7]

The pace at which the 'monoculture' spread accelerated through the 1990s as a consequence of the collapse of the Soviet Union and of the technologies and ideologies of globalization. Today the dominance of neoliberal capitalism means that mainstream development operates within its parameters. The organizations set up in the wake of the Bretton Woods Agreement of 1944, the International Monetary Fund (IMF) and the World Bank, have long since succumbed to neoliberal economic policies, most notoriously demonstrated in the 'conditionalities' imposed upon governments seeking development loans. A cruel paradox lurks here. The very organizations established as the engines for economic stability and growth within capitalism have now been transformed into the bodies that preside over the glaring inequalities and instabilities resulting from the transfer of wealth from 'underdeveloped' to 'developed' states.

This is not, however, the whole story of development since World War II. While the IMF and the World Bank operate out of the government district of Washington, their geographical proximity indicative of their shared interests in global governance, the United Nations headquarters is in New York where more cosmopolitan agendas can be at work. Although more often honoured in the breach than the observance, the UN has nevertheless fostered the development of a global rights framework, founded upon the Universal Declaration of Human Rights (1948) and the Convention on the Rights of the Child (1989) and supported by accompanying legal bodies. The governments that are the signatories are the same ones whose economic, domestic and foreign policies mostly undermine the intentions of those documents. Development agencies, in particular NGOs, frequently find themselves caught between the contrary pulls of these two global agendas: on the one hand the neoliberal economic frame that increasingly determines the policies of nearly all governments around the world and, on the other, the rights frame with its emphasis on dignity, equality and justice. Helen Cahill, writing in Chapter 3, draws on the discourse of rights to underpin her work on gender in Vietnam. The first Article of the Declaration at once sets us on a collision course with capitalism and more especially with neoliberalism:

> All human beings are born free and equal in dignity and rights. They are endowed with reason and conscience and should act towards one another in a spirit of brotherhood.[8]

The aspiration is magnificent even as the realization is grotesque. Article 19 carries a special charge for practitioners of Theatre for Development, especially when the authorities seek to prevent TfD activities even though their governments have signed the Declaration:

> Everyone has the right to freedom of opinion and expression; this right includes freedom to hold opinions without interference and to seek, receive and impart information and ideas through any media and regardless of frontiers.[9]

These are the two contradictory tensions experienced by development agencies today. The political reality of the world they inhabit means that their operations are judged according to perceived notions of value for money, growth and economic benefit while the rights framework underpinning these activities measures their worth according to wholly different, people-centred criteria. From the largest global NGO to the smallest grassroots TfD project these contradictions sooner or later come into play.

## Education through theatre

Although Theatre/Drama in Education and the many and varied branches of community theatre are not the subject of this particular volume, it is impossible to consider the advent of TfD without viewing it as part of a wider movement that gathered momentum after 1968 for using theatrical practices for educational purposes. John O'Toole, for instance, draws upon this legacy to frame the capacity building projects he presents in Chapter 3. In his introduction to *Learning through Theatre* Tony Jackson gives a baseline definition for this area of practice: 'Essentially TIE seeks to harness the techniques and imaginative potency of theatre in the service of education.'[10] As has already been noted, some theatre had been doing this ever since there was theatre. Now, however, explicitly educational purposes were linked to its practice:

> Its *raison d'être* lies in its function, first, as a method of education and therefore with a justifiable claim to be seen as an educational resource within the school system, and, second, as an art form in its own right but one that is peculiarly suited to its specific audience and age range (and that, in theatre, is almost unique).[11]

Jackson points up the tension at the core of all applied theatre practices: that between the 'applied' and the 'theatre'. The two functions are not necessarily incompatible but those funding the work according to the efficacy of the application may not be sympathetic to the resource demands of the art form while arts organizations may look to the beneficiaries of the particular application to supply the required cash.

While Theatre in Education (TIE) addressed itself to children, usually within the context of formal education, the methodology became available for application to adults and children alike, whether in formal, informal or non-formal educational settings. The core notion (Vygotsky, Bruner, Illich, Freire, et al.) was that effective learning depended upon engaging with the lived experience of the learner. Theatre which is the bringing together of the experience of the actor with that of the character is an ideal method of achieving such an engagement, especially when the actors are the learners: children, community members, participants in a process of development. Because TIE's fortunes have always been closely linked to the state of formal education, it is not surprising that it enjoyed its greatest flowering during the period of economic boom and social democracy in the English-speaking, Anglo-Saxon world. The progressive, child-centred educational theories of the 1960s offered the conceptual framework to support TIE while the healthy condition of the public sphere provided the necessary resources. Conversely, the economic turbulence of the 1970s, leading to the rise of neoliberalism with its accompanying shrinking of the public realm, ushered in a period of decline which has accelerated since the crash of 2007. Today the national curricula of neoliberal regimes, driven by the utilitarian demands of literacy, numeracy and science, have more or less expelled drama/theatre from the territory of formal education. Even if there is a backlash against grading and 'banking'[12] education in the years ahead, those charged with funding provision in a minimalist state may be unable or unwilling to resurrect TIE.

Yet while the influence of TIE in the arena for which it was intended has waxed and waned, it has left its mark upon the broader field of applied theatre:

> Applied theatre usually works in contexts where the work created and performed has a specific resonance with its participants and its audiences and often, to different degrees, involves them in it. . . . Those practices existing (some rather reluctantly) under the umbrella of applied theatre might include: community theatre, community performance, theatre for social change, popular theatre, interventionist theatre, drama in education, theatre for integrated rural development, participatory

performance practices, process drama/theatre, prison theatre, theatre
in health/education, theatre for development, theatre for conflict
resolution/reconciliation, reminiscence theatre and so on.[13]

Essentially all these areas benefit from the methods of TIE with
appropriate adaptation to the varied contexts in which they are exercised.
Ironically, given the current state of formal education in utilitarian,
neoliberal regimes, it may be time, as Williams suggests, for TfD to
give something back to TIE. Just as the ideological commitment of the
initial TIE movement to help to create a better world frequently became
diluted or downright contradicted by some of the later practitioners
who accepted funding in return for creating uncritical performances
in the service of education authorities, so too much of applied theatre
has shifted from social intervention to therapy. Rather than offer a
social critique through the exposure of contradictions, much applied
theatre practice is geared towards an agenda of domestication; helping
those with 'problems' to fit back into society on society's terms – 'pro-
social' behaviour. This is a deficit model where the participants are
lacking something in their lives, typically confidence and the capacity
for empathy. Applied theatre, it is hoped, supports the growth of these
attributes, leading to the recovered participants playing a fuller part
in society. Though the territory of official drama therapy is zealously
guarded, much of this type of practice is *de facto* therapeutic with the
facilitator in the role of therapist and the participant as patient.

The precise genealogy of TfD may always be a matter of dispute
but what is clear is that, towards the end of the 1960s, a confluence of
cognate practices involving education through drama/theatre occurred.
Chris Vine described the effect of importing Augusto Boal's Theatre of
the Oppressed techniques into the work of Greenwich Young Peoples
Theatre in the 1980s:

A real sense of excitement was generated both by its theory and by the
descriptions of Boal's methods, particularly his use of Image Theatre
and Forum Theatre, forms which encourage the spectators to intervene

directly, in the first to 'speak' through images made with actors' bodies and in the second to 'act' in the place of the main protagonists.[14]

Explicitly or implicitly Boal's influence is to be felt throughout the field of TfD as the case studies in this volume indicate.

## Philosophical underpinnings of TfD

The philosophical bedrock of TfD is Marxism. By this I mean that it fits within the frame of critical social analysis inaugurated by Karl Marx. Unless we believe that human social structures and the relationships that support them are capable of being changed, there is no point in embarking upon a TfD process. It is grounded in the premise that the world needs to change, can be changed and that the means of making change is human agency. Following Hegel, Marx identified dialectics as the driving force of change: 'For any present state of affairs was in the process of being negated, changed in [*sic*] to something else. This process was what Hegel meant by dialectic.'[15] While Hegel gave Marx his dialectical method, the former's philosophical conclusions were, for Marx, a dead end because of the priority given by Hegel to thought over material reality. For Hegel contradiction could ultimately be resolved in the mind of man and where that failed, God would supply the answer. In the last of his *Theses on Feuerbach* Marx gave a resounding rejection of this position: 'The philosophers have only interpreted the world in various ways; the point is, to change it.'[16] TfD practitioners, knowingly or otherwise, adopt Marx's view that change itself arises from a dialectical encounter between the understanding developed through lived experience and the capacity to construct alternatives; that inherently theatrical process of an encounter between reality and imagination: 'Men make their own history, but they do not make it just as they please; they do not make it under circumstances chosen by themselves, but under circumstances directly encountered, given and transmitted from the past.'[17] Taking due account of context is a central feature of TfD as Andrea Baldwin demonstrates in her contribution to Chapter 3. In claiming TfD as a method for instigating social change we must acknowledge Bertolt Brecht's role in its genesis. He took Marx's theories of change and applied them to the theatre: 'I wanted to take the principle that it was not just a matter of interpreting the world but of changing it, and apply that to the theatre.'[18] Brecht developed a theatrical aesthetic explicitly aimed at the creation of performances which examine social contradictions and where and how pressure for change might arise.

Brecht died on 14 August 1956, less than 2 weeks before the Berliner Ensemble's opening in London of his production of *Mother Courage and Her Children*. His plays and theories only became influential in the English-speaking world during the 1960s when translations began to be readily available. This coincided with the growth of the drama/theatre education movement. Even then attention was paid almost exclusively to his post-1933 plays, the Minor Pedagogy of 'compromise forms', rather than to the Grand Pedagogy of the *Lehrstücke;* those plays which he created between 1929 and 1933 in the years after he took on a formal study of Marx and before the Nazi election victory forced him into exile. These were the productions Brecht called the theatre of the future as opposed to the forms foisted upon him by geopolitical circumstances that turned him into an itinerant writer divorced from any control over the means of theatrical production. The theatrical experiments of this period featured a number of elements which have subsequently become defining characteristics of TfD. Many performances of the *Lehrstücke* took place outside designated theatre spaces in schools, community halls and at trade union meetings. This move was not undertaken to improve access or in the name of inclusion but rather to put theatrical practice in the hands of those whom Brecht thought were most likely to use it to support their own and society's development:

> The bare wish, if nothing else, to evolve an art fit for the times must drive our theatre of the scientific age straight out into the suburbs, where it can stand as it were wide open, at the disposal of those who

live hard and produce much, so that they can be fruitfully entertained there with their great problems.[19]

In other words, like TfD, the theatre happens in the field at the place and time where its representations are most relevant to all who participate in its processes. Latin American popular theatre, in particular, has developed the significance of location by embedding performance at the heart of a specific community, as the case studies of Marcia Pompeo and Eugene van Erven demonstrate. As a consequence this move also entails working with those whom Boal was later to term 'non-actors'. Although Brecht was both playwright and producer of these experiments, the material was tested, amended and re-produced in the light of the experience offered to him by the workers and children. The further implication of the move out of theatres which Brecht began to embrace with these plays concerned the role of the audience. In this kind of theatre 'the audience is a collection of individuals, capable of thinking and of reasoning, of making judgments even in the theatre.'[20] Brecht's notion is a precursor of TfD's oft-declared aim of triggering a discussion among its audiences around the issues which are impeding self-development. In labelling the *Lehrstücke* as his Grand Pedagogy, Brecht was consciously foreseeing these experiments as the theatre of the future. The Grand Pedagogy 'abolishes the system of performer and spectator',[21] opening the productive forces of play to 'non-actors'. As with many subsequent forms of TfD there were only to be participants: 'These experiments were theatrical performances meant not so much for the spectator as for those who were engaged in the performance. It was, so to speak, art for the producer, not art for the consumer.'[22] In these plays education happened through the process of production, thereby laying the foundations for TfD some 40 years and a world war later.

It was not only the contexts of production which marked the *Lehrstücke* off from what had preceded them, both in the European theatre in general and in Brecht's own work specifically, but also the intention behind them in line with his recent study of Marx: 'Briefly, the aristotelian [*sic*] play is essentially static; its task is to show the world as it is. The learning-play is essentially dynamic; its task is to show the world as it changes (and how it may be changed).'[23] For Brecht the term 'Aristotelian' covered a multitude of theatrical genres from those which are in effect propaganda for the *status quo* to those which advocate reform of existing social institutions without a fundamental or revolutionary questioning of the institutions themselves. In the latter category would come much of the work of Ibsen and other proponents of naturalism. Therefore in order to depict change it was necessary to develop a non-naturalistic aesthetic that allowed actors and audiences to question the surface appearance of social interactions. This was the motivation behind the evolving 'epic' style throughout his work. It is these plays and experiments which were the harbinger of much of the subsequent practices in TfD, including Boal's development of the 'spect-actor'. Brecht's development of *Verfremdungseffekte*, the making strange of the familiar, was directed towards creating a state of critical curiosity in audiences – a counter-hegemonic device which opens up the gap between appearance and reality so that the deep structures of social inequality and injustice can be exposed. In the world of global, viral propaganda, marketing and media manipulation, this process becomes a vital ingredient of any TfD project with aspirations to induce changes in sociopolitical structures. Practical and theoretical study of Brecht's performance aesthetics is a fundamental element of any training for facilitators.

His presentation of the contradiction or crisis as the moment in which change might occur is a forerunner of Boal's Forum Theatre where a crisis is presented to the spect-actors in order for them to decide in action how to resolve it. This process of resolution is about using theatrical means to rehearse actions which will subsequently be adopted beyond the acting space. In terms of the process which Paulo Freire described as 'conscientisation',[24] Brecht's theatre is the first stage of consciousness-raising with the whole process completed by whatever social action is undertaken by the audience or, in the case of the *Lehrstücke* where there is no audience, the participants in the theatrical learning. Brecht shares with Freire the core belief that learning can only emerge out of an encounter with lived experience rather than the absorption of abstract knowledge: 'Taught only by reality can/Reality be changed.'[25] This is a core concept in TfD where the process starts with the material that participants bring to the project. NGOs that conceive of theatre as a means of improving the quality of their message delivery to communities find themselves from the outset at odds with that methodology. The tension between the sponsor's intention for the work and the participants' contextualized understanding underpins the process of the case studies developed in subsequent chapters. The colonial model whereby knowledge is the property of the centre to be disseminated to the unfortunates on the periphery is anathema to practitioners of TfD.

In terms of the ideological underpinning, Augusto Boal stands in relation to Paulo Freire as Brecht does to Marx. Boal took what he learnt from Freire and applied it to theatre. The debt is announced through the title of Boal's seminal work *Theatre of the Oppressed*,[26] consciously echoing Freire's original, *Pedagogy of the Oppressed*.[27]

The dialectical process of change is a *leitmotif* throughout Freire's work, placing him squarely in the line of post-Marxist critical theorists. Not only does his notion of the dialectic make him an essential source for understanding the purpose of TfD, but also the way in which he perceives transformation as a dialectical process links his thinking to a theatrical practice which is grounded in the dialectical relationship of reality to imagination:

> Transformation of the world implies a dialectic between the two actions: denouncing the process of dehumanization and announcing the dream of a new society.[28]

Like Brecht before him, Boal was a theatre artist who emigrated from the confines of formal theatre in order to develop a theatre for social change among the people for whom change was most urgent – the non-actors of the 'oppressed' classes. Forum Theatre with its 'spect-actors' is located in a clear developmental line from the *Lehrstücke* where Brecht worked with school classes, workers' choirs and trade union assemblies. As Marx located the motor for revolutionary change among a newly conscientized working class, so Boal sought to use his Theatre of the Oppressed as a 'rehearsal of revolution'.[29] Just as Marx's analysis of the roots of revolutionary change has been criticized for being too much a product of a specific historical moment, so Boal's theatrical analysis, conducted through the medium of Forum Theatre, has come to appear too rigid, too simplistic and too much a product of work with the 'oppressed' sectors of Brazilian society during the years of military and oligarchic dictatorship. In particular, the requirement that any potential 'spect-actor' can only replace the oppressed person in a given scene raises a number of problems. In the contemporary world, especially without benefit of strategies for highlighting contradictions between surface reality and deep structures, it is frequently uncertain who is 'oppressor' and who 'oppressed'. The reification of a fixed binary between the categories may make for clear definitions for structuring Forum Theatre but all too often creates a distortion of lived experience where any one of us may move between oppressor and oppressed functions many times even in the course of a single day. Furthermore, by placing the responsibility for social change upon society's victims, the 'rules' of Forum Theatre, applied rigidly by overzealous disciples, run the risk of excusing those in positions of power in the *status quo* from having to change their attitudes and behaviours. Instead this becomes yet another task to place at the door of the already over-burdened 'oppressed'.

All too easily this can become another instance of objectifying the 'other' in order not to face the need to make changes to the 'self'. The very term Theatre for Development falls foul of the same tendency. Much of what is undertaken under the labels of Community Theatre and Theatre in Education pursues the same methodologies as TfD. If the project is conducted among the poor of what used to be called a Third-World country, it is likely to adopt the latter label but if it is taking place closer to home, it will choose one of the others, since 'development' is what we do to others, not what is done to us for we are already developed. Yet, though there are contradictions and paradoxes at the heart of TfD, it remains a viable means of contributing to social and political change according to the terms laid out by Marx and Freire, and transposed to the context of theatre by Brecht and Boal.

## African theatre for development

If the route by which Boal's theories and practices entered the UK discourses of Theatre in Education is quite clear, the penetration of this body of work into African practices of what was commonly labelled Popular Theatre is rather more opaque. The birth of theatre used in development in Africa is usually credited to the *Laedza Batanani* campaign of the 1970s in Botswana. The instigators of the campaign, Ross Kidd and Martin Byram immediately encountered the contradiction between intention and form which has bedevilled much TfD work ever since:

> On the one hand, there is concern to show people that they themselves can dramatize their own problems. On the other hand, in order to convey the complexity of the issues and show the contradictions in the social conditions, a certain degree of professional performance skill is needed. Initially the *Laedza* campaigners opted for the first and went to great lengths to persuade villagers that they could act and sing and operate puppets; but it is now generally agreed that the performances which resulted became message-orientated: 'Build pit latrines', 'Support your headman', 'Co-operate!' – which is all in the end a sort of development moralism. There was little in the way of a detailed social analysis in which the villagers could participate.[30]

Learning from this experience, as Michael Etherton goes on to describe, Kidd and Byram were soon developing an innovative, participatory approach in the course of the project:

> However, in 1977, Kidd and Byram carried the process of getting the audience to participate to its logical – and in this instance very

successful – conclusion. They engaged in some community work among the Basarwa (formerly called the Bushmen) in the west of Botswana across the Kalahari desert [*sic.*] Even in the initial discussion with the villagers, the Basarwa were encouraged to drift into role, thus dramatizing the problems they were attempting to articulate. The whole village group, sitting round the fire, became increasingly involved in improvising their problems, by showing, through characterization, exactly what was supposed to have taken place when they met the government authorities. Byram and Kidd accepted roles of the outsiders who were responsible, in part, for the Basarwa's backward state. The men were able to halt the improvisation they were taking part in at any time, in order to discuss the implications of each little scene and how their role in it might be changed. Understanding grew as they re-enacted certain situations, this time changing their own behaviour. Every man around the fire in that remote scrubland was simultaneously actor and audience in the 'play' of his life.[31]

In the space of 3 years Byram and Kidd's work in Botswana enacted the process which TfD has been undergoing ever since: trying to free itself from message delivery by discovering strategies for genuine participation. The final chapter of Etherton's *The Development of African Drama*, titled 'Theatre and Development', written before the term TfD had been coined, strikes a markedly more optimistic note about the possibilities for the genre than David Kerr writing in 1995:

> many of the problems which were identified in the *Laedza Batanani* campaigns could only be understood within the context of Botswana's dependence upon the Southern African migrant labour system, and the social anomie and marginalization deriving from it. By concentrating on disparate constraints divorced from the underlying structural causes of underdevelopment Theatre for Development often obscured issues for the rural poor rather than clarifying them.[32]

These two views of the efficacy of TfD span the so-called lost decade of development, the 1980s. By the time Kerr was writing neoliberalism was approaching its zenith and the depoliticization of the genre has resulted in far more modest ambitions being articulated in relation to the specific concerns of the funding organizations which themselves form part of the neoliberal economic paradigm. Notwithstanding the retrospective scepticism about the political trajectory of much of African TfD, Kerr highlights the importance of the *Laedza Batanani* initiative in setting the template for the subsequent development of the genre. Out of the 1978 Molepolole workshop he identifies the core elements which came to characterize most TfD projects:

- a general introduction to popular theatre for the whole group;
- intensive work by the participants on one of the four performance skills (drama, dance, song, puppetry);
- information gathering in the villages;
- preparation and rehearsal of the village performances;
- performing in the village;
- evaluation and preparation for follow-up programme.[33]

However, much of the radical potential of this form was dissipated by both political and practical concerns. In practice most TfD projects were sponsored by NGOs that were staffed by adult education extension workers without theatre experience. Consequently the theatrical process was reduced to role-play, usually of a crude two-dimensional variety frequently depicting the 'good', modernizing NGO worker triumphing over the 'bad', backward, indigenous peasant. Such depictions suited the agendas of the neo-colonial governments and their expatriate colonial sponsors. By representing the poor as deficient in character, the fault for the oppressive conditions in which they lived could be laid at their own door, rather than that of the systems under which they laboured and through which government elites and international financiers secured their own fortunes: 'This results in a development strategy based on changing the poor rather than the system of oppression which makes them poor.'[34]

Kerr looks more favourably upon the work of the group that set up a TfD collective at Ahmadu Bello University (ABU) in Zaria, Northern Nigeria. They had the benefit of learning from the experiences of the

TfD projects in Botswana and Zambia, as well as a series of international workshops in Zimbabwe and on the Indian subcontinent. Furthermore the specifically theatrical influence of Boal was beginning to be felt in addition to the learner-centred pedagogy of Freire. Consequently the workshops they conducted in the late 1970s and early 1980s attempted to achieve ever closer relationships with the chosen communities from which the audiences for the work were drawn. The emphasis of the projects moved from 'finished' theatrical products to an open-ended process where performance might serve as the research method to articulate the direction of the increasingly important dimension of follow-up. For instance in the *Wasan Bomo* project with landless farmers the farmers themselves rehearsed the means of resisting the expropriation of land, discussed the strategies and refined them in the next rehearsal. As Kerr points out, the process was significant for the opportunity it gave to the 'oppressed' to get into the mind of the 'oppressor':

> By having actors among the oppressed community of landless farmers and petty marketeers acting out more privileged roles, such as that of the Sarkhin Masawa (chief of the market) or a police inspector, the actors were able to think their way into the strategies and practices of the dominant class. . . . The elimination of over-optimistic or idealized methods of resistance is an essential step in the process of achieving solidarity among the subaltern classes.[35]

In 1989 the ABU collective morphed into the formally constituted Nigerian Popular Theatre Alliance which continues to be active under the leadership of Oga Abah and Jenks Okwori. It remains the most important and influential TfD organization in West Africa.

At the opening of his chapter on TfD in *African Popular Theatre* Kerr establishes a connection between TfD and the tradition of travelling theatres:

> A frequent aspiration of the university travelling theatre movement has been to interact with non-academic theatre campaigns aimed at

community renewal, particularly in the rural areas of Africa. This wider mode of drama is commonly referred to as 'Theatre for Development'.

There have been two major sources of Theatre for Development: the colonial tradition of theatre as propaganda, and another more radical tradition of community theatre.[36]

I would rather reposition Kerr's analysis to suggest that the two sources of African TfD are the university travelling theatre movement and the more conventional one, common to TfD elsewhere, of NGO-sponsored projects designed to address development issues. The former places its emphasis on theatre aesthetics while the latter grew out of the need to improve the efficacy of development communication. During the forty years of these approaches, like parallel lines disappearing into the distance, they have appeared to draw ever closer to each other. The travelling theatre groups have looked for ways of improving their dialogue and research with the communities where their performances have occurred. NGO-based TfD has slowly come to realize that much of the efficacy of development communication lies in the quality of the theatre structures in which that communication is located.

The university travelling theatre movement was active across Anglophone Africa from the 1960s onwards with some organizations proving to be more durable than others. In Nigeria the pioneer was the Ibadan Travelling Theatre, drawing upon the indigenous forms of Yoruba Opera and the Concert Party. Though based firmly in scripted material the company developed a repertoire which included locally authored plays, sometimes written in Pidgin. On the eastern side of the continent the most significant organization during this first phase was the Makerere Free Travelling Theatre of Uganda which was active from 1965, attracting major funders and taking its programmes to all parts of the country. In the 1970s the driving force was Rose Mbowa who oversaw the political and aesthetic direction of the group. Though successful in breaking 'out of the strait-jacket of the art theatre', 'the impressively elaborate logistics of the tours (fleets of Land-rovers, lengthy rehearsals in Kampala, copious costumes and so on) tended to prevent a completely fluid interaction between performers and community.[37] In 1969 the University of Zambia Drama Department, under the guidance of Michael Etherton, built the Chikwakwa Theatre with the expressed intention of making types of theatre accessible to the rural population on the fringes of Lusaka and beyond. 'In its home base the theatre company developed a theatre style in which modern dialogue was integrated with traditional performing arts such as dancing, singing and music, traditional elocution, masquerades, etc.'[38] The group toured to different provinces throughout the 1970s with a focus upon local languages and art forms. Particularly important in relation to the evolution of TfD were the accompanying workshops which provided a site for interaction between the university students and local community animateurs. Etherton took his experience of establishing Chikwakwa to ABU where a similar model of combining a campus-based theatre with touring to specific areas enabled the later development of the Nigerian Popular Theatre Association under the direction of Oga Abah.

For the movement in the 1980s the best documented case study is that of the Marotholi Travelling Theatre of Lesotho by Zakes Mda.[39] The case studies which Mda analyses show a progressive move away from performing *for* rural audiences, through performing *with* rural audiences, to performing *by* rural audiences. It is a study of how university travelling theatre became, in effect, TfD. In reflecting upon his experience he poses one of the perennial problems of the genre:

> Theatre-for-development practitioners, in their dramatization work with local communities, should create a balanced situation that will result in optimal intervention. Optimal here refers to the most favourable or desirable condition. Optimal intervention would therefore mean the best compromise between the opposing tendencies of participation and intervention.[40]

However, the judgement about the appropriate point of balance, the fulcrum between participation and intervention, tends to be made by those making the intervention rather than the recipients of that intervention. Just how contentious this might be in practice is revealed by Mda's own words immediately afterwards:

> This finding places a great responsibility on the catalyst. It confirms an assertion previously made in this study that catalysts must have a higher level of social consciousness than the villagers. Without this higher level of social consciousness – and of critical awareness – they cannot play their interventionist role effectively, and the villagers will remain unconscientised through theatre.[41]

While I agree without hesitation about the need for facilitators of TfD to possess both an acute sociopolitical consciousness and sophisticated theatre skills, the hierarchy of intelligence implied by the statement is worrying, especially when compounded by the use of the word 'catalyst'. A catalyst typically is an agent which produces a chemical reaction while itself remaining unchanged. The facilitator who supposes that she can enter the process without undergoing personal change is likely to be a person dangerously immune to processes of change wrought by dialogical encounters, as Rodrigo Benza's case study in Chapter 5 vividly reveals. The realities of class and educational background adumbrated by Kerr tend to pour some cold water on the very notion of 'optimal intervention':

> Even more problematic is the class position of university students, who form the bulk of travelling theatre workers. By origin, many students are from working-class or peasant backgrounds, but in their aspirations and training they are impelled towards a bourgeois life style. This class limbo often makes the students somewhat marginal to their society and capable of wild vacillations of ideology. The radical ambitions of student performers, linked to an ultimately petty-bourgeois world-view, often produce theatrical policies which waver between unacknowledged elitism and a romantically immature ultra-leftism.[42]

Fuelled by her experience of participating in the *Hammocks to Bridges* workshop in Kumba, Cameroon, under the direction of Hansel Eyoh,

Penina Mlama offers similar scepticism about much of the facilitation of African TfD:

> In fact it has been debated whether it is proper for Popular Theatre [her term for TfD] to operate with an external team going into a community and trying to work with people to solve their problems. This is frequently the case in Africa, where the Popular Theatre workers are often expatriate or middle class theatre artists and university lecturers.[43]

It may be more than a coincidence that the two case studies in this book which draw attention to the dangers of a gulf between facilitators and participants (Kennedy Chinyowa in Chapter 3 and Veronica Baxter in Chapter 6) both emanate from African contexts. Mlama also makes the link between Travelling Theatres and TfD, seeing the latter supplanting the former in the evolution of popular theatre:

> Although the travelling Theatre approach is still in practice in some parts of Africa today, the more progressive theatre artists abandoned it in the 1970s for the new approach referred to as Theatre for Development and more recently Popular Theatre.[44]

In the event, once the fruit salad of terminologies settled down, it has been TfD which has tended to replace popular theatre as the term of choice. Mlama's definition of what she calls popular theatre indicates how thoroughly Freire's concepts have entered the discourses of TfD, underpinned by core Marxist precepts:

> Popular Theatre is intended to empower the common man with a critical consciousness crucial to the struggles against the forces responsible for his poverty. It is an attempt to enable the masses to break free from the culture of silence imposed on them and reawaken or strengthen their latent culture of resistance and struggle, which needs to be part of the process to bring about their development.[45]

Whether any art-based methodology can empower anyone is a moot point since the methodology must be linked to an ideological intention before critical consciousness is aroused. It may be a means available to those wishing to break from the 'culture of silence' imposed first by colonialism and then by neocolonialism but the wish itself must be present before the TfD process can be put at the service of changing the world in favour of more just societies. Though not articulated as such, it may be that Mlama's preference for 'Popular Theatre' over 'Theatre for Development' reflects her belief in the socialist intentions of a process grounded in the histories and aspirations of the grassroots while the apparently innocuous, politically neutral term that has come to dominate the field has proved to be a stalking-horse behind which Western, top-down agendas of neoliberalism have subverted the transformative potential of the genre.

Mlama's assessment of African TfD's inability to build upon the outstanding example of people's mobilization through community theatre, the Kamiriithu Community Education and Culture Centre, has proved prophetic as TfD's political ambitions have shrunk to the limits of the single issue NGO agendas with their Western notions of right living:

> The coming to a standstill of the Kamiriithu theatre endeavour . . . brings us to yet another significant issue which Popular Theatre in Africa has yet to resolve. This is the issue of giving Popular Theatre an organisational base that would ensure the long term sustenance of the popular theatre process.[46]

The story of Kamiriithu has been told and analysed in many places such as Chapter 12 of *African Popular Theatre*[47] and most notably by Ngugi wa Thiong'o himself in Chapter 2 of *Decolonising the Mind*.[48] Suffice it to say here that its ghost looms large over the history and current practice of TfD where the possibility of such large-scale, high-profile community engagement seems ever more remote. Etherton also concludes *The Development of African Drama* with an analysis which identifies the lack of people's organizations as the major stumbling-block to the use of theatre for social critique and political action:

> Unlike Latin America, where unofficial radical political and cultural organizations already exist, in Africa there seems to be an absence of

any effective organizational framework to provide continuity – apart from the ruling or dominant political parties. Theatre work needs to be keyed into organizations which are concerned with raising consciousness and strengthening people's culture, rather than with acquiring and holding on to political power. The drama may well become a key *methodology* for developing thought across a broad front as a basis for future collective action; but the drama group, the theatre company, the university drama department are all politically inadequate organizations.[49]

Etherton's reflection sets the landscape for African TfD at the end of the last century. As a methodology in the hands of organizations whose concerns lay primarily outside the theatre process, TfD is conceived as a tool which may help in addressing the issues which form the agenda of the NGO and its efficacy is judged not in theatrical terms but according to its impact on the specific issue. Depending upon the attitude and aspiration of the NGO, the TfD process may be turned towards domesticating or transformative ends but, given the realities of funding sources within a neoliberal paradigm, the latter is considerably less likely.

## Asian theatre for development

In the sense of a coordinated or homogenous movement on this continent, there is no such thing and the following section will, therefore, merely offer some examples of influential work from that region. Once again given the dominance of the Anglo-Saxon world in colonial and neo-colonial history, it is not surprising that much of the attention given to TfD relates to the Indian subcontinent and the British-based International Non-Governmental Organizations (INGOs) that operate there. There is, however, one organization outside that orbit whose presence must loom large in any consideration of the achievements of TfD – that is the Philippine Educational Theater Association.

# The Philippine Educational Theater Association (PETA)

Founded in 1967, PETA is fast approaching its fiftieth anniversary. Its longevity contains many lessons in sustainability for the myriad TfD organizations that have come and gone in that time. Maribel Legarda, PETA's current artistic director, articulated the purpose behind its founding:

> In short, PETA's aim was to develop a new and liberating theater pedagogy that would lead to the creation of original Filipino dramaturgy at both professional and community levels. The synergy of these two initiatives led to the birth of the national theater movement Cecile Guidote envisaged.[50]

One of PETA's abiding strengths has been the cross-fertilization of these two levels: professionally trained artists have ensured that the work done in and by communities is not allowed to take any aesthetic shortcuts while the pedagogic demands of learning through theatre have been thoroughly respected in the Freirean-based processes of the workshops. Thus PETA has not suffered from the typical shortcomings of TfD where theatre artists are assumed to be capable of working as applied theatre facilitators despite an absence of specific training and NGO extension workers with little or no theatre training are assumed to be capable of crafting and running a workshop. The term used to describe the core personnel of PETA who disseminate their workshop programme nationwide is 'artist-teacher'. This evenhanded term neatly encompasses the dialectical nature of the interaction between the art and pedagogy without a hint of preferring one axis over the other. While the concept of the artist-teacher was articulated and occasionally implemented in the early days of the British TIE movement, it never achieved the centrality and substance with which PETA has been able to endow it. Legarda is also clear about the role history has played in the forging of the steely and unflinching purpose that has guided the organization through the inhospitable, choppy waters of the years since its foundation:

> PETA was founded during the Marcos dictatorship. This experience of making theater under such conditions sharpened the group's stance: it was no longer enough to assert the importance of cultural identity, asserting the right to a Filipino national theater; the theater also had an obligation to oppose dictatorship. The content and form of both its aesthetic and pedagogical work were shaped by the conditions of the time.[51]

In any organization a potential threat to its continued efficacy comes from a loss of impetus when the vision of founding members dies or retires with them. PETA has limited this effect by its annual summer schools from which new members are regularly recruited to fill gaps and enable expansion. As a consequence of their participation in the Basic Integrated Arts Workshop (BITAW) method, these recruits enter the organization with an understanding of its aims and a strong commitment to its purposes. The scheme was worked out through the 1970s and bears the marks of Freire's influence upon its intentions:

> This methodology has shown the value of art in freeing individuals steeped in a culture of silence to realize their creative potential and in the process *release, explore,* make them *aware, select, master* and *apply* this potential for growth.[52]

The phrase 'culture of silence' is a direct quotation from Freire while the emphasis on 'freeing' endorses van Erven's categorization of this work as 'theatre of liberation'.[53] Where Freire supplies the core pedagogical influence, the theatrical input comes from Viola Spolin with her stress upon improvisation.[54] By themselves, however, this combination of education and art would not have provided the BITAW process with its unique and sustainable characteristics. These emerged when 'staff realized that educational theater or theater that aims to develop human resources and creativity cannot ignore socio-economic realities that affect individuals and communities'.[55] It was this grasp of the connection between the workshop process and the context in which it was set that gave focus and immediacy to the BITAW structure, inspiring the OAO framework which shaped all subsequent workshop activities. The first O is for orientation; this covers the identification of the intention for the particular project which itself emerges from pre-workshop research into the issues, stories and histories of the community and is itself modified by the 'exposure trips' undertaken by participants as part of the workshop process. A is for artistry which is the means of expression for effective communication to an audience. The PETA prescription of integrated arts involves the participants being able to employ music, dance and visual art forms in addition to the theatrical process at the core. PETA constantly stresses the importance of using Filipino art forms as part of the process by which workshop participants are able to discover aspects of their origins and identities. This is the significance of the term 'national' for them which should not be misunderstood as the type of jingoistic patriotism currently active in European and North American discourses. The second O is for organization, referring to the experience of working as a collective, involving leadership, delegation and, above all, solidarity. In this way the workshop forms a bulwark against the otherwise overwhelming drive for competitive individualism sponsored by neoliberal relations of production.

Central to all PETA's activity is a belief in the creative potential of every human being:

> All of their efforts have a common thrust – to draw out from the participants the reservoir of their creative energies, to tap their inner resources and to help them give form and expression to their inner selves. In other words, it is an Integrated Creative Arts seminar-workshop. It is not meant to make professional artists and performers out of the participants but help them grow into creative persons no matter who they are, where they are and what their occupation is, for how important it is to be creative as a person, as a community, as a people.[56]

Lest it seem that such a statement is merely another in the plethora of verbiage which has fetishized 'creativity' to the point where it is almost meaningless, the authors are quick to offer their definition of how and why the concept lies at the root of their endeavours:

> To be creative, one has to open up the mind to new vistas. It means finding exciting alternative solutions to problems. It involves having goals, objectives, commitment – an inner vision which one passionately and indefatigably pursues. Being creative entails training in how to be resourceful.
>
> Creativity, moreover, means learning to be sensitive to one's inner self, and therefore, being sensitive to others. Inevitably, it involves a sensitivity to the universal human condition that binds all men.[57]

This core belief in the possibility of art to enable the profoundest expression of what it is to be human is articulated by Peter O'Connor in Chapter 7 as the 'wonderment of feeling alive' which is, itself, an echo of Brecht's Appendix to Paragraph 45 of *The Short Organum*: 'Every art contributes to the greatest art of all, the art of living.'[58]

While, as van Erven makes clear, PETA's significance on the world stage extends well beyond the specific territory of TfD, part of their enduring importance for the field resides in their understanding of the connections between political action and self-realization through art:

> Its major contribution to world theatre has been the development of a total political theatre package that includes performance, training, and long-term interaction with target groups. Finally, it must be credited with emphasizing the necessity for networking on the local, regional, national, and international level as the one and only key to sustaining a genuinely effective theatre of liberation movement.[59]

These connections are manifest in the way in which Legarda reflects upon the Dulaang Smokey Mountain project where PETA facilitators worked with the children who attempt to survive on Manila's giant, smoking refuse dump:

> The Smokey Mountain experience illustrates how PETA continually adapts its strategies in theater-in-education to situations where formal educational systems are virtually non-existent. In the Smokey

Mountain case, theater was education. This reality requires the PETA artist-teacher to step out of the artistic confines of a conventional theater ensemble into the arena of development work, where one reinvents theater not only as a means of self-expression but as a venue for imagining, proposing and actualizing change.[60]

By asserting that 'theater was education' she articulates, like van Erven's case study in Chapter 9, PETA's theatre not *for* but *as* development for both its participants and its audiences. She does, nevertheless, identify a discrete arm of PETA's programmes as TfD. There may, therefore, be something of a contradiction in aspects of PETA's relations with development agencies:

> PETA intersects with development agendas through its participation in various human rights advocacy campaigns for women, children or young people. Our participation is expressed through the development of performances and informances that tackle these concerns and through the development of a curriculum that integrates the study of these issues within a theater process.[61]

Their current TfD project, *Rated PG*, illustrates the potential for contradiction between drawing the material out of lived experience and delivering a preconceived message to an audience. The topic is positive discipline and the need to stamp out corporal punishment in home and school. PETA's networking skill is attested in its range of partners – the Psychosocial Support and Children's Rights Resource Center, terre des hommes Germany, the German Federal Ministry for Economic Cooperation and Development – and in the number of local government zones with which the project interacted. This project is grounded in an advocacy campaign so the message is always likely to be at its core:

> The campaign's launching platform is a theatrical play on positive discipline. PETA called for script proposals in preparation for the development of the play. Three script proposals were shortlisted and evaluated based on the content and mounting feasibility. The clarity of the message and handling of the corporal punishment issue were given importance in judging the proposed scripts.[62]

Aside from the 'product' implications of starting the project with a script, it is difficult to avoid making a link between the presence of a development NGO and government funders and the requirement to put the message if not above, at least separable from the medium. PETA's integrity and longevity put them in a better position than most to resist these dangers but, even for PETA, they lurk within the contradictions of TfD.

## TfD on the Indian subcontinent

As in previous examples it is impossible to divorce the growth of TfD from the colonial history which precedes it. The British imposed their version of Victorian schooling and with it came the cultural and theatrical forms of the mother country. Postindependence the legacy was an urban, bourgeois elite who sought to imitate the culture into which they had been educated, and a rural peasant mass for whom this culture was entirely alien. These divisions showed up in particularly stark ways in Bengal, in many ways the cultural centre of the Raj, with its thriving literary, musical and theatrical centre of Calcutta. At the same time rural Bengal was home to many indigenous or folk forms, some of which, notably *Jatra*, were revived as part of the nationalist movement. Although its origins lay in religious performances, the form has long since become entirely secular. Its capacity to adapt to changing social patterns, together with its open-air performances geared to large crowds, has made it an ideal form for the promotion of social messages and in part explains the pre-eminence of Bengali (today this means West Bengal and Bangladesh) popular theatre on the subcontinent.

Popular theatre in India predates independence with the formation of the Indian People's Theatre Association (IPTA) in 1941 by the cultural wing of the Communist Party of India. Two main forms of popular theatre emerged from the impetus provided by IPTA: street theatre and social action theatre. The former took a declamatory style of theatre out into the streets of towns and cities, as exemplified by Utpal Dutt's use of *Jatra* to promote the communist ideology in Bengal. Social action groups (SAGs) quickly realized the importance of going beyond one-off workshops or 'parachute' visits into communities. Typically SAGs address themselves to small, rural villages which lie beyond the reach of any mainstream media. Outside any issues relating to the specifics of a performance, the presence of a performing group, be they outsiders, members of the community or a mix of both, creates a moment of celebration for that community; a validation of its existence and a tribute to its capacity to survive. Jacob Srampickal makes an important distinction between independent NGO groups and those which are sponsored by the government:

> In India, where the government participates in development theatre it is necessary to distinguish between the themes and the methodology of government sponsored plays and SAG plays. Basically, themes like nation-building, civic education, health, family planning, agricultural extension, co-operative education, community development, literacy, land and agrarian reforms, resettlement, social welfare, university extension, employment creation, radio schools and media usage are dealt with in the plays of the SDD [Song and Drama Division], the Department of Advertising and Publicity and the publicity divisions of state government.

> But the themes dealt with in the SAG plays are often more fundamental. For instance in India, land is wealth. Therefore, the patterns of landholding and the land ceiling acts have immense implications for the landless people.[63]

Broadly, this distinction reflects the binary posited by Kerr in relation to TfD in Africa: namely that it can be used for either domesticating or transformative ends. If the funders, as is almost inevitably the case, are part of the established, neoliberal system, the intention for the work will be to improve the operation of that system rather than to change it. In this respect TfD in the neo-colonial countries of Africa and the Indian subcontinent shares similar problems around the dangers of being co-opted by funding agencies or the NGOs dependent on those funds. Intention is everything and frequently those intentions are masked behind pseudo-Freirean rhetoric and empty jargon of participation. As Srampickal declares, even where intentions are transparent they may not relate to the priorities of the community – a particular danger where groups come from outside that community and from a different class, caste or set of cultural assumptions:

> SAGs have initiated post-performance discussions, seminars and workshops for the audience, to help them understand the dimensions of the problems. By comparison, the SDD appears to be merely selling messages to the poor.

> SAG theatre practitioners are conscious that there needs to be a sharing of visions, ideologies and strategies with the people. However, often these visions and ideologies are not really compatible with the concrete situation and mind-set of the people and if the people do not comprehend, the sharing turns out to be an imposition.[64]

Besides the domesticating agendas of governments and funding agencies and the risks of cultural imposition, there is another immediate and very real barrier to the promotion of transformative work.

> However, when the play turns out to be an indirect attack on the upper castes, their land-grabbing patterns and other exploitative measures they react violently. Often the electricity supply is cut off and stones thrown at the actors and the crowd. Several groups have been chased away by heavies in the landlords' pay. Hardly anyone will have a man-to-man confrontation with the animateurs of the SAGs. For the landlords know only too well that what the SAGs are trying to put across is factual. Hence they use strong-arm tactics.

> The local government officials are often in league with the landed gentry and the exploiters. They too try to frighten away the SAGs. And the SAGs have to play it safe. For if the local government officials do not give them a good report, the SAG quota of foreign contributions may be discontinued.[65]

Such an instance is recounted by Michael Etherton in the course of his child-rights TfD activity with Save the Children:

> Camaraderie grew among the various groups who were developing improvisations. Then, quite suddenly, the people in the independent Bangladesh NGOs who were hosting our workshop received threats of violence from some rich young men in powerful village families. They accused us of undermining the 'cultural values of Bangladesh'. We had clearly come up straightaway against the powerful vested interests in the village.[66]

Among all these problems and disincentives there are, nevertheless, dedicated groups and facilitators who commit themselves to long exposure with the poorest rural communities and to the long-term training of those who might sustain the activities in their own communities. The best of these efforts are usually grounded in storytelling processes which put the lived experience of the workshop participants at the centre of the project as a precondition for dialogue between social activists and community members. Even among the groups who work in this committed manner, and certainly among those whose work is defined by short-term, project-based activities, there is an enormous deficit in the area of follow-up and impact assessment as Munier and Etherton pointed out in relation to the child-rights work on the subcontinent.[67]

It is clear from Srampickal's analysis of the limitations of the SAGs that any TfD process which intends to make a transformative difference to the lives of those it touches must fulfil a number of criteria such as long-term activities with specific communities which set the agenda for the work, effective evaluation and impact assessment strategies, and a willingness and capacity to forge common cause with non-theatre organizations which share similar concerns:

> The historical, economic and political factors underlying a particular situation need to be explored. This is how the poor come to know that the real causes of poverty and underdevelopment are not the ignorance and weaknesses or the wickedness of the rich but the structural

relationships which keep them powerless and exploited. They can come to realize that the real problems are not lack of proper drinking water, illiteracy, superstitions, large families and malnutrition, but exploitation, victimization, injustice and corruption. The former are only symptoms of the real problems.[68]

Srampickal's repeated assertion of the 'real' runs the risk of aligning him among those who impose their ideology regardless of the context and concerns of those being addressed. The key point here in relation to a TfD process is the way in which that process can forge a link between 'symptom' and 'problem'. To those afflicted by them these 'symptoms' are life-threateningly real and no TfD process should dismiss them lightly. However, a long-term relationship between facilitators and community may enable that process to go beyond addressing the specific issue into the territory of deep structures, of causes and effects.

## Jana Sanskriti

Jana Sanskriti was founded by Sanjoy Ganguly in 1985 in a rural location outside Kolkata; perhaps the most important contemporary manifestation of the rich Bengali theatrical legacy. His company embraces many of the challenges laid out by Srampickal above. Ganguly is unambiguous on the importance of connecting with other organizations in the cause of sustainable social change:

> theatre of empowerment is a long and arduous journey. It does not end with the performance. We could see that it is our responsibility not only to make the people think, but also to mobilise such thoughts towards action. That is why it is sometimes necessary to work in collaboration with other groups who have the same political objective but do not necessarily work through the medium of theatre. We have always tried to collaborate with such groups, and continue to do so today.[69]

Though theatre and politics, especially in TfD, are inextricably linked, theatre is not politics. If the theatre is able to provoke an action leading to change, that provocation can only bear fruit if there are agencies beyond the theatre who can take it forward into areas such as policy, rights and the law. Ganguly constantly stresses the significance of the relationship between the performers and the audience, picking up on Freire's notion of dialogue. As much as the audience may learn from the actors, the actors are shaped even more by the experience of their long exposure to the village communities among whom they ply their trade:

> He [one of the actors] had seen that the activities of Jana Sanskriti – Forum Theatre, Image Theatre – were a continuous and evolving process, helping the artist to develop not only his artistic potential but also his social consciousness. It extends his role beyond the arena of the theatre, taking the artist close to the people, making him part of the people, of the greater human self. The artist is then not alienated from the people: he and the people are one and the same.[70]

This is the core of the commitment which takes Jana Sanskriti's work beyond what Ganguly terms 'propaganda' theatre where messages are addressed to audiences in the form of monologues, into a dialogue where the performance is an expression of the growing understanding which emerges from the relationship forged between artist and community. The rhythms and working methods of the company are a far cry from the single issue-based project emanating from an external agency and it is in the contrast that the possibility for effecting change lies. Ganguly echoes Freire in articulating the need for a process which enables grassroot communities to analyse and act upon the structural inequalities that may not always be apparent on the surface of daily encounters:

> Perhaps the most important thing to note here is that Forum and the kinds of behaviour it stimulates can lead to strategic change, which goes beyond simply addressing tactical proposals to address a particular situation. The latter may overlook key contextual features or other factors which would ultimately render intervention less or non-effective: strategic thinking means that people can understand the whole situation in the long-term; and this leads to real 'deliberative action'.[71]

As Ganguly makes clear at every point, the seminal influence upon his artistic and political development is Boal. He has established the Jana Sanskriti Centre for the Theatre of the Oppressed and is the foremost exponent of Forum Theatre on the subcontinent. He found in the rural communities of West Bengal and later more widely in India, an echo of the conditions which led Boal to develop the Theatre of the Oppressed poetics in response to his experiences of poverty and oppression under the Brazilian dictatorship. Similarly, Ganguly speaks about cultures of silence and sees Boal's influence as a 'liberation', picking up the term regularly employed in South American contexts to describe movements opposed to the ruling *status quo*:

> through Theatre of the Oppressed I have seen how the strength of endurance in the oppressed people gets converted to the strength to bring about change, a liberation from passivity and muteness.[72]

His processes draw upon the existing, time-honoured qualities of the host community and then exploit them through the function of the 'spect-actor' for the purpose of transformation; sustainable because rooted in the lived experience of that community. It is the long-term commitment between company and community that gives credibility to claims of sustainable transformation associated with the TfD process:

> Theatre of the Oppressed possesses the capacity to enable people to challenge the cultures of monologue; its processes include both individual and group/community development from within, through rehearsal, collective scripting, performance and interactive engagement with spectators, and subsequent long-term ongoing collaboration with those spectator communities.[73]

## Natya Chetana

Natya Chetana which means 'theatre for awareness' was founded in 1986 by Subodh Pattanaik in Orissa. The initial impetus came from a group of graduates looking for work and deciding to engage in social work through drama and still today the company consists of volunteers who devote themselves to TfD in return for subsistence and a vocation. Initially the group followed the inspiration of Safdar Hashmi's street theatre. Though Hashmi himself was beaten to death by Congress Party goons on 1 January 1989 while his company, Janam, was performing a play about the government's repression of the labour movement, Natya Chetana is one of those 'clear and hopeful signs that Hashmi's death may convince progressive Indian artists to forget their differences and unite to realize Hashmi's vision – a truly people-oriented Indian theatre of liberation movement'.[74] In 1990 the company founded Natya Gram, a 'theatre village' as its base and clear statement of its intention to persist with its mission, described today on its website as:

> To explore and develop theatre and artistic abilities for reviving own cultural roots and highlighting socio-political-economical themes for supporting people's movements leading towards a self-reliant society with equal justice and right.[75]

Another major influence in the development of the company's ethos and workshop style was Badal Sircar, whose Third Theatre took performances out of the proscenium arch and into the streets of Kolkata to instigate political debate among its audiences during the turbulent 1970s. But his importance for a group like Natya Chetana is summed up by Chris Banfield writing before Sircar's death:

> his ambition has long been to reach the 'real' audience of India: the villagers. Increasingly this is happening not through the performance of his plays . . . but through his leading of workshops that have sought to liberate the emotions and creativity of the participants, however unfamiliar they may be with 'theatre' or his working process. The trust and enthusiasm that Badal Sircar is able to engender within the workshop situation and the obstacles to expression he dismantles, are functions of an unswerving honesty and integrity, qualities that others have envied, and few in an Indian, or for that matter any other, context have matched.[76]

Along with Sircar, the other formative influence on the group's workshop aesthetic was PETA. Natya Chetana had visits from trainers from both to guide and support the evolution of the company. From these inputs Pattanaik understood the importance of integrity and continuity in workshop practice as well as the strategy of making use of local, indigenous culture in areas such as music, costume, dance and storytelling. The special characteristic for which the company is now known is its 'cyclo-theatre'. Early on in the development of the group, Pattanaik decided to concentrate their efforts in the rural villages of Orissa and to work repeatedly with the same communities over a long period. To serve this end the company uses bicycles as their preferred means of transport in order to overcome issues of accessibility where roads are largely non-existent:

> The style of theatre by Natya Chetana is a novelty and is known as 'CYCLO-THEATRE'. This new way of attempting a theatre is developed by experiments travelling a definite span of time and passing many trial and errors. Participants of CYCLO THEATRE go to remote places where the people are being oppressed socially, economically, culturally and politically even after fifty years of independence. In other words their psycho status remained unmoved and were [*sic.*] being exploited. The participants visit such remote places and conduct a cultural survey on the local cultural expressions, the traditional forms and the local problems and sort them out on priority basis. Then a theatre workshop is followed up.[77]

## Michael Etherton's child-rights TfD

Etherton's career has enabled him to adopt some unique perspectives in relation to the growth and development of TfD. Not only does it span the geographical territory of Africa (East and West), Europe and Asia, it also encompasses the contrasting experiences of the academic and NGO worlds. This was the range and depth of understanding he was able to bring to his work on TfD for Save the Children UK on the Indian subcontinent. Most unusually, a seasoned academic and practitioner of TfD found himself in a senior position with a major INGO. Here, at last, was the chance for TfD to make its presence felt at the heart of an organization's strategy, rather than being a mere bit-part on the fringes of a particular project. That said, he still had to find the right point of entry for TfD into the current discourses of the organization. His choice of child rights for the framework within which to develop a particular style of TfD proved prescient. All the governments of the countries within the region for which Etherton was policy adviser are signatories of the CRC which enabled Save the Children to hold local community-based organizations (CBOs) to account, specifically in relation to Articles 12, 13 and 15. These cover both the right of children's opinions to be heard and their right to choose the medium through which they are expressed. Consequently a space existed into which TfD made by children and young people fitted and, as the INGO whose mission is most associated with children and young people, Save the Children was the obvious organization to sponsor this activity.

This work coincided with the wider NGO movement which sought to change the emphasis within development from needs to rights. The words themselves are indicators of an attitude towards 'the other'. Needs have been determined, historically, by those with the power to satisfy them. Powerful nations determine who 'needs' to have Western style parliamentary democracy imposed upon them. Traditionally, INGOs decided which set of needs they were going to meet. Rights, however, shift the emphasis away from the donors to the participants in a development programme. Instead of the grace and favour principle of 'needs', recipients of development aid could now assert their 'right' to material resources and cultural freedoms:

> Development activists are now moving into the much more radical notion of children and young people co-opting adults around their agenda, rather than adults getting children to participate in adult

agenda. This process, initiated by Save the Children UK, is part of a much wider movement among children, not only in Asia but worldwide.[78]

Once the young people set their own agenda many of the assumptions which adults make about them are overturned. In words which encapsulate many of the principles and desires articulated by practitioners who have been exposed to the power of theatre in the hands of participants, Etherton hints at the moral dimensions unearthed by the specific dynamic of people-centred theatre, whatever the material circumstances:

> TfD is a dramatized expression of a shared humanity, in this case by children in communities in many different countries around the world. It leads directly to the heart of Child Rights. I am constantly inspired by very poor children's collective ability to express what is good, what is bad, what is right and fair, an understanding that transcends their poverty, disadvantage and exclusion.[79]

In relation to sustainability, Etherton suggests that the TfD process where it is made by children according to their own self-determined agenda can give rise to the creation of children's organizations as has happened in India and Nepal. The skills summoned to produce an effective TfD process are mostly also those required to form a well-managed, child-centred organization.

Etherton's reflections upon the specific qualities that emerged in the course of his work with young people take us back to the origins of the genre in the aesthetics of Brecht and the pedagogy of Freire: 'The central idea of Child Rights TfD is to emphasise the neverending [*sic.*] process of improvisation and analysis.'[80] This notion of the dialectical relationship of creativity to analysis lies at the core of theatre in the service of social change and is manifest in the case studies selected for this book.

Given his unique dual perspective, Etherton is well qualified to understand the mutual suspicions which lurk in both the theatre and development 'camps' as he identifies the tension that has surfaced throughout this brief examination of theatre's relationship with development:

> Some political theatre activists see NGOs negatively, whether these NGOs are international, national or local. They are seen as part of the development industry, a destructive economic force that continues to marginalise individuals and communities. NGOs promoting TfD, therefore, are seen as having the ultimate purpose of promoting compliance in the existing world order. An independent theatre, by contrast, enhances the collective cultural will and the desire for profound change in the world order.

> On the other hand, INGOs themselves see no future in TfD if all it does is produce more and better political theatre. They would embrace theatre if it produced significant social change.[81]

Perhaps there are two fundamentally different processes at work here. TfD with development agencies must accept the limitations that come with the purpose of the INGO: to improve an aspect of human society within the existing world order; a clean supply of neoliberal water is better than no water at all. Those who use TfD not *for* but *as* development are committed to a vision of theatre either as a rehearsal for a revolution which will overthrow the capitalist system or as an evolution which will educate humans into forming societies based on different principles from the monetary ones that currently prevail.

## Latin American theatre for development

A number of factors have given rise to a different set of conditions from those prevailing elsewhere in the world in which TfD has grown and been shaped in Latin America. The colonial legacy, though clearly evident throughout the continent, is less immediate than in most parts of Africa and Asia. Iberian colonization of the Americas took place some 200 years earlier than the British and French versions with much greater mixing between Native Americans, transported Africans and Europeans than occurred in Africa and Asia. Independent nations in Latin America formed a hundred years earlier than the decolonization process elsewhere. Consequently, there has been a longer period in which national identities and class and ethnic identities within the nation could be formed.

In the postwar period US national security policy, attempting to preserve a favourable climate for its business and ideological interests, has ensured the presence of a common, external 'enemy' to unite the peasants and working classes across the continent. Successive US governments have given military and financial backing to a series of oppressive dictatorships, frequently installed over the corpses of the previous, democratically elected regimes. In such a landscape the call for social and political change was unlikely to fall on deaf ears. The major catalyst for such a call was the successful revolution in Cuba which saw Fidel Castro take control at the head of a communist government in 1959. The Cuban Revolution produced two macroeffects in Latin America: US policy took on a harder, more paranoid edge as it sought to ensure that communism or even socialism, did not take hold anywhere else, leading to increased support for neo-fascist regimes, and people's movements were encouraged by the example of a successful outcome that resisted US efforts to destroy it.

This is the context in which the movement which has attracted the label Nuevo Teatro Popular came into being in the 1960s and which has framed TfD ever since:

> The New Popular Theatre is characterized not only by a rich variety of expression, but also and more importantly perhaps, by the various forms of collective processes and non-hierarchical organizations through which it could maintain a close connection to its social context. It also developed consciously as an international cultural movement, a series of regional and hemispheric networks that have operated through tours, exchanges, and festivals.[82]

This is the value of forming the kinds of organization, both theatrical and pedagogical, the absence of which Etherton and Mlama lamented in Africa. The movement has exhibited a further strength, similar to PETA, of maintaining a close, mutually nourishing relationship between professionals and community:

> There are two major and relatively autonomous tendencies within the Nuevo Teatro Popular: the grass-roots theatre, which is sometimes known as 'theatre of popular participation' or 'community theatre,' and the artistic theatre, which is made up primarily of trained theatre professionals. The two tendencies have always intersected and interacted, with crossovers by artists between the two types. Professionals have worked as directors or consultants with nonprofessional, grass-roots projects and groups, while professional artistic groups have also included and trained nonprofessionals.[83]

It is worth remembering that Boal himself intersected these 'tendencies', being a director at the Arena Theatre in São Paulo before developing his Theatre of the Oppressed methodology.

Across the hemisphere there is a vigorous history of festivals and meetings (*encuentros*) where all the various strands involved in community theatre come together to share performances, theories, organizational problems and consciousness-raising around current political issues. Post-revolutionary Cuba took the lead in organizing international festivals in the 1960s and today they are ubiquitous. By the 1990s many grassroots theatre organizations were attached to adult education programmes. However, these programmes need to be understood within the Latin American context where education is thoroughly politicized. Liam Kane differentiates 'adult' from 'popular' in order to clarify exactly what is meant:

> What distinguishes popular education from 'adult', 'non-formal', 'distance' or 'permanent' education, for example, is the belief that in the context of social injustice, education can never be politically neutral: if it does not side with the poorest and marginalised sectors –

the 'oppressed' – in an attempt to transform society, then it necessarily sides with the 'oppressors' in maintaining the existing structures of oppression, even if by default.[84]

Here there is another link particular to Latin America: the conceptual framework afforded by Freire's learner-centred pedagogy which Boal adapted for theatrical purposes. Popular educators schooled in Freire's method are unlikely to find it hard to accept the popular theatre system of Boal as an important methodology to support their work. The close links between popular education and TfD in Latin America have raised the public profile of the former while assisting the sustainability of the latter.

The significance of grassroots popular education organizations is heightened by the relative absence of the university sector from this area of work, although Chile and Mexico offer partial exceptions. In Brazil, for instance, even though it is the land of Freire and Boal, community theatre has struggled to get onto the curriculum of universities due to the elitist prejudices of their managements. Recently, however, inroads have been made with the work of Marcia Pompeo Nogueira (see Chapter 4) at the State University of Santa Catarina in Florianopolis. Besides installing community theatre in the undergraduate and postgraduate curricula, she has also established strong links with local communities through the setting up of a facilitators' network, FOFA. Following her lead, her former doctoral student, Marina Henriques Coutinho, has blazed a path for community theatre in UniRio with student placements in the previously off-limits *favellas*. Gradually the global significance of the light shone by Freire and Boal is penetrating the gloomy portals of academe. However, at its core this work can never be subsumed into universities because it belongs where its audiences are found:

> The clearest relationship of the Nuevo Teatro Popular is with its audience, which is both an assembly of spectators and a constituency. Audiences are not there merely to be played to, or talked at, but to be engaged in a dialogue that goes well beyond the limits of a single

performance. The group establishes the basis for the dialogue by reaching out to learn about the community and understand it.[85]

An outstanding example of such a company is Teatro Escambray who left Havana in 1969 to work for the revolution in a part of the country where it felt it was most needed. The Escambray region of central Cuba was chosen because it was designated as economically 'backward' and had been the site of counterrevolutionary activity throughout the 1960s. In working closely with grassroots organizations, training professionals and community members, and developing community-based theatre it was to prove a pioneer but it distinguished itself from other independent collectives engaging in collective creation by its close links with the Communist Party of Cuba. To this day the company supports the state and enjoys state support. Another feature which was to prove paradigmatic was the establishing of a permanent base, Cumanayagua, in the heart of the community. All over the hemisphere this model has been followed with companies becoming closely associated with the immediate locality in which they are situated. In Latin America not only is community theatre by, with and for the community, it is also very much *in* the community. Teatro Escambray, while rooted in the community, has held firmly onto an international perspective as evidenced by its recent tour of children's theatre and workshops in Venezuela.

Since Teatro Escambray's formation there have been similar companies created throughout the hemisphere. The Centre for the Theatre of the Oppressed in Rio (CTO Rio) is the guardian of Boal's legacy and ensures through its training programmes that the TO methodology continues to inform the work of community theatre organizations and networks both in Brazil and beyond. Boal's death is still too raw and recent to allow CTO Rio to relax its grip on that methodology and to encourage dialogues between TO and other strategies. For the moment its approach to Forum Theatre is that of the zealous disciple who regards the words of the prophet as sacred even though Boal himself constantly asserted the need for flexibility and spontaneity. However, theirs is only one influence in the rich mix of possibilities created by those who have followed in Teatro Escambray's footsteps. The model of long-term commitment to a particular place has characterized the work of some of the hemisphere's most effective groups such as Teatro La Candelaria from the Candelaria suburb of Bogotá, Pombas Urbanas from the Cidade Tiradentes district of São Paulo and Catalines Sur from La Boca in Buenos Aires. As times have changed, governments have gone from dictatorships to democracies, and US influence has waned, so political issues have altered their complexions. The need to voice the concerns and aspirations of 'the oppressed' remains the *raison d'être* but the manner of doing so and the targets for reform may have changed.

An outstanding example of the health of the sector is afforded by the project, *El Quijote Latinamericano* created in 2009. Seventy actors from twelve countries took part in a production where different scenes were created by community theatre companies from Argentina, Bolivia, Brazil, Chile, Colombia, Cuba, El Salvador, Guatemala and Peru. Cervantes' novel, *Don Quixote*, was adapted for the stage and for contemporary Latin American discourses. Quijote's adversaries are the various faces of the neoliberal system of oppression as encountered by impoverished communities throughout the hemisphere. The willingness to cooperate across national boundaries, to share expertise and to create in two languages, Spanish and Portuguese, as well as incorporating local cultures into the music, dance and costumes, is typical of a movement which has never been hamstrung by unnecessary distinctions between community theatre, popular theatre and theatre for development. From the experience of creating the *El Quijote* project the Latin American Network of Community Theatres was born. *Caja Lúdica*, the subject of Chapter 9, is a member of this network.

Julie McCarthy offers a concluding reflection on her experience of working with various NGOs in Brazil and Peru:

> If participatory development is to facilitate change it must develop long-term strategies to challenge power inequalities at individual,

organisational and community level. What is needed is a critical methodology that not only addresses inequities, but also strives to understand how those inequities arose and what maintains them. Empowerment can only occur when individuals, groups and communities are aware of the power relations in multiple aspects of their lives. Although social change begins with the individual who is first able to take action in her own life, it is vital for participatory practice to strike a balance between a focus on personal transformation and the development of a sense of agency, enabling the individual to take collective action to produce change at a wider scale.[86]

While I agree wholeheartedly with the sentiment, there is, following Freire, no shortage of companies and facilitators working with 'a critical methodology'. As for 'change at a wider scale' many countries in Latin America are now experiencing attempts at such a change. However, even where there is a government determined to reform ancient patterns of patronage and corruption as in Brazil, the process is painful, uneven and fiercely resisted. Nevertheless part of the will to change comes from grassroots communities which have experienced the life-affirming force of collective creation through theatre. Weiss' summary of the achievements of the movement tells much, but not all of the story:

> The Nuevo Teatro Popular is unquestionably a counter-hegemonic movement. It has defined itself as such both literally and indirectly. Its groups have exchanged artists and have been active in festivals, workshops, and encuentros throughout the hemisphere since the earliest efforts to create new national theatres, to restructure the organization of dramatic production, and to expand the boundaries of theatrical creation into new geographic areas and new constituencies, always challenging the norms, the formulas, and the frameworks proposed by the dominant sectors.[87]

This frame of reference may prove more suited to the second half of the twentieth century than to the twenty-first. Community theatres have been accustomed to adopting an oppositional stance in relation to the prevailing government or supporting it in the Cuban case. Today there are regimes in countries such as Bolivia and Brazil which call for more nuanced responses from popular theatre. While social inequalities continue to abound and the function of creating spaces for the voices of the people is as urgent as ever, new possibilities may be opening up for more dialogical approaches to the traditional sources of oppression. Liam Kane's assessment of the Landless Rural Workers Movement's (MST) relation to the Labour (PT) Government in Brazil could readily apply to the popular theatre movement as well:

> On the evidence so far, the MST appears to have maintained its radical edge while taking full advantage of the changed political conjuncture. It is clearly in charge of its own education programme, with its own educators, courses, schools and materials, and, from a position of strength, has managed to negotiate (limited) state support and recognition without yielding autonomy.[88]

# Fool's Play or Juggling with Neoliberalism

## Culture

The antagonism which I depicted above in the contrast between the dominant neo-liberal economic frame and the United Nations rights frame surfaces again when considering the relationship between development and culture where Theatre for Development (TfD) plays a significant role. 1988–97 was declared the World Decade for Cultural Development by the UN. Unfortunately, this period coincided with the full unleashing of the 'free market' ideology of the Reagan/Thatcher axis which promoted market forces above any other measurements of worth. Besides the direct effect of reducing public money for 'cultural activities' available to governments and NGOs, the indirect influence of the neo-liberal agenda has been wholly hostile to the aims and aspirations of the cultural aspects of development. Neoliberalism asserts the dominance of economics and finance over every other area of human activity and requires that the myriad ways in which humans relate to each other – the very stuff of culture – are reduced to the codes of monetary exchange: 'what do I get out of this? How much is it worth to me? Can I afford it?' These kinds of question are now routinely applied to areas of life such as education and health from which they were formerly exempt. In such a climate it is not surprising that those experiences that do not lend themselves readily to monetary analysis feel the chill winds of neglect and indifference howling around them. The Office of the World Commission on Culture and Development at UNESCO produced a report in 1996 called *Our Creative Diversity*. UNESCO President, Javier Pérez de Cuéllar, concluded his Foreword as follows:

We have a long way to go. We have not yet learned how to respect each other fully, how to share and work together. This truly exceptional time in history calls for exceptional solutions. The world as we know it, all the relationships we took as given, are undergoing profound rethinking and reconstruction. Imagination, innovation, vision and creativity are required. International partnerships and interaction are an essential ingredient for creativity in problem-solving, a quality that requires a willingness to frame bold questions instead of depending on conventional answers. It means an open mind, an open heart, and a readiness to seek fresh definitions, reconcile old opposites, and help draw new mental maps. Ultimately it will be the honesty of introspection that will lead to compassion for the Other's experience, and it will be compassion that will lead us to a future in which pursuit of individual freedom will be balanced with a need for common well-being, and in which our agenda includes empathy and respect for the entire spectrum of human differences.[1]

Meanwhile back in the 'real' world of neo-liberal politics, the Reagan administration had led a withdrawal of right-wing governments from UNESCO, along with a portion of their UN funding. To this day the United States remains outside UNESCO and remains resistant to the very notion of human rights. Just as the new century might have been starting to face up to the challenges and opportunities of globalization in relation to cultural exchange, migration and confronting the depredations of the monoculture, the World Trade Centre attack of 11 September 2001 provided a backward-looking, Reaganite regime with the opportunity to create a 'war on terror' where violence replaces thought, suspicion is the default response to 'the Other' and the very notion of public good is devoured by deregulated private greed from which ordinary people are suffering in large measure today. This creed of privatization impacts profoundly upon those agencies and activities, such as TfD, which are concerned with promoting collective rather than individual responses to lived experience and which are bound up with processes rather than products. As governments look to private individuals and corporations to fill some of the gaps caused by their

withdrawal from the public sphere, such funds as are still available to
the cultural sector are increasingly directed at high-profile products
that produce some media glory for the donors to bask in. The daily,
invisible grind of long-term, process-oriented TfD does not sit too high
on such an agenda. Where public sector funding does linger on, it is
almost always closely tied to instrumentalist outcomes such as reducing
youth offending rates or cutting the numbers of teenage pregnancies. In
short public money is not available to give 'the oppressed' an experience
of finding their own voices through a theatre process. Such applications
are a long way from the vision enshrined in the UNESCO sponsored
Universal Declaration on Cultural Diversity (2001). Article 1 states:

### Cultural diversity: the common heritage of humanity

Culture takes diverse forms across time and space. This diversity
is embodied in the uniqueness and plurality of the identities of the
groups and societies making up humankind. As a source of exchange,
innovation and creativity, cultural diversity is as necessary for
humankind as biodiversity is for nature. In this sense, it is the common
heritage of humanity and should be recognized and affirmed for the
benefit of present and future generations.[2]

As a key methodology of community culture, this raises the question
of whether TfD has a default conservative stance as the guardian of
endangered cultural practices. Once again TfD appears on a fault-
line: this time between the modernizing, homogenizing, Westernizing
tendencies of the state-sponsored development industry, designing their
programmes in order to make 'them' behave like 'us', and those who
regard a people-centred, cultural practice as the bulwark against the
McDonaldization, Disneyfication of the planet. Neoliberalism's signal
'triumph', aided by compliant and frequently sycophantic mainstream
media, has been to reposition all human transactions and interactions
in terms of the marketplace; buyers and sellers. In this process culture
has ceased to be the vehicle through which each of us makes meaning
of our lives, and has become a commercial transaction. 'We' are without

culture until 'they' – the entertainment-industrial complex – sell it to us to fill our void:

> as an act, consummating purchases can never express the breadth or depth of meaning that inheres in heritage culture or that we invest in our own creations. But the particulars of what is purchased are incidental to the main impacts of the act – enriching the consumer cultural industries and placing our roles as consumers at the center of our lives and communities. By reducing culture to commerce, globalization robs us of so much: our connection to our own histories with their reservoirs of resilience and creativity; our ability to reconceive the past for the benefit of the future; the ease of exploring our boundless creativity.[3]

Even since these words were written the pace and reach of globalization has so increased, particularly in the media sector, that the invasion of consumer culture threatens to hollow out ordinary people's capacity to make their own meanings and to fill the void with the rancid prejudices of a small gaggle of media oligarchs. Adams and Goldbard link our capacity to make culture explicitly to the core pedagogy of Freire with his insistence on the importance of each person being in a position 'to name their own world':

> Community cultural development practice is based on the understanding that culture is the crucible in which human resilience, creativity and autonomy are forged. As everyone knows, an unexamined life is indeed possible: any of us might move through our lives in a trance of passivity, acted upon but never acting as free beings. The root idea of community cultural development is the imperative to fully inhabit our human lives, bringing to consciousness the values and choices that animate our communities and thus equipping ourselves to act – to paraphrase Paulo Freire – as subjects in history, rather than merely its objects.[4]

This description of culture carries vital echoes for the TfD process which at its best is always built on a dialectical relationship between the creative and the critical. The double meaning is wholly intentional when participants in a TfD workshop are offered the opportunity to become actors in their own stories. It is a process which moves participants from a place as objects of development, victims of the culture of silence, into the limelight as subjects developing social actions on their own terms. The so-called safe space of the workshop provides a location where the normal power relations and hierarchies are suspended so that alternative ways of relating to each other can be tried out. Whether the experience of active agency changes anything outside the territory of the workshop depends upon the particulars of the context; not least whether the TfD process is linked to a community organization which can act in the 'real' world upon the initiatives emerging from the workshop. As a collective act of creation the TfD event does at least provide an experience of solidarity, increasingly rare among the dominant discourses of individualism, from which the participants may draw strength to confront the barriers to their chosen path of development.

If it is the cultural moment, the right to make meaning, which is all important, what is the purpose of taking that moment forward into an art form? Why does everyone need the chance to be active as an artist?

> Culture underpins all choices, all outcomes. It contains the means of expressing all thoughts and emotions. It enables all associations. And within this encompassing realm, the purest and densest meanings are conveyed through art, through individual and collective creations driven by the desire to express and communicate, unencumbered by extraneous objectives.[5]

If culture is as important as this to human relations and activities, why has it struggled to find a central place in the policies, strategies and action plans of governmental and NGO development agencies? Whatever the reasons, they have had and will have a significant impact upon the use and misuse of TfD by those agencies. Tim Butchard's 1995 report for the British Council, 'The Arts and Development', laid out the position starkly: '. . . the arts remain a Cinderella activity, a glimmer of colour in the sombre world of development theory, but starved of the status, the resources and the intellectual attention they deserve.[6] Helen Gould and Mary Marsh found that position only slightly improved by the time of writing their 2004 report 'Culture: Hidden Development', where they write of the simultaneous importance and invisibility of culture in the work of the development sector. By the mid-1990s, in the face of the manifest failures of the sector, particularly in relation to combatting the spread of HIV/AIDS, development theorists were starting to acknowledge the significance of culture and indigenous knowledge systems although practical impact was still patchy and frequently haphazard:

> In the late '70s and early '80s it became clear that many of the development strategies introduced into the Third World by the western powers were flawed, largely because they had failed to take into account the cultures of their target populations. One symptom of this failure was that resources placed at the disposal of the higher echelons of many developing societies failed to trickle downwards to those who needed them and, instead, supported stagnant pools of privilege and self-serving oligarchies.[7]

Gould and Marsh identified two distinct modes in which culture operates in relation to development – modes familiar to TfD practitioners – culture as a tool for achieving outcomes beyond the realm of the art form and culture as a process, engaged in for the intrinsic benefit of the experience:

> Cultural approaches are being applied in the development arena in two observable ways:
>
> **As a tool:** cultural approaches are used in an instrumentalist manner and are generally message-based. The tool-based approach is generally intended to inform, although it is sometimes used in such a way so as to allow or try to encourage some degree of participation, but ultimately its outputs are usually pre-determined by those controlling the development process.

**As a process:** cultural approaches are the basis of a liberationist approach that endeavours to explicitly address issues of shifting power and strengthening people's control over the development process. It starts from people's own experience and involves a participatory creative process, the output of which is not pre-determined.[8]

Interestingly, Butchard a decade earlier, even though writing for an arts rather than a development organization, champions the cause of practices such as TfD in 'instrumentalist' not 'liberationist' terms:

*The arts and community development* covers the mobilization of the arts to communicate social messages and values, and to raise the quality of life for disadvantaged sectors of the community. Types of activity include: *theatre for development* (TFD): using theatre to raise health and living standards, to alleviate injustice or abuse, and to change social attitudes;[9]

Perhaps the notion of engaging in a TfD process *as* rather than *for* development could not then, and perhaps still not now, be 'sold' to development agencies as a worthwhile deployment of resources. Nevertheless it was becoming apparent as we entered the new century, even to mainstream organizations at the heart of the neo-liberal discourse, that culture had to assume a more central position in development if any social changes were to be achieved. Gould and Marsh quote from Arjun Appadurai's report to the World Bank in 2004, 'The Capacity to Aspire, Culture and Public Action':

We need a sea change in the way we look at culture in order to create a more productive relationship between anthropology and economics, between culture and development, in the battle against poverty. This change requires us to place futurity, rather than pastness, at the heart of our thinking about culture. . . . This does not mean that we need to forget about culture in its broadest sense, as the sense of tradition, the fabric of everyday understandings, the archive of memory and producer of monuments, arts and crafts. Nor do we need to slight the idea that culture is the fount of human expression in its fullest range, including the arts, music, theatre and language. Culture is all these things as well. But culture is a dialogue between aspirations and sedimented traditions. And in our commendable zeal for the latter at the cost of the former, we have allowed unnecessary, harmful and artificial opposition to emerge between culture and development.[10]

Appadurai unerringly taps into the limitations of the Western development paradigm of what culture means. The dominance of economists and accountants has fuelled the perception that culture is represented only by commodities with a monetary value. In turn commodification leads to a static view of culture where, almost by definition, it refers to knowledge that has become fossilized in artefacts. Thus culture belongs to the past even as development does to the future and the possibility of a dialectical understanding of the two has dissolved in a fruitless, binary antagonism. Gould and Marsh go on to suggest that this stand-off may indicate something more than involuntary misunderstanding. Their investigations raise the possibility that it is the very structure of the development industry that wilfully contributes to this destructive state of affairs by refusing to factor into its strategies those cultural elements which would make the developers' task more complicated, but without which development is certain to fail:

> The other, more insidious, possibility is that culture is invisible because cultural plurality is inconvenient for development. It is far easier for the machinery of development to function in a world where cultures do not get in the way of political and economic progress; where communities share a set of universal values which make them respond uniformly to change. Furthermore, culture is part of the landscape of human rights which makes it doubly uncomfortable – not only are people diverse in language, thought, belief and identity, but it is part of their inalienable rights to remain so.[11]

This analysis links the commercialization and commodification of culture to the processes of an accelerating globalization. Now that the market for products is global, the mechanisms for achieving worldwide sales require the destruction of diversity at the hands of the monoculture. The marketing gurus at McDonalds may insert a couple of lettuce leaves and a slice of tomato into burgers destined for southern European outlets but the core production process remains unhindered by any real sense of local culture. Transferred into the realm of education this becomes, in O'Toole's eloquent phrase coined in the next chapter, 'the world-wide privileging of monological, disembodied and acquiescent, non-reflective pedagogy'.

At the same time, there has also been a growing awareness among development practitioners of the importance of looking at human behaviour in relation to any ambition to stimulate social change; so much so, indeed, that the expression 'behaviour change' has come to replace 'social change' in much of the development discourse. Twenty years ago Butchard was alert to the implications of making behaviour change a goal of development though agencies have been much slower to react: 'if a change of behaviour is sought it can only be achieved through painstakingly engaging the emotions of an audience, and then empowering individuals to make decisions for themselves'.[12] This type of process is part of the 'inconvenience' of culture in development articulated by Gould and Marsh. Therefore development agencies that take hold of the notion of behaviour change look for a way of making the concept manageable within their existing structures. One way of doing this is to isolate behaviour in relation to a particular issue rather than seeing it as part of the whole cultural nexus of a given society. Consequently a TfD practitioner may find herself employed on a project using theatre to raise awareness of how HIV/AIDS spreads. A participant-centred, story-based approach may reveal how the transmission of the disease is intimately related to questions around gender and power in that community but the project will lack the scope and resources to delve into the implications over a protracted period.

> The main problem with the focus on behaviours is that the majority do not occur in isolation; they occur as a result of social and cultural interactions. If development activities are to demonstrate 'change'

in general and 'behaviour change' in particular, it is imperative that development planners and practitioners recognise the extent of the influence of culture in the establishment and expression of behaviours. It is time for the importance of culture as a foundation of behaviour to be acknowledged, and for culture to provide the basis for the 'change' objectives of development.[13]

People are awkward, cantankerous creatures; persistent in their diversity; absurd in their beliefs; dogged beyond reason in their passions. The economists and politicians of development would have them predictable and pliable to the log-frames and intentions of planning. If people cannot fit into the system, they must be coerced or persuaded to alter their behaviour until they do. Before despair takes hold the Indian environmental activist, Vandana Shiva, reminds us that there are voices even in the inner sanctum of economics who understand the folly of the exclusively instrumentalist approach:

> Nobel prize-winning economists Joseph Stiglitz and Amartya Sen have admitted that GDP [*Gross Domestic Product*] does not capture the human condition, and have urged the creation of different tools to gauge the wellbeing of nations. We need to create measures beyond GDP, and economies beyond the global supermarket, to rejuvenate real wealth. We need to remember that the real currency of life is life itself.[14]

## Familiar dangers

In view of the ubiquitous grip of the neo-liberal model of capitalism on all areas of human activity in almost every part of the globe, it is necessary for TfD practitioners to work out strategies with workshop participants to enable critical consciousness of this situation to inform but not control the operation of that workshop. The notion of hegemony – leadership and control of a society through the presentation and manipulation of ideas rather than by coercion – is as old as language-based societies. However, it was Marx, writing in

*The German Ideology,* who gave the concept its specific political edge for modern times:

> The ideas of the ruling class are in every epoch the ruling ideas: i.e. the class which is the ruling *material* force of society, is at the same time its ruling *intellectual* force. The class which has the means of material production at its disposal, has control at the same time over the means of mental production, so that thereby, generally speaking, the ideas of those who lack the means of mental production are subject to it. The ruling ideas are nothing more than the ideal expression of the dominant material relationships grasped as ideas; hence of the relationships which make the one class the ruling one, therefore, the ideas of its dominance. The individuals composing the ruling class possess among other things consciousness and therefore think. Insofar, therefore, as they rule as a class and determine the extent and compass of an epoch, it is self-evident that they do this in its whole range, hence among other things rule also as thinkers, as producers of ideas, and regulate the production and distribution of the ideas of their age: thus their ideas are the ruling ideas of the epoch.[15]

The force of this argument, articulated by Marx in the mid-nineteenth century, by the twenty-first has become overwhelming. While the production of ideas may, essentially, be as it was then, the distribution of them has changed out of all recognition. The invention of the internet and satellite technologies has enabled instant, global distribution. While it may be argued that access to distribution means that ideas other than the ruling ones may also be disseminated widely, in practice the control of the mass media and the technologies of surveillance ensure that the grip of the dominant goes largely unchallenged. In recent times there are two particular phenomena which give an especially monolithic quality to the appearance of hegemony. One is the 'end of history' trope which, since the demise of state communism, sees 'the triumph of capitalism' as an indication that there is only one political ideology current in all societies. The other stems from the ease and immediacy of access to a bewildering quantity of information, resulting in 'information overload'. The effect of the latter is to swamp consciousness, leaving the victim trying to 'know' so much that she can understand almost nothing. From the rulers' perspective this is an ideal state since it robs citizens of any capacity for critical consciousness.

Habitual, daily exposure to the same set of ideas renders them 'normal' and their acceptance and rearticulation becomes 'common sense'. Consider, for example, the myriad ways in which business has taken over the airwaves in the last 50 years. Whereas stock market values, dividends and company profits were once the province of the financial pages of a few broadsheet newspapers, today they can feature as the first item on broadcast television and radio bulletins. The pronouncements of a new phenomenon, the credit rating agency, are given pride of place without any interrogation of who these people are and whose interests they represent. Predictably their measures of the 'success' and 'failure' of whole nations are based solely on the usual neo-liberal criteria: a shrunken public sector; dividends to shareholders and the all-powerful GDP. This wisdom is disseminated worldwide through the touch of a button as 'breaking news', free of debate or critical intervention of any kind.

Bertolt Brecht developed his *Verfremdungseffekte* as part of his strategy for evoking a state of critical consciousness in his spectators. It was the aesthetic choices made at his typewriter and in the rehearsal room which enabled him to present a social situation which appeared on the surface to be normal as extraordinary in order that it would be inspected for its underlying reality. He refers constantly to 'Aristotelian' theatre as the opposite of his own 'epic' theatre and the fundamental distinction is between an aesthetic which deals in surface appearance as reality, for instance naturalism, and his aesthetic of realism which is concerned to uncover the hegemonic surface to reveal the contradictions beneath. In his Appendix to the 'Short Description of a New Technique of Acting which Produces an Alienation Effect' Brecht wrote:

> The A-effect consists in turning the object of which one is to be made aware, to which one's attention is to be drawn, from something

ordinary, familiar, immediately accessible, into something peculiar, striking and unexpected. What is obvious is in a certain sense made incomprehensible, but this is only in order that it may then be made all the easier to comprehend. Before familiarity can turn into awareness the familiar must be stripped of its inconspicuousness; we must give up assuming that the object in question needs no explanation. However frequently recurrent, modest, vulgar it may be it will now be labelled as something unusual.[16]

This process refers both to the manner in which the moment is structured on the page or, in the case of a TfD workshop, the scenario is developed with the participants, and to the way in which the actor confronts the situation in performance:

> To transform himself from general passive acceptance to a correspond-ing state of suspicious inquiry he would need to develop that detached eye with which the great Galileo observed a swinging chandelier. He was amazed by this pendulum motion, as if he had not expected it and could not understand its occurring, and this enabled him to come on the rules by which it was governed. Here is the outlook, disconcerting but fruitful, which the theatre must provoke with its representations of human social life. It must amaze its public, and this can be achieved by a technique of alienating the familiar.[17]

An example of structuring a whole play according to the aesthetics of counter-hegemony is provided by *The Good Person of Szechwan* (Brecht 1994).[18] In order to provoke an awareness of the ironies and contradictions between bourgeois notions of goodness and capitalist notions of success in business Brecht creates the 'double' character of Shen Te/Shui Ta. This non-naturalistic device enables him to make both morality and business 'strange' to the audience while simultaneously exploring the dialectical relationship between both concepts for Shen Te produces Shui Ta and is produced by him. Rather than offering a simplistic agitprop piece about the villainies of capitalism, Brecht has adopted an aesthetic that allows him to require audiences to confront contradictions at the heart of the deep structure of their society. Brecht's theatre aesthetic anticipates Paulo Freire's pedagogic aesthetic of 'codification'. This is the system by which learners are encouraged to organize key themes around images, ideas, words, etc. which have the effect of opening up the structures of oppression for discussion, analysis and, following a phase of praxis, action. A common element with both Brecht and Freire is the notion of distance, the 'detached eye', that enables learners or TfD workshop participants to explore their lives with both the emotional integrity of lived experience and the critical analysis necessary for understanding that experience in relation to the governing forces of their society. Codification works much like *Verfremdung* as a counter-hegemonic strategy for 'defamiliarising' a world which the rulers would have us accept at face value:

> By understanding the codification's 'deep structure' the learner can then understand the dialectic which exists between the categories presented in the 'surface structure' as well as the unity between the 'surface' and 'deep' structures.[19]

## Fooling as facilitation

We can, however, look back beyond the twentieth century for theatrical models for creating critical consciousness in audiences. As I've argued elsewhere[20] the fool has a long history of offering alternative perspectives upon the stage action in order that the playwright can expose the characters to the ironies and contradictions lurking in the deeper layers of the worlds they inhabit. Here let one example from the early modern period suffice to illustrate the point. In Shakespeare's *King Lear*, the central relationship at the heart of that play is that between King Lear and his Fool. If we take the Fool out of consideration, we are left with a play about a protagonist whose resignation from office unleashes a tide of political violence that sweeps away his family and his wits, leaving him to die, broken and mad. The Fool, however, as Lear's antagonist, offers a critical commentary which frames the action of the play within a broader set of discourses around hierarchy, rule, folly and finally the nature of man(un)kind. In relation to the practice of TfD the Fool acts as a semi-detached facilitator, 'pointing' the action in order to stimulate the critical consciousness of the audience. He is able to undertake this role because he is 'all-licensed': that is, he has a special dispensation from the monarch to interpret the world just as he sees it. He is, in fact, the embodiment of counter-hegemony; a venerable ancestor of the TfD facilitator. When Lear starts to experience the breakdown of conventional relations between father and daughter, king and subjects, he asks: 'Who is it that can tell me who I am?' (I,4,229). The Fool immediately supplies the answer: 'Lear's shadow' (I, 4, 230). Typically for the utterances of folly, the answer operates on many levels. In terms of the playhouse 'shadow' was the common word for actor. The one who can reveal Lear's identity is the actor who plays his role. Without an actor the character is silent. In drawing attention to the split between character and actor, however, the Fool is also opening up the whole discourse of kingship that so preoccupied the age. Lear is starting to be made aware of his vulnerability as an ordinary mortal. The monarch as a function or role is immortal: like the character upon the page it goes on forever. But the particular person who dons the costume is subject to the laws of time and chance. Paradoxically that immortal presence can only exist through the mortal performance of the actor. In this way the Fool launches an investigation into the limits and contradictions of Tudor Absolutism.

The way in which Balwant Gargi describes the functions of the Vivek or Fool in that popular Bengali form of *jatra* is redolent of Shakespeare's presentation of both Lear and his Fool:

> When a character does something wrong, the Vivek turns up to warn him in song. If a king is doing an injustice, the Vivek suddenly appears to check him. Dressed like a madman – his eyes glazed, his head and feet bare, his beard tangled – he wears a robe of black, saffron, or white. His movements are sharp and conclusive. He enters the gangway on the run and disappears in the same way. The Vivek has a definite dramatic

function. He comments on the action by his song, externalizes the feeling of the character, plays his double and puts questions to him. He is everybody's shadow, a running commentary on actions and events. He lives in the past, present and future.[21]

As a description of Lear's Fool this is uncanny; not only the synchronizing of functions but also the devices of song and playing with time. In discrete, popular cultures from distant continents the same need is identified for a figure who supplies critical consciousness as a means of countering the injustices of the powerful.

The person who 'shadows' Lear throughout the play is the Fool, and it is he who persistently attempts to tell Lear who he is. One of the journeys Lear undergoes through the play is that from king to fool. In other words he becomes his own fool, marked by that actor's disappearance from the play. The protagonist becomes his own antagonist. The facilitator has been made redundant due to the awareness of the participant. The moment of the Fool's departure is signalled by counter-hegemony's triumph of inversion:

*Lear:* We'll got to supper I' th' morning.
*Fool:* And I'll go to bed at noon. (III, 6, 84–5)

At noon no shadows are cast. Lear will cast no shadow having both absorbed folly into his persona and entirely divested himself of his role. In one of his songs the Fool, in a reprise of Feste's epilogue to *Twelfth Night*, reminds us of the imperfect, fallen state of the world: 'Though the rain it raineth every day' (III, 2, 77). The Fool, like the TfD facilitator, reminds the audience/participants that whatever society they wish for or attempt to create must take account of the realities of both human and other nature.

Brecht took up this notion of the Fool as commentator and antagonist in *The Caucasian Chalk Circle* where, in the original production he directed with the Berliner Ensemble, he cast Ernst Busch as both Azdak, the Fool, and as the Singer. Not only is there a foolish frame around the story which recounts the 'foolish' action of Grusha in adopting a royal baby and of Azdak in harbouring the fugitive Grand Duke, but there is also a playful device whereby the commentator's actions can be commentated upon for both the onstage (participants in a TfD workshop) and offstage audience. Brecht's own note on the casting of Azdak reveals his understanding of Azdak's line of theatrical descent, as well as a possible autobiographical confession:

> It is essential to have an actor who can portray an utterly upright man. Azdak is utterly upright, a disappointed revolutionary posing as a human wreck, like Shakespeare's wise men who act the fool. Without this the judgement of the chalk circle would lose all its authority.[22]

Transposed into the contemporary world of TfD, *The Caucasian Chalk Circle* can be read as a scripted play in the form of a development project. The issue to be analysed through theatre is the appropriate allocation of land by ancient right or by current productivity. The Singer as facilitator uses dramatized story as the means of organizing the analysis. The play is then offered to the community for discussion and to assist with the decision it has to make about the use to which the valley will be put, even though that decision is heavily influenced by a facilitator who has veered a long way towards intervention at the expense of participation. Brecht does, after all, give us a play, not a TfD workshop but, uncannily, it offers a partial model of what was to be developed some 30 years later. Lest the foolish facilitator be mistakenly thought of as the 'solution' to unjust societies, the Singer is careful to declare his limitations in the parting words of the play:

> And after this evening Azdak disappeared and was never seen again.
> But the people of Grusinia did not forget him and often remembered
> His time of Judgment as a brief
> Golden Age that was almost just.[23]

In the 'safe' space of the workshop right can triumph and justice become a reality but beyond that charmed circle 'the rain it raineth every day'.

## Facilitation as fooling

The desire to create a bridge between the performance and the world beyond the theatre was also a primary motive for Augusto Boal's creation of the Joker. Today this figure is invariably associated with the operations of Forum Theatre but Boal developed the concept much earlier in the 1960s as part of his formal theatre practice with the Arena Theatre in São Paulo. Following Brecht he was searching for methods that would cement a level of political engagement between performers and spectators: 'The first problem to be solved consists in the presentation within the same performance, both of the play and its analysis.'[24] Mady Schutzman's description of the functions of the Joker takes us straight back into the orbit of the combined figure of the Singer and Azdak:

> This Joker, *curinga*, in Portuguese, has a polyvalent role as director, master of ceremonies, interviewer, and exegete, representing the author who knows story, plot development, and outcome as no individual character can. Through all his various roles, the *curinga* was responsible for performing a commentary on the performance within the performance.[25]

Boal's concept for the Joker also took into consideration the need to offer that commentary beyond the performance in a manner which would appeal to the audience. In this respect Boal is adapting the time-honoured role of the fool who commutes between stage and auditorium even as the trickster in the founding myths of many cultures moved between the worlds of gods and men:

> We propose a 'Joker' who is a contemporary and neighbor of the spectator. For this it is necessary to restrict his 'explanations'; it is necessary to move him away from the other characters, to bring him close to the spectators.[26]

Here already, even before the moment when the 'spect-actor' emerged, Boal is contemplating how the action of the play can be mediated.

Furthermore, there is an aesthetics of mediation announced by the very name given to the function; the Joker. Besides connecting the figure to that ancient, crosscultural lineage of folly in the theatre and beyond, the title also announces the Joker as the wild card in the pack – the one who knows the rules of the game but also knows how and when to break them. As function rather than character she is both the most and the least powerful of the players: worth (as *King Lear* shows) as much as a king or worth nothing. Coming closer to the spectators in the manner advocated by Boal also raises cultural issues about the provenance of the particular person who takes on this function as part of the continuing debate about the relative merits of 'insiders' and 'outsiders' in the process. Mlama reflects on her experience of being in an 'external team':

> This is frequently the case in Africa, where the Popular Theatre workers are often expatriate or middle class theatre artists and university lecturers. It has been argued that the differences in class between these people and people at grassroot level prevents [*sic*] a meaningful realisation of the Popular Theatre goals. However, it should be noted that people from outside or within a community can play an effective role if they understand their role in Popular Theatre as being primarily that of animateur, facilitating critical analysis of issues; ensuring participation of all interest groups; broadening views where they are too narrow or restricted; facilitating discussion without imposing one person's ideas.[27]

In Brazil and more widely across Latin America CTO Rio has been running courses in the training of Jokers for some years. Bárbara Santos offers a comprehensive insight into the elements that underpin the training programmes:

> Like the Joker in a card game, the Joker in T.O. has multiple functions. The Joker should be able to participate as a performer, rehearse and stage Forum Theater, facilitate workshops and courses in T.O., write and/or co-ordinate the collective production of theatrical texts, conceive a

play's aesthetics and serve as master of ceremonies at a Forum session, stimulating dialogue between spect-actors and the audience.

The Joker in T.O. is an artist with pedagogic and political functions who helps people to understand themselves better, express their ideas and emotions, analyze their problems and seek their own alternatives to change or solve them. The Joker doesn't need to have answers but should be able to formulate questions that stimulate the suggestion of alternatives to each question presented during a Forum Theater play.

The Joker should be an expert in diversity, with multidisciplinary background and attitude, possessing knowledge of theater, popular culture, pedagogy, psychology, politics and as much else as possible. Beyond that, a Joker must have sensitivity, the ability to communicate with and coordinate groups, heightened perception, common sense, energy and the ability to synthesize.[28]

For all its ferocious inclusiveness, this list of functions and personality traits nevertheless masks a contradiction at the heart of the Joker function in Forum Theatre – that same contradiction which Mda has presented as a binary opposition between participation and intervention. If TfD is simply about securing the participation of neglected and 'oppressed' communities in a theatrical process, about the retelling of stories already known to the community as an act of celebration, it takes its place alongside the community play and other participatory forms and is essentially indistinguishable from them. The politics of social change is a fundamental element of TfD and in the Forum Theatre process today so beloved by TfD facilitators, the Joker is the custodian of an interventionist politics of social change grounded in the lived experience of the community. The TfD facilitator as Joker is the distinguishing feature that sets TfD apart from the other practices which huddle together under the applied theatre umbrella to shelter from the neo-liberal storm. If during the Forum Theatre process the Joker sees herself merely as the conduit for the fullest possible democratic participation between the play and its audience, this feature can become buried under the good intentions of inclusiveness. In his later reflections on his work in *The Aesthetics of the Oppressed* Boal is clearly conscious of the dichotomy, though he attempts to have his cake and eat it:

> It is true that the joker in a Forum Theatre session, for instance, must maintain his or her neutrality and try not to impose his or her own ideas. BUT *only after having his or her camp!* The Joker's neutrality is a responsible act and arises after having made a choice, after taking the side of the oppressed; the substance of the Joker is doubt, seed of all certainties; the end is discovery, not abstention.[29]

There is, therefore, a precondition to the job description and person specification that Santos sets for the Joker: namely, that a Joker must be someone who brings a counter-hegemonic understanding to the theatre practice. Neutrality, even supposing such a state is possible, is only neutrality within the sphere of what is fundamentally a Marxist frame. I am uneasy with the concept of neutrality even on these terms. It is commonplace to hear a facilitator described as a catalyst in TfD discourse. In chemistry a catalyst is a substance introduced among other substances in order to induce an interaction between those substances without, itself, undergoing a change or participating in that interaction. A facilitator who behaves like this with human participants is a dangerous practitioner. Facilitation requires a constant, dialectical flow between facilitator and participants. In any meaningful exchange of experience and understanding conducted as a dialogue both parties are engaged in a process of changing and being changed by that encounter. If only one party is open to the possibility of alteration, we are in the territory of the monolithic expert imparting higher level knowledge to those less intellectually gifted. The terms of the exchange need to be as equal as possible once the shared objectives (in Freire's term, 'co-intentionality') have been agreed. In setting those objectives the political position of the facilitator comes into play in dialogue with those of the community. The relationship between ideology and art is articulated with characteristic directness and purpose in the Philippine Educational Theater Association (PETA) workshop manual:

It is necessary for the facilitator to be socially aware and responsive and have an unequivocal viewpoint about the world and the society in which she lives. This viewpoint, manifest both in her art and in her judgment, should likewise be reflected in the sharing of ideas, comments, and suggestions as she helps out the participants in their theater games and production activities.

Social awareness, however, is not enough. The facilitator should have a working knowledge of play-writing, directing, acting, creative music, choreography, and designing to be able to develop the theater pieces that the participants will produce. Yet she should not forget for a moment that her aim is to help develop and not to do the work for the participants. If the facilitator does everything for the participants, neither skill nor knowledge is acquired. The skill of the facilitator as a mentor should be developed to encourage a learning process neither rote nor spoonfed but evocative.[30]

Given the very close links between popular theatre and TfD, particularly in Latin America, together with an underlying intimation that, were these terms to merge, TfD might regain some of the political edge surrendered through its accommodations with the catch-all of applied theatre, Liam Kane's assessment of the function of popular educators in Latin America carries a powerful charge for a reconsideration of what facilitation means in TfD contexts:

The educators' role thus differs from that of traditional teachers. Instead of being the experts and sole arbiters of right and wrong, they are aware of their limited understanding and of the need to inspire people to articulate their own view of the world. They need to have the ability to engage people in dialogue, ask challenging questions, provoke analysis, summarise and synthesise discussions, throw this back at participants for verification and further analysis – all backed up by a variety of appropriate pedagogical techniques (for which popular education has rightly become famous). It would be a mistake, however, to see the 'popular educator' as a mere 'facilitator', given the implied neutrality of this latter term. While they do fulfil some of the roles of a facilitator, popular educators are clearly more interventionist: though there is no predisposition to transmit a particular set of ideas, they start with an a priori political commitment to the organisation, have a clear idea of its main aims and objectives and in bearing the major responsibility for the eventual shape of the learning process, have a major influence over what is likely to be learned. As participants in a collective process, they also have a right to contribute their thoughts on the issue under discussion.[31]

These words can be transposed with very little adaptation into the discourses of TfD. It is interesting that Kane sees facilitation as the opposite of intervention, somewhat akin to describing the Joker as a master of ceremonies. It may be that the very word 'facilitator' is no longer suitable to describe the person(s) who animates a TfD process. The field has long been beset by contending terminologies and arid disputes over the territory indicated by a preference for a particular term over others, so I am loath to be a party to a request to create yet another. But in his introduction to Boal's *The Rainbow of Desire*, Adrian Jackson comes close to expressing a similar unease over the word:

> The joker's function is not that of facilitator, the joker is (in Boal-speak) a 'difficultator', undermining easy judgements, reinforcing our grasp of the complexity of a situation, but not letting that complexity get in the way of action or frighten us into submission or inactivity. Things aren't always what they seem, it says; let's try and do something about them.[32]

'Things' not being 'what they seem' takes us back to Brecht and links the joker with the counter-hegemonic aesthetics of *Verfremdung*. A core function of the Joker is to make the world of the participants 'strange' to them in order that they may view it with fresh eyes. In so doing they observe matters previously overlooked since hegemony works through absences: what areas of contemporary reality never arise in parliamentary debates? What are the unchallenged starting assumptions that ignore alternatives in the questions posed by broadcast journalists? The Joker provokes the participants into interrogating that which has previously gone unnoticed. The source of the problem with facilitation probably lies with its etymological root: *facile* means 'easy' and that which is facile is simplistic, unrealistic; its awkwardness mediated to smoothness. The Joker who draws her credentials from the line of folly is the opposite: jagged, uncompromising, with a Socratic nagging method designed to strip away illusion and false consciousness.

Faced with such an immense battery of responsibilities, we might ask what person in their right mind would take on this TfD business? Part of the answer may be that such a person would not be 'in their right mind' for a degree of madness is a key ingredient. Once more Brecht gives us a clue to a vital element in the make-up of the Joker, naivety. The capacity to be astonished by the familiar not only describes part of the Joker's persona, it also alludes to a capacity which she tries to develop in or transmit to the participants. Some late notes reflecting on his career indicate the centrality of the concept of the naïve in Brecht's work:

> My whole theory is much naïver than people think, or than my way of putting it allows them to suppose. Perhaps I can excuse myself by pointing to the case of Albert Einstein, who told the physicist Infeld that ever since boyhood he had merely reflected on the man running after a ray of light and the man shut in a descending lift. And think what complications that led to! I wanted to take the principle that it was not just a matter of interpreting the world but of changing it, and apply that to the theatre.[33]

In Brecht's mind his central, core concept of theatre for change (TfD before the phrase had been coined) was intimately bound up with a disposition to naivety. The naïve are the repository of that critical consciousness that is the prerequisite for change. Peter Brooker has highlighted the centrality of naivety in the development of Brecht's *oeuvre*:

> The 'naive' therefore fittingly joined together contraries; it was a look, a posture, an attitude of mind; it implied an intelligent simplicity, innocence and shrewdness, joining the conceptual and concrete, the

popular and philosophical. A naive attitude would estrange the familiar, and problematize the self-evident, signalling a dialectical movement from the ordinary and everyday to the original and innovatory. It was thus, in short, a summary gest of Brecht's transformative, utopian perspective upon art and life.[34]

## Only connect

Many of the qualities listed here are also closely associated with clowning, in particular the jumping from one level of reality to another, seemingly discrete but actually connected one. This question of making connections is especially pertinent for TfD where one aspect of the practice concerns methods of connecting the macro politics of development with the micro stories of grassroots communities. The connector in this process is the Joker. It's not possible to facilitate a TfD process without an understanding of what development is and how it operates, any more than a prison theatre practitioner can work without some knowledge of the prison system or a TIE company without experience of the organization of a school. As a result of globalization we now live in a highly connected world where decisions taken in the airconditioned offices of New York, London or Beijing impact directly and quickly upon the lives of rural labourers in sub-Saharan Africa or South-East Asia.

It is very rare for the actions and words of those at the grassroots to affect the policy and decisions of those who are elected to represent them. Such is the lack of connection between the political class and the mass of the population that increasingly questions are being asked about the viability of the nation state maintained on the present scale. For the moment, however, it is part of the business of facilitating a TfD process to support a community in its analysis of what it can do for itself and where it is being thwarted by systems beyond its control. TfD is the process of enabling communities to explore the barriers to their self-development, be these internal or external. For instance, today almost all 'developing' countries seek to alleviate their dire economic circumstances, themselves often caused by the rigged structures of the World Trade Organisation, by begging for loans from the IMF or the World Bank. These loans are forthcoming on condition that the country signs up to the usual neo-liberal prescription of stimulating economic growth by cutting government spending on public services, redirecting subsistence agriculture towards cash crops for export and providing large incentives to foreign transnational corporations. Typically those communities with whom a TfD facilitator/Joker will be working do not experience any benefit from these loans. Instead they discover that their previous entitlement to free primary education has disappeared or, if that education is technically 'free', it now comes with a requirement to pay for a uniform, books and materials which puts it out of the reach of ordinary members of that community. In this scenario it is girls especially who become the casualties with families only able or willing to send boys to school. The physical environment might also be the victim with forests cleared to make space for growing cash crops. This process leaves women with long journeys to collect firewood, too little time for other tasks in the home, thus rendering them vulnerable to domestic abuse. At this point a TfD workshop to tackle domestic abuse is proposed.

If the facilitator lacks awareness of the macro-structures of development, she will tend to isolate abuse as a problem local to that community and confine her explorations to the stories which are directly related to abuse. A broader knowledge, together with a *penchant* for the counter-hegemonic, is needed to trace some of the causes of the abuse back to their sources at national and international levels. In this example there is often a further problem when the workshop only has the victims of the abuse as participants. It is all too common, especially on the Indian subcontinent, to come across all-women programmes designed to raise awareness of female rights around issues related to domestic abuse. If the workshop is well-run, those who have participated experience a raising of their confidence, a willingness to speak out, a sense of empowerment. These outcomes are splendid in the 'safe' space of the workshop but, if there has been no corresponding process with the abusers whom the NGO probably finds much harder to engage in a TfD workshop, these women will return to the 'real' world context of their abuse where nothing has changed with regard to the source of the abuse. In all likelihood they may be more vulnerable to abuse now because they are inclined to speak out against it. This type of scenario is not unrelated to the dominant aesthetic mode of TfD, Forum Theatre. In Forum Theatre as with so much applied theatre activity, the focus is on the victims of domestic, social or political injustice. The Forum actors present an instance of an oppression to the audience which they then replay in order that members of that audience can transform themselves into spect-actors by intervening in the action to alleviate, resolve or overturn the oppression. According to the rules of Forum Theatre as administered by CTO Rio, it is only the oppressed person who can be replaced by the spect-actor. Besides limiting the problem-solving creativity of the audience to a single character's perspective, this restriction also puts all the responsibility for solving the oppressive impasse onto the hardpressed victim of the oppression. Conveniently the perpetrator(s) of the situation is absolved from such demands and carries on with their oppressive behaviour. As in the domestic abuse example above, those with the power to change a given situation are the ones being left out of the transformative process. As long as the oppressor – husband, policeman, IMF – is excluded and the 'other' disengaged from the dialogue, the oppressed can carry on rehearsing the revolution and repeating the age-old vicious circles of power until the crack of doom. A truly radical TfD is one which opens up spaces for dialogues with the oppressors on both the micro and macro scales. Here the playful figure of the Joker is central, for her function is to find the play in any situation; by this I understand all three meanings of play: the play which rehearses and transforms experience into alternative modes of being; child's play where participants are helped back into contact with those instincts for playing typically suppressed in adulthood; and finally, perhaps most importantly, play in the sense of the movement, the flexibility in all living things. Systems are about fixing people into rigid positions; nailing them down through labels like bluecollar worker, banker, ethnic minority person. Jokers are about unfixing people, concepts, built environments so that new capacities emerge, real identities are created and the imagination can discover new configurations. Just as the trickster was a shape-shifter (Christ risen from the dead), so the Joker plays with notions of fixity to change the shape in which the oppression is presented in order that it may suddenly become amenable to alteration. However monolithic the system may appear – state communism, global neoliberalism – the Joker is trained to find the play, and, finding it, to shake that system until it settles into a more people-centred shape.

## Hitting the target

This question of changing the shape of the oppression encompasses a further critical element in the total TfD process, the target audience. Theatre is a process of communication between actors and audiences. The quality of that communication determines what and how the audience understands what is emanating from the performance space. Where a workshop or project is only intended for participants without an audience dimension, this is drama, not theatre. Those embarking upon a TfD programme need to be clear about the destination of the work and if a theatrical communication to an audience beyond the participants is intended, those participants must be equipped with the necessary skills in the manner stressed by the PETA workshop method. TfD diverges from mainstream, formal theatre not in having an audience but rather in having a target audience. Whereas formal theatre is usually attended by a more or less random cross-section of people, bound only by the willingness and ability to purchase a ticket, TfD seeks a specific audience which those involved in the production determine need to be exposed to the matter of the performance. In this scheme the process moves from the workshop phase into the production phase and a key question before the production can be embarked upon is: who constitutes the appropriate audience for what is about to be developed? Too often this is a neglected area of the process, resulting in a performance to whoever has the time or inclination to show up; usually other members of the community from which the participants derive. This often results in an audience being presented with images and actions with which it is already familiar. If that audience is large and a general community celebration ensues, the process is deemed uncritically to be a success. It is difficult to see what constitutes development in this instance for the audience is witnessing what it already knows. However, if the dramatized stories of the participants have revealed that the barriers to development in relation to a particular issue are located within the community, then a community audience is appropriate provided that those members associated with the problem are to be found in that audience and mechanisms are in place to hold them to account through open discussion and other follow-up actions.

In many instances, though, the location of the levers of change is outside the community from which the performance is generated. Part of the Joker's role is to help to identify where the greatest possibility for change lies and then to make sure that participants build into their process strategies for enabling the performance to evolve into a provocation for a dialogue between itself and the target audience. If the performance depicts an oppression or social injustice in action, the audience should comprise either those who need to be made aware of it because they have the power to remedy it, or those who are the oppression, or both. This targeting is one aspect of making connections between the micro and the macro. Given the ways in which power operates within systems it is highly unlikely that the ultimate source of the problem or oppression will be accessible to grass-roots participants or even to the Joker. However, a series of chain reactions might be set in motion in this way. For example, where members of the target audience complain that they are themselves the victims of oppression from further up the chain, the next phase of the TfD project would be to develop a performance with the target group to set in front of those higher up in the power chain, and so on for as long as it takes.

This is a long-term, ripple-effect cascade of engaging outwards from the epicentre of the issue with the Joker as the fluid element who can run up and down the ladder of causality in response to E. M. Forster's dictum in the epigraph to *Howards End*, 'only connect'.

The way in which that connection is made is intimately tied up with the counter-hegemonics of the Joker. If target audiences are made to feel like sitting targets with the actors using the privilege of performance to launch tirades of wet sponges at their defenceless faces, there will be no development. The audience may have been made uncomfortable but that discomfort will leave them wishing to escape the confrontation and return to their comfort zones of oppression as quickly as possible. Instead, the Joker proceeds obliquely, guiding the actors into the wiles of irony and paradox so that humour ingratiates the performance with its audience who only gradually discover that, having laughed, they are now laughing at themselves. The objective of the Joker is to bring the performance to the point where the audience is confronted with a contradiction so fierce, so blatant that something must be done and they are the ones who have to do it. Contradiction is the motor of social change but most contradictions are bubble-wrapped so thickly in hegemony that they are not apparent. The function of the Joker, orchestrating the actors, is to peel off the layers until the audience are in the unavoidable presence of that which requires them to change. Cultural anthropologist Lewis Hyde gives a similar key role to contradiction in loosening the fossilizing accretions of hegemony:

> Individuals who never sense the contradictions of their cultural inheritance run the risk of becoming little more than host bodies for stale gestures, metaphors, and received ideas, all the stereotypical likes and dislikes by which cultures perpetuate themselves.[35]

The Joker's role with both participants and audiences is to encourage and enable them to 'sense the contradictions' in their presently fixed positions in order that they can become susceptible to change. She is thus a walking, talking *Verfremdungseffekt* at the heart of a methodology which is about process, becoming and fluidity. It does not accept the binary of oppressors and oppressed but seeks out the contradictions in the situations of both so that all involved may be exposed to the dynamics of change. Political systems of all colours try to fix people into roles which serve that system even if such service may be at the expense of the person. As Lear observes: 'a dog's obeyed in office' (IV.6.159). While those who participate in a TfD project may have revolutionary intent, the desire to replace one system with another, the process itself is concerned with unfixing all systems, providing a liminal space in which all social organizations may be re-examined.

I was recently privileged to be invited to co-facilitate a workshop to train members of 'O Movimento dos Trabalhadores Rurais Sem Terra' (MST) to act as animateurs with children and adults in their settlement communities. This was one of those all too rare moments when a TfD process is allied to an organization with the capacity and will to sustain and take forward the initial insights opened up by the brief moment of the workshop. An atmosphere of play, dance and physical freedom was created from the outset by using Brazilian musicians to launch each day's work, together with traditional songs that served as reminders of the cultural heritage that all the participants carried within them. The subgroups of participants built up stories from individual life-maps before selecting or amalgamating them into short performance scenarios. The context of the workshop meant that we were lucky to be working with a group with a well-developed critical consciousness and a sophisticated understanding of Freirean pedagogy. This resulted in the pieces being put together with mostly just technical, theatrical input from the facilitators since there was an uneven practical experience of theatre from group to group. When each group presented their scenes to the others there was an appreciative sharing of the way in which the stories and images revealed important realities in their lives; be these personal – separation from family members who joined the urban migration in search of a livelihood – or more sociopolitical – deforestation by illegal gangs. At this point I asked the audience whether they had seen anything here that they did not already know. They had not. I suggested that there was little purpose in their presentations, however adept, since no new element had been introduced which might bring about any change in the prevailing conditions. I encouraged them, or perhaps rather demanded, there being only a few working hours left for this phase of the workshop, that they return the following day with their scenes restructured so that they presented the audience with a contradiction. Remarkably most of the represented scenes did just that. The deforestation play now concerned the contradiction between environmental protection and earning a living. The migration play explored the social conditions which made the break-up of families inevitable. The audience mood had gone from the celebratory to the thoughtful. We had not had any time to attach this journey from propaganda to contradiction to the workings of a Joker who could have guided the audience/participants towards the next challenge that their TfD could face. However, my co-facilitator, Marcia Pompeo, is engaged in a much longer process with the MST training groups which will encompass this aspect. Propaganda is the material, concrete and ideological, with which we are already familiar. It is the position where we are secure, knowing who are friends, who enemies. It contains our creed, our allegiances, our habits of mind. Contradiction is a much less familiar land where nothing is as it first appears, where what is taken for granted is taken away, where negotiation with the strange other replaces a cosy chat with the self.

In his notes to *The Threepenny Opera* Brecht coins the phrase 'complex seeing' as a way to articulate the type of response required of both playwright and audience:

> But this way of subordinating everything to a single idea, this passion for propelling the spectator along a single track where he [*sic*] can look neither right nor left, up nor down, is something that the new school of play-writing must reject. Footnotes, and the habit of turning back in order to check a point, need to be introduced into play-writing too.

> Some exercise in complex seeing is needed – though it is perhaps more important to be able to think above the stream than to think in the stream.[36]

Transposed from the aesthetics of the theatre text to the more improvisational ones of TfD, the task of turning back and providing footnotes falls to the Joker. Like fools before her, she inhabits that twilight space between actors and spectators, functioning as the lubricant in the dialectic that produces a response in the audience to the provocations of the performance which in turn produces an altered response in the action. Boal's concept of the spect-actor is one concrete manifestation of this dialectical call and response but not the only one. Complex seeing is the enemy of hegemony. Ironically, in view of his intentions, Boal's Theatre of the Oppressed in general, and Forum Theatre in particular, has exerted a hegemonic grip on TfD which often results in practitioners resorting unthinkingly to the default mode of Forum Theatre regardless of the specifics of the context in which they are operating. If a Joker is doing her job properly, no set of theatrical aesthetics and no set of human relations should exert hegemony for long.

## The joke of contradiction

Increasingly towards the end of his life Brecht ceased to talk of his theatre as epic and, instead, described it as dialectical. His analyses drew attention to the manner in which a contradiction in a given character or social depiction was produced dialectically. Thus Shui Ta is not the opposite of Shen Te but is rather produced by Shen Te as a necessary but not inevitable response to a specific set of circumstances. The contradiction lurking within, like the grit in the oyster, emerges recast as the next set of possibilities. The water in which this oyster swims is irony so the pearl, though produced by the oyster, is able to set itself in an ironic relationship to its progenitor. This is the process and tone which Brecht attempts to capture in his Appendices to the *Short Organum*:

> The theatre of the scientific age is in a position to make dialectics into a source of enjoyment. The unexpectedness of logically progressive or

zigzag development, the instability of every circumstance, the joke of contradiction and so forth: all these are ways of enjoying the liveliness of men, things and processes, and they heighten both our capacity for life and our pleasure in it.

Every art contributes to the greatest art of all, the art of living.[37]

The art of TfD is best captured in that phrase, 'the joke of contradiction'. Contradiction alludes to the primary structural principle for its processes and 'joke' to the manner or aesthetic within which that structure is set. Above all TfD is a process without end. The binary of process against product is redundant here for the process produces the performance which itself is the means, the research method, by which the next phase of the process emerges and so on *ad infinitum*. It is no more and no less than the means by which art can enhance the experience of living and, as such, should not be denied to any sector of the population.

Part Two

# Case Studies

# Capacity Building Theatre
## (and *Vice Versa*)

John O'Toole, Au Yi-Man, Andrea Baldwin,
Helen Cahill and Kennedy Chinyowa

This chapter explores the educational connections of Theatre for Development (TfD) and how the capacities to create, structure and manage the artistic forms and apply them in their contexts are generated. The chapter starts with a review of some of the main themes and trends within the field in thinking about education and capacity building. The second, longest section provides case study evidence of some of what is happening. Since the contexts of TfD are so varied geographically, culturally and socially – as the previous chapters have demonstrated – instead of using one case study, we are using four to identify, examine and compare them, looking at the commonalities and a few of the divergences in what are widely used approaches to education and training for TfD. A common thread to provide some measure of coherence and comparability is that, to a degree, all the case studies are concerned with consciousness-raising about HIV-AIDS. In all of these case studies the researcher and writer is a participant-researcher, involved in a leadership capacity in their project. All have been asked to identify the main aspects of their project that relate to building capacity of the participants and leaders, and to identify the challenges as well as the progress and successes of the projects.

The third section analyses some of the main convergences and divergences of these four projects, comparing their approaches to capacity building and identifying some of their successes and challenges.

# Section 1: The educational landscape

## Background

In the 40 years or so since TfD began to cohere both as a generally accepted term and as a movement, some notion of education has been deeply embedded in it, and educational training structures and institutions have usually framed it. TfD has had strong roots from the start in universities, such as Makerere (Uganda) and Nairobi (Kenya) where for more than a generation intellectual playwrights like Ngugi wa Thiongo and Ngugi wa Mirii[1] (*I will Marry When I Want* 1977), directors like Opiyo Mumma[2] and theatre studies experts like Patrick Mangeni[3] (*A Theatrical Alternative for Child Survival* 1996; *One Earth One Family: Drama and Environmental Education* 2001) have turned their minds and hands to using their art form, as all the titles suggest, to create some form of change and transformation – to educate. The same is true of TfD's more recent close relative, applied theatre. Like many useful inventions, this term and movement emerged or gelled around the same time independently in a number of places, notably the two University Centres established the same year (1992) in England (Manchester) and Australia (Griffith in Brisbane), both tertiary institutions with strong educational establishment.

Drama-in-education or educational drama, one of the antecedents of applied theatre and another close relative of TfD, has been solidly anchored in traditions of school pre-service and in-service education, delivered mainly through education colleges and faculties. The Big Idea behind drama-in-education is that it exists not just to teach students about drama and how to do it, but that drama itself has a pedagogical, transformative or dialogical purpose and effect – therefore in both broad and narrow senses is educational. This Idea, in that traditional setting, carries the corollary that it requires some kind of specialized training or teacher-education to do it. The confluence of drama-in-education and TfD has also over the years led to many university-generated projects, such as South Africa's Dramaide outreach project, that initially used an innovative but not always fully integrated mix of drama graduates and nurses.

Not all TfD has had such an intellectual pedigree. The Philippines Educational Theatre Association[4] used the child scrap pickers on Manila's garbage mountain as performers, not only to give the children themselves a sense of pride, but also to vividly portray to its adult audiences the social injustice. Kenyan Victor Nyangore[5] chose and persuaded the mothers and grandmothers in his village to co-create and perform a play aimed at changing their village's culturally sanctioned practices concerning water and sanitation, where strangers would have been ignored. Wa Thiongo and wa Miri had untrained villagers performing their play in the local community education centre.

However, especially in the early days, NGOs looked to a more obviously professional source of theatre-making to transmit their messages about health, sanitation, the environment, social justice and democracy (didactic communication was in those early days the dominant purpose in their using theatre); they tended to turn either to established theatre companies, or to acting academies, and ask them to put together a bunch of actors to take to the road. A kind of Boy Scouts bravura sometimes accompanied these early initiatives, such as the early efforts of the now long-established Natya Chetana theatre commune in Orissa, India: 'Messengers on bicycles: pedalling cultural awareness . . .'[6] The assumption seemed to be that professional actors should be up to the job, as they were trained for it – though in fact the professional stages and theatre audiences they were trained for were often far removed from the rural village or urban favela they were heading into.

Over the years, there has been a long-standing debate (not only within the arts) about the relative appropriateness of the terms 'education' and 'training' to describe adult professional learning contexts. In theatre/drama contexts, this has been a lively dispute between those who primarily 'train' dramatic artists and those who primarily 'educate' teachers.[7] In economically developed countries the tensions between these two visions have over the years often been manifest in the field of Theatre for Young Audiences. Young people's work usually has lower status and funding than 'adult' work and often involves touring away from custom-built theatres. The mix of artists working either in its purely performative forms or in the more interactive genre of theatre-in-education has, from my own observation over many years, tended to be young and energetic, not always experienced and not always fully dedicated either to young people or to community-based work. Those tensions and that territorial pedantry have been thoroughly problematized by the arrival of applied theatre, and the global proliferation of tertiary courses in it; not wholly however, as these courses are roughly split between theatre/arts and education faculties, where the old divisions are sometimes still spiritedly maintained. What has emerged is a much better-formed concept of dedicated theatre workers recognizing this kind of theatre-outside-conventional-theatres as a worthy career path and lifelong endeavour (significantly, most of the applied theatre courses are at masters level).

## Capacity building

Since then, a new terminological buzzword has appeared in TfD, adopted from the development and NGO contexts where it has been current for much longer: 'capacity building'. The new demands that this term implies match well the changes that have happened to TfD.

Over the years our understanding of the needs, demands and constraints of TfD work has changed, at least in the field, and rather more slowly in the NGOs themselves. The imposed one-way transmission of messages and fly-in-fly-out propaganda has become discredited though it is still practised.[8] The problems and dangers of not being part of and not fully understanding and responding to the local context have been – and still are – vividly highlighted in the literature.[9] In the mid-1990s, Dramaide exemplified the bridge from the old approach to a new one. They had a message play to deliver about the dangers of HIV/AIDS, but realizing that a Zulu adult audience would be culturally resistant to strangers preaching at them to change their sexual habits, they targeted the schools with it, then workshopped with the more impressionable child audiences performative ways the children might be able to get that same message over to their parents.[10]

Message-based TfD has nowadays been replaced with a more dialogical vision, where communities consult with NGOs about their needs, and theatre workers are brought in, often on a longer term basis, to generate projects and programmes that respond to the need. The theatre workers most often use the increasingly popular dialogical and interactive theatre techniques such as forum theatre and process drama, and often employ local performance forms.[11]

Nine years ago, the writer of one of the case studies that illustrate this chapter, Au Yi-Man, was introducing fieldworkers of an international NGO in China to applied theatre techniques. She found that they were all expected to attend or have attended 'capacity-building' courses – of which hers was one, but not one of their basic training courses. They had diverse backgrounds, some with master's degrees, some with little educational experience. There were no specific requirements for her course, but she began to wonder not only what 'capacities' needed to be 'built' in order to create effective NGO applied theatre workers, but also what they brought to the training themselves – and more particularly did not bring (though she was careful not to fall into 'deficit' thinking – what Ira Shor[12] calls a 'zero-paradigm'). Naturally they needed knowledge, skills and understanding in applied theatre – that was what they had come for, and they brought differing levels of familiarity with some form of drama, even some applied theatre. She also began to notice several other significant factors: that they brought differing levels of confidence, status and experience in their working contexts; that they generally expected they were there to be 'filled' with new knowledge and skills by the teacher transmitting it, much of it through teacher-talk; they tended to be strongly dependent on the teacher as a figure of authority and the sole purveyor of knowledge; and they believed that this knowledge would be in and of itself sufficient.

Of all these she was most struck by the last: what appeared to her to be a distinct deficit of capacity in the fieldworkers to reflect critically on their teaching or their learning, as would be expected in some Western settings with which she was familiar. Dialogical teaching and reflective practice were unfamiliar to the participants from their own education and training, and sometimes quite alien concepts – the Confucian tradition of the pupil sitting at the feet of the master was still strong for them.

She shared these reflections with me, and over the next few years we shared and discussed them with other experienced drama and applied theatre educators, some of whom were familiar with Chinese and South East Asian contexts. From these discussions, a matrix of two intersecting dimensions or axes emerged, which we use briefly in this chapter to analyse the four case studies, and which Yi-Man is using in depth to analyse her ongoing work with NGO capacity building in China.

To amplify the model:

## Axis 1: Levels of capacity

We think one can usefully categorize practitioners' levels of capacity in applied theatre, with its implications for training. This axis is not a continuum, but falls fairly naturally into five distinct levels, separated by barriers where trainees/workers/leaders seem to need some aid or spur to get them over the hurdle and up to the next level. Most people seem to pass through these levels in this order (and many starters don't get beyond levels two or three).

The first level is *Readiness*. Even to make a start, workers in TfD must have an openness to experiencing and experimenting not only with a dynamic art form but with a new pedagogy; a willingness to encounter disruptions to their expectations and familiarity. In many cases too, they must be ready to shed some assumptions relating to their prior experience or understanding of drama and theatre. Once those conditions of readiness are met, the first hurdle requirement entails an active willingness to engage in an ensemble in the teaching setting, to manage emotions, techniques of empathy and reflective distancing, and to teach or be taught dialogically.

The second level is *Experience* (direct and personal). It is difficult if not impossible for practitioners to understand fully any form of participatory theatre, appreciate its potency or manage their own clients effectively in it, unless they have undergone the dramatic experience themselves – the particular aesthetic combination of embodied learning, emotional engagement, cognitive reasoning and reflection. On occasion, these two first levels may be simultaneous or even reversed, where the first encounter with participatory theatre is through an unexpected and unprepared-for experience, that must then be processed and reflected upon to generate the desire and impetus to continue. The hurdle requirements to get beyond those preliminary requirements are sufficient confidence and enough basic skill to extrapolate from the experience and implement the next stage themselves.

The third level is *Adoption*. At this level the practitioners apply within their own practice the new structures, strategies and techniques that they have experienced, and become used to managing the pedagogy in their own familiar context. Here there is often a major barrier to further progress. It takes time, practice, considerable embedding of the understanding, a sophisticated ability, and a further leap of confidence to move beyond this phase towards autonomy.

The fourth level of prowess we have labelled *Ownership*. Practitioners at this level have acquired the ability to take the structures, strategies and techniques and modify and re-create them in both familiar and new learning contexts. This stage not only demands increased control of the medium, but the ability to cope with trial and error, and to reflect on and learn from their errors rather than be deterred by them. To get beyond this stage, workers must not only be able to demonstrate in a diversity of contexts their autonomy as reflective learners and teachers, but must also have the opportunity to demonstrate the top level, their *Mastery*. This is where practitioners become leaders, with the ability to take on the task of engaging and instructing others, playing a mature part in the developing praxis and scholarship, and creating networks of support. So there is also in this level an element of logistical opportunity (sometimes opportunism): the ability to identify potential TfD contexts where applied theatre skills and structures could be valuable, and work within those contexts to make it happen.

Along with these levels, we have identified another dimension of the *kinds* of knowledge which are necessary, and/or which can occur in applied theatre training. There's more to it than just knowledge of applied theatre techniques, and in some settings the most urgent need may be to develop an ability to reflect, or to teach dialogically, or to have a personal level of public self-confidence, any of which may be untypical in terms of the trainees' own education and culture.

## Axis 2: Kinds of knowledge

Obviously the first necessary knowledge base is *applied theatre knowledge*. There are several dimensions to this:

*Understanding:* understanding of the nature, purposes, advantages, strengths and limitations of applied theatre and its relationship to its contexts.

*Techniques:* understanding of the structures and procedures of applied theatre, and the ability to design effective applied theatre programmes or components.

*Skills:* the ability to manage and teach effective applied theatre programmes or components.

The second kind of knowledge is *Professional knowledge*: increased understanding of the worker's own professional context and how to apply theatre strategies and techniques within it. The third kind of knowledge is *Personal knowledge*: increased cognitive and affective understanding and knowledge of self, others and the external world, including self-confidence. The fourth kind of knowledge, which we might label *Social awareness*, also entails a number of distinct dimensions:

increased understanding of social process;
improved ability to manage social interactions and communications in their professional context, including public settings;
shared situated understandings emerging from the learning context.

The fifth kind of knowledge is *Pedagogical knowledge*: understanding of the new pedagogy involved in TfD, its philosophy, techniques and implications – especially dialogical, communal and democratic teaching. The sixth kind of knowledge, without which none of the others can be fully operative, is by no means a given for TfD workers and may have to be instilled as much as any of the others: this is *Reflective capacity*, the ability to reflect on one's teaching and improve one's own practice as a result.

In the next part of the chapter, we share four case studies in capacity building in TfD, which vividly illustrate these requirements. Each is a training context in an economically developing country, working with NGOs and concerned with capacity building for practitioners. The case studies differ in the level of priority and explicit attention they are able to give to capacity building. Two of them, coincidentally, almost share their title.

## Section 2: Scenes in the landscape

### Case study 1: *Butterfly effects*, by Helen Cahill

This was a medium scale one-off TfD project for a women's NGO in Vietnam, taking place over the period of 1 year, with the intention of developing some autonomy and capacity among the participants to continue it after the project's conclusion. The writer of this case study designed the whole programme and was the principal trainer.

# Overview of the project

The *Creating Connections gender rights and HIV prevention* programme was commissioned by the Vietnam Women's Union, a mass organization of 14 million members. Within the context of escalating HIV rates in Vietnam, a key aim was to improve the capacity of women and girls to talk about sexual and reproductive health. The underpinning presumption was that mothers needed the knowledge and confidence to teach their children about these matters, and that both adult women and adolescent girls needed to learn how to negotiate for their own sexual safety. The Women's Union provides clubs and educational activities at commune level throughout the country, and wanted to pilot a gender rights and sexual and reproductive health curriculum within this context. Thus my commission included the development of a year-long club curriculum for adolescent girls, and another for mothers of adolescents. The clubs were to be led by local facilitators and to run for 2 hours at monthly intervals. The facilitators were experienced trainers accustomed to leading clubs within the Women's Union, but they were new to the issue of sexual and reproductive health, and to use of participatory and drama-based pedagogies.

Prior to developing the programme, I conducted focus groups with women and girls, in both urban and rural areas, and a key informants' workshop with Hanoi-based Vietnamese health professionals working on reproductive health issues. I ran a two-day consultation workshop to investigate the trainers' perceptions of the viability of various participatory learning strategies. During this exploratory workshop participants sampled each of the learning conventions I anticipated using in the programme. These included both the information-giving activities, a range of critical thinking and problem-solving activities built around scenarios gathered in the focus groups phase, as well as variations of classic naturalistic role-plays, forum theatre exercises and surrealist theatre exercises. In the following data story I report on ways in which participants engaged with both the content and the methodologies during this exploratory workshop, and the way in which they embraced them for use in the *Creating Connections* programme once it went to a full pilot in three provinces.

## Data story 1: Consultation workshop

The women introduce themselves as people who have expertise as trainers and programme managers. But they are new to teaching about Sex. I explain the evidence-base which highlights that participatory methods are fundamental to the effectiveness of prevention education. I explain that we will learn through doing, not just telling. We will use stories and scenarios to enact and explore the circumstances we wish to be able to address. We will create and enact the conversations we wish to make possible

I see the doubt in the room. Both the topic and the medium are new. *Women in Vietnam do not talk about sex. Vietnam women are shy to do role-play.* I invite them to sample and give feedback on each of the strategies. I explain that I will cut, keep or modify based on their experiences of the various learning strategies. They agree to engage in the experiment. They are excited about the possibility of change, but as yet unsure as to what it might mean, and somewhat nervous about its implications for them as trainers.

First we sample thematic games. The gameplay tickles the doubting space. They become giggly. The circle of reserve is recharged as a space for exchange. I ask them to find key messages in the games. Now they are serious. They speak their moral purpose. They name their cultural strengths. *We must use our collective strength. We must serve our nation.* They find metaphors in the game. *We must pass messages accurately. We see in the game the way they get lost. We must not lose our message.* It appears that their readiness is enhanced. They already have a deep moral commitment to social change, and now they also have the beginnings of some confidence in the potentially pleasurable nature of the proposed teaching methodology. They are beginning to experience the power of the dramatic medium to engage people in a collective and supportive manner towards their subject matter.

We form small circles to discuss scenarios garnered from the focus groups. *The girl is upset. There is blood on her dress. She does not know what is happening. She is told to go home and ask her mother.* They explore what it is the mother could have said, if only the clock would wind back. They talk about what a good mother could do, should do. *This we must change, the shyness and the shame, from our own mothers, and the grandmothers before.* They talk furiously. They are hard to interrupt. *This talking together brings us strength. We like these talking circles based on the scenarios. We can teach like this using the games and the talking groups.* Their experience of the participatory medium is enriched. They discover that it is not as alien to them as they had anticipated. Talking circles are women's business.

They have generated considerable advice in relation to the scenarios discussed. I point to the difference between advice and action. *We can tell this mother what she should do, but how will it be for her to do it?* I set them to role-play in pairs. The mother is to explain menstruation to her daughter. They role-swap and role-reverse, trying on the different positions. Did they notice this was role-play? There was no audience. They express their frustration about the task of speaking frankly, as yet not ready to focus on the methodology. *This is so hard for us to speak.* I ask if it is the role-playing that they find hard. They are quick to dismiss that suggestion. They explain it is not the role-playing they are struggling with; it is the gender norms which put a taboo on what they can speak about. It is the script not the performance which they are struggling with.

At this stage they are experiencing the programme as their participants would. They are learning about the medium from the inside.

I introduce the Hidden Thoughts convention as a way to explore the norms that confine their talk. I invite a pair to show their scenario. Then we add on the layers: *What is this mother (and her daughter) thinking or feeling but not saying out loud?* The alter-ego device helps them to articulate the cultural norms and expectations that shape the fears and desires of their characters. I ask if they can use this Hidden Thoughts device, when they are the trainers. Yes. *This method is good for the Vietnam culture. We must save face, but this one lets us speak what is behind the face. We can ask the questions in this way of the Hidden Thoughts. This is a good way for us to ask the question with comfort.*

We return to the scenario, using a modified form of forum theatre to coach the characters, and craft and explore possible ways for the mother to talk openly with her daughter. *It is good this method. First you cannot find the solution, but when you see someone try, you can learn. You can learn your own fear.*

Their experience with the form gathers. They are excited about the way the naturalistic role-play exposes the struggle, with the way the Hidden Thoughts convention has them show their insight into what holds the challenges in place, and the way in which the coaching and replaying of the scenes generates a sense of connectedness and camaraderie.

As the workshop progresses, we approach the more sensitive matter of contraception. Use of condoms is a key teaching point, for the programme aims to reduce HIV transmission. Family planning is provided by the state in Vietnam, with the Intrauterine Device the most common method. However condom use is stigmatized, and associated with sex workers. How do we normalize them as an option? How can the dramatic medium be harnessed to prove to them that they can talk openly about condom use? I select a surrealist convention for them. They will play in role as Celebrity Condoms interviewed by the TV chat show host. Once they are cast as contraceptives, they flaunt and strut, boasting about what they, as heroic condoms, have to offer the world. As they perform, they find a new voice, a transgressive voice. That which cannot be said by a woman, can be said by a condom! Raucous laughter recharges the room. Within this surrealist performance mode *We like this game. We can talk about sex like a man.* I see this as a collective shift in identity as they find a flight path to lift them (fleetingly) away from the restrictive social norms that confined their prior talk.

At the end of the workshop I consult them about what should be included in the programme. They want to include all the different types of drama-based activities they had sampled, including games, simulations, role-play, forum theatre and surrealist play. Their enthusiasm for adoption is palpable, generated by the experience as participants within the activities. They are full of enthusiasm about what this type of programme may bring to their club programme. They are having fun! And they are learning.

## Programme development and 5-day training

Following the consultation phases, I developed a detailed course manual to guide delivery of a comprehensive participatory sexuality and gender rights programme for mothers and girls. I worked with a Vietnamese counterpart, who was a medical doctor and sexuality expert. We then co-facilitated a 5-day training of trainers during which participants got to sample and experience all activities in the programme. Alongside the sampling process we spent time discussing each key activity, addressing issues for them in their anticipated role as facilitators, and developing a set of notes to guide practice. On the final day of the training, the participants led activities from the programme, demonstrating their capacity to step into the facilitator's role. During this phase they worked as coaches, giving each other formative feedback guided by the quality criteria that had been developed across the previous 4 days. Stepping into the 'coach' role also assisted them to internalize the pedagogical goals of the activities and to develop a sensibility about what mastery might look like. By the end of the training they had established that they could go forward and lead the programme. They were ready for a full trial.

They reported that the sampling process had assisted them to engage with the pedagogy from the inside and develop a sense of what happens for the learner. This experiential learning fostered a sense of ownership.

They experienced for themselves the moments of engagement and transformation that can be produced, particularly through the drama-based activities. They found that this direct experience increased their optimism about the potential of the programme. They also found it useful to watch the way their two master facilitators had run the activities. *There are many things to see that are not written in the manual.* Once the participants took on the facilitator role they faced the challenge of embodying theory in action. They were both nervous and delighted. They were delighted because they discovered that it is exciting to lead these activities and have participants respond through the tasks. Working in role as coach was also a useful part of the training. They found that when they had to give feedback to each other, this forced them to make their experiential learning more explicit. *You have to explain what is good or what is needed to make it work better.*

## Data Story 2: Observation of women's club in Ha Nam province at programme 6-month mid-point

Midway through their delivery of the 12-month programme, I returned to Vietnam to observe the clubs in action. I observed a mother's programme in the rural area. Two facilitators ran the games and scenario-based exercises with confidence. Their biggest challenge seemed to be to get the women to stop talking when they wanted to move them on to a new activity. As the workshop progressed, I saw to my delight that they had made conical paper hats for the performers who were to take part in the Celebrity Condoms exercise. They had embellished the activity by adding the comic phallic costumes. The players clowned in role as condoms. The observers shrieked with delight and asked to play the game again so they could all have a turn. It seemed that the facilitators had exerted not only a high degree of ownership, but also a degree of mastery as they claimed control of the theatrical medium.

## Outcomes

The workshops I observed illustrated that the facilitators had adopted and adapted the methods, and were able to produce positive responses from their own participants. *Creating Connections* was piloted in three provinces. Focus group and pre- and post-survey data were collected, showing mothers were more satisfied with their capacity to relate to their children, and girls and mothers were more likely to initiate talk with friends and family members about gender-based violence, HIV and STIs.[13] The trainers reported a high level of programme fidelity in their delivery. This in itself can be regarded as a significant outcome relating to *adoption* of the approach. Fidelity research within the field of prevention curriculum identifies that facilitators commonly default to use of didactic methods and fail to deliver the participatory methods that have been demonstrated to be integral to effectiveness, indicating that adoption and ownership are common barriers which in themselves work against the possibility of developing mastery.[14]

At the completion of the 12-month pilot, the Women's Union commissioned a boys' programme and a 6-month extension to the existing programmes in response to requests from the clubs which did not want to disband. Subsequently the programme came to the attention of U.N. bodies co-ordinating responses to HIV in the Asia-Pacific region. UNICEF, UFPA and UNESCO worked together to fund variations of the programme for Cambodia, Myanmar, Laos, Nepal, Bangladesh and Indonesia.

## Conclusion

Learning can show up as a rapid transformational shift, a sudden flourishing within productive conditions, a butterfly effect. This was the line of flight seen in the Celebrity Condoms exercise. But the butterfly does not wing for eternity and the line of flight in the butterfly phase should not be confused with mastery. The transformative moments did not indicate mastery over either the restrictive social norms pertaining to open talk about gender and sex, or the dramatic form. They were moments of creation, moments of becoming and as such part of the long slow process of social change. A true liberation from restrictive social norms would mean that the speaker could replicate their freedom of speech in any social context, rather than just within the protected and permissive space provided within the workshop environment. However, the evaluation showed that the programme did increase the participants' comfort to talk about sexuality and gender rights, and in this lies the promise of accelerating change.

The facilitators were able to lead the programme with a high level of fidelity. They were keen to extend and to replicate the programme, which in itself indicates a high level of ownership. It would be unrealistic to expect that they attained a high mastery of facilitation of the various dramatic forms, but nonetheless, they provided a rich-enough opportunity for their participants to engage through these modes. Indeed, their participants found the experience so useful, enjoyable and engaging that they did not want to disband their clubs. Perhaps in this situation, the HIV prevention programmers in the Women's Union would consider *opportunity* (for participants) to be more important than *mastery* (on the part of the facilitators). True educative mastery addresses the integral connection between environment and organism, between gestation and hatching, between hatching and flight. It would be unrealistic to presume that either of these forms of mastery would be produced within the conditions of the training and programmatic interventions. However, the facilitators did take forward the drama-based methods and identified that they would continue to use them in their programmes. This high level of adoption and ownership may foster the development of mastery and a further internal sharing of such approaches.

## Case study 2: *Life Drama*, by Andrea Baldwin

This is a rather larger-scale project than the first, though it started on quite a small scale, eventually taking place over several years in Papua New Guinea (PNG), also with the intention of developing capacity for autonomy and continuation. Like the first, its aim is to help the community properly understand HIV-AIDS in an attempt to contain the spread of the disease and assist its sufferers. The writer of the case study was involved in the programme from the start, and one of its initiators and workshop leaders.

## Introduction

*Life Drama* began as an experiential learning approach to sexual health education in PNG. The government-sponsored approach, 'awareness-raising', was clearly not working. Relying heavily on written materials in a country where over 860 languages are spoken, and the vast majority do not read or write in any of them, the results of the awareness campaign were not surprising: over 90 per cent of people had heard of HIV and/ or AIDS, but there was no evidence that people were adopting safer sexual behaviours.

I was approached by an NGO, and delivered a workshop in which improvisation games were used to explore three themes: the HIV virus, transmission and prevention, and discrimination against people living with HIV/AIDS. The one-day workshop in Lae, with participants from 12 NGOs, was enthusiastically received. I returned to Australia and approached Professor Brad Haseman for assistance to develop a programme for HIV education in PNG. Partnerships were formed and an application was made by Queensland University of Technology (QUT) Creative Industries Faculty to the Australian Research Council, with the National AIDS Council Secretariat of PNG as principal industry partner. Word spread quickly in PNG and a number of individuals approached the embryonic research team on behalf of their organizations, seeking to participate. The *Life Drama* programme evolved in PNG over 4 years, from 2008 to 2011, and culminated in a Train-the-Trainer programme conducted in Port Moresby and Goroka in 2012. This case study considers three groups of learners involved in the Train-the-Trainer programme: community educators, teacher educators and co-trainers.

## Community educators

The Train-the-Trainer group in Port Moresby consisted of community educators: people who by virtue of leadership roles in the community and/or educator roles in community organizations were in a position to teach others about sexual health. This group included a number of peer educators who were volunteers in a service run by the university; peer educators working with sex workers; officers from the National Capital District Council; two community development officers from mining companies; women's leaders; youth leaders; church leaders; a police officer; a teacher; and several freelance theatre workers involved in delivering community education. A total of 24 (16 men and 8 women) completed the train-the-trainer programme as Community Educators.

The original selection criteria for the group were:

a.  At least some experience of teaching or delivering education, and a mandate to do so in their current work environment;
b.  Some knowledge of sexual health, HIV and STIs;
c.  Some knowledge of and skills in drama, theatre or performance;
d.  Personal commitment to and enthusiasm for learning to use drama for HIV education.

In practice, however, it was difficult to know who would turn up for the training, and hard to turn away anyone who did. In the interests of partnership-building, it was necessary to trust organizations to make decisions about the most appropriate representatives to train. The result was a group that had disparate levels of motivation and commitment, and varied greatly in terms of existing knowledge of HIV, previous experience with theatre generally and applied theatre in particular, and experience and mandate as an educator. Most learners were at the first level of readiness. About one-third of the group were at level two: experience, having had at least some prior drama experience. This included six who had participated in early *Life Drama* development workshops.

At the end of the week, the group showed a remarkable move into the beginnings of level three: adoption – willingness to participate in the structures of applied theatre, and some capacity to conduct exercises. However, although the training emphasized adapting the techniques to other contexts, it was clear most participants did not feel a high level of confidence to do this – they had not yet achieved ownership. The group as a whole reported learning in the areas of Applied Theatre, Pedagogy and (to some extent) Reflective Practice.

There was an extensive discussion at the end of the workshop, about whether or not the training had provided enough for the individuals to conduct similar experiential learning activities with their client groups. Some of those with the fewest resources available to them said it was up to individual efforts, and felt confident about using their new *Life Drama* skills for HIV education. Others warned of the danger of burnout, and said a systematic programme of resources and support would be needed to roll out HIV education through *Life Drama* in a meaningful, effective way.

## Teacher educators

The University of Goroka trains secondary teachers. It is the only university in PNG which delivers a mandatory HIV programme for all undergraduate students. The course is taught by lecturers from across the faculties, as well as support staff from the Student Health Service. The teacher educator group consisted of 13 of these lecturers, as well as a graduate student, two administrative staff and a nurse from the university health service. Also included were a male and a female lecturer from Madang Teachers' College, engaged in training primary school teachers, and two educators from an NGO. A total of 27 (15 women and 12 men) completed the train-the-trainer programme as teacher educators.

The group had a much higher level of education, and more experience as teachers, than the community educator group. The teacher educators tended to work in more formal education settings, and to have more sophisticated ideas about pedagogy. This was balanced by a generally lower level of experience with theatre and performance, resulting in a lower level of confidence to engage with this form of experiential learning. The example set by a pro vice chancellor, who attended the first morning and threw himself into the activities with gusto, was of enormous help in overcoming some initial anxiety in the group about committing to performative learning. The group had a high level of readiness, but only six felt they had experience in drama.

Commitment to the training was high, with no absenteeism or dropout, and enthusiastic adoption. Interestingly, when asked to work in small groups on the last day to conduct exercises with the rest of the group, all showed distinct evidence of ownership: not one exercise was used in exactly the way it had been taught. Instead the group integrated the new activities with their previous teaching strategies, and applied these new hybrid activities to specific areas of teaching they envisioned in the future. The early childhood teachers adapted an exercise to be played with a group of children, while two educators from the health service conducted a role-play about family attitudes to school-based sex education.

The group reported learning in the areas of Applied Theatre, Professional Knowledge of using applied theatre within their existing roles, Pedagogy and Reflective Practice. A few people also reflected on social knowledge, having gained new knowledge about the content material (HIV) or having gained confidence in their role as an educator.

Most participants felt confident they had gained ownership, and would be able to use the *Life Drama* training in education work. However the two community educators echoed the concerns of the community educators' group in Moresby: that without a mandate from their organization, organizational support, a peer network, and additional resources, they would be unable to conduct this work on an ongoing basis – mastery was some way off, logistically at least.

## Co-trainers

The four PNG co-trainers, who worked alongside the Australian lead trainers, are graduates of the University of Papua New Guinea theatre programme. All are lecturers, or senior educators with NGOs. As with the teacher educator group, these trainers fill roles both as formal educators at universities, and as community educators in their own communities, where their employment and social position command respect.

It was the vision of the Australian researchers that these co-trainers would eventually take over *Life Drama* in PNG, but it has been more difficult than anticipated to gain recognition for the programme and attract the funding required to place it on a sustainable footing. Political turmoil in the country, instability in the administration of the universities, staff turnover within funding agencies and partner organizations, safety and security concerns, and the unreliability of PNG telecommunications, have all contributed to these difficulties.

In addition, people with a high level of skill and experience may not wish to be 'deployed' to roll out a programme in accordance with a predetermined vision, even if they have been involved in developing both the programme and the vision. All four co-trainers are now pursuing options for higher degrees, three of them through QUT.

There is a need to consider the goals and motivations of individuals: capacity building cannot be dictated by the organizations seeking to 'build capacity'.

## Knowledge and understanding

- Applied theatre: All participants were excited by the experiential aspect of applied theatre – 'involving head, heart and body'. The idea of an emotional experience producing learning was novel. The methodology was well accepted.
- Professional knowledge: At the start, there were significant gaps in the HIV knowledge of even some experienced HIV educators, particularly about the difference between HIV and AIDS, and the potential for people living with HIV/AIDS to lead healthy lives. The train-the-trainer programme helped to correct some misperceptions, particularly among the community educators. There were some very astute reflections on the participants' own teaching contexts, among all three groups.
- Personal knowledge: While there was a general sense of greater confidence in the teacher educator group than in the community educator group, this confidence was tied to the individual's perception of their position and available resources. A number of staff in the teacher educator group were not in teaching roles but rather in administrative or health service delivery roles within the university. These participants had less confidence in their ability to conduct *Life Drama* training, than those lecturers whose day-to-day role included working with groups of students.
- Social learning: This training explicitly encourages reflection on social organization and processes, particularly the status of women in society.
- Pedagogical knowledge: Participants were excited (though in some cases a little daunted) by the idea of participatory pedagogy.
- Reflective capacity: Most participants in all three groups showed great capacity for reflecting on their own practice and contexts.

# What helped learners move

All groups of participants reported that the structure of the training programme, including the daily workshop structure, was a key factor in helping them overcome inhibitions, engage with the experiential learning process, and build knowledge and skills.

Reflective practice was a vital component of learning. Group debriefs were considered highly culturally appropriate, given the extent to which PNG culture emphasizes orality and community.

# Barriers

The main barrier to learning, raised by all groups but particularly the teacher educators and the co-trainers, is that the dominant pedagogical model in PNG is not participatory. Teachers, pastors and politicians are granted 'expert' status, and others are required to sit and listen. Students are not encouraged to experience, reflect, discuss, challenge, question or display independent thought and creativity. Participants reported a sense of excitement at discovering a new, participatory pedagogy, but were also somewhat daunted by its novelty and in some cases felt students would be reluctant to embrace it.

Gender inequity may be a significant barrier to participatory learning in other contexts in PNG. Both female co-trainers reported having more difficulty than men in establishing their authority as educators, and gaining the trust and respect of learners, particularly outside formal learning settings.

# Conclusion

The *Life Drama* programme recognizes that HIV transmission is not all about the behavioural choices of individuals – contextual factors are generally more powerful than individual knowledge, attitudes and behavioural intentions. This is why we work with groups, and the exercises specifically encourage reflection on social norms.

Theatre for Development cannot focus only on individual trainers. Our Train-the-Trainer programme demonstrated that an individual may have readiness and experience, and show willingness to adopt and adapt, but unless systemic supports are in place they are unlikely to achieve mastery.

## Acknowledgements

The *Life Drama* team gratefully acknowledges the support of the National AIDS Council Secretariat of Papua New Guinea, the Australian Research Council, the University of Papua New Guinea, the University of Goroka and the QUT, in enabling this research. A more extensive history of *Life Drama* can be found in Baldwin.[15]

## Case study 3: *Drama for Life,* by Kennedy Chinyowa

This third case study is rather different from the two above, in that it is not directly based in the field, in a specific community. Like the second study, it is large scale and continuing: an ongoing university postgraduate course in South Africa with students from across Sub-Saharan Africa. It started like the first two specifically to address HIV-AIDS but has since diversified, and the student/practitioners, many of whom are experienced TfD workers before they attend the course, deal in their practicums with a wide range of TfD purposes and causes. In this case study, unlike the others, the writer was not involved in the programme's original design, but has been involved in its operation as a lecturer and administrator of the programme.

# The context

The *Drama for Life* (DFL) programme based at the University of the Witwatersrand in Johannesburg, South Africa, was born out of the need for capacity development in HIV/AIDS education through applied drama and theatre practice. The programme began as a Southern African Development Community (SADC) initiative aimed at integrating the efforts of theatre-makers, facilitators, performers, directors and managers in empowering young people and local communities to take responsibility for the quality of their own lives in the context of the HIV/AIDS pandemic. The programme, which is the first of its kind in terms of offering a comprehensive package in applied drama and theatre training within the SADC region, became fully operational in January 2008 with an intake of 27 postgraduate students selected from the SADC region.

The main aims of the *DFL* programme, as outlined in the initial report that paved the way for its launch, were as follows:

> To enhance the efficacy of applied drama and theatre as a sustainable medium for HIV/AIDS education as opposed to short-lived projects that are rarely documented and assessed for impact.
>
> To train master trainers in applied drama and theatre who will train other trainers at national level, who will in turn train at-school and out-of-school youths, who will eventually reach out to their local communities with interventions on HIV/AIDS.
>
> To improve awareness of the impact of HIV/AIDS among youths who cannot relate the relevant facts to their own lives in terms of behaviour change.
>
> To integrate applied drama and theatre into existing educational and national structures, school curricula and teacher training institutions within the SADC region.[16]

The programme's success or failure was dependent on the acquisition of knowledge and skills in applied drama and theatre by the master trainers whose academic and practical training was intended to enable them to be effective in HIV/AIDS education across the SADC region. This meant that the programme needed to demonstrate its point of departure from previous HIV/AIDS initiatives by training the master trainers in 'best practice' HIV/AIDS intervention strategies. Such training would depend on the readiness of the trainees to experiment with the new pedagogy, their capacity for embodied learning coupled with empathy, distance and reflection, the ability to apply the new strategies and techniques to other contexts, taking ownership and responsibility for initiating change and being able to help others to help themselves.

Although *DFL* still focuses on enhancing the capacity of young people, theatre practitioners and local communities to take responsibility for the quality of their lives in the context of HIV/AIDS education and advocacy, it has since broadened its scope to include other related social development questions such as human rights, social justice, cultural diversity, gender equality and conflict management. The *DFL* organizers have realized that the continued spread of the HIV/AIDS epidemic is not divorced from other broader struggles and structural issues.

## Approach to pedagogy, training and capacity building

The *DFL* programme's pedagogic approach focuses on how the theory and practice of applied theatre can be used for purposes of activism, education, development and therapy. To this end, the courses offered at both honours and master's degree level are meant to be process oriented rather than product based. During the period of academic training, workshop-based approaches are employed in order to equip students with the skills and knowledge required in applied theatre. The programme places emphasis on practice-based research training for HIV/AIDS education and other related themes. *DFL* scholars are required to identify, motivate, plan and carry out applied theatre interventions within selected local community settings. The course also enables students to engage with multiple roles as applied drama teachers, facilitators, practitioners and caregivers. The practical projects run concurrently with academic training in the theory and practice of applied drama and theatre. Students are expected to relate the knowledge and skills learnt in class to the site specific contexts in which they undertake both individual and group projects.

Indeed, examples of research projects undertaken over the past few years show that students have focused mainly on the social challenges affecting communities as a result of the HIV/AIDS epidemic. For instance, Clayton Ndlovu[17] worked with the Khaya African Arts group from Zimbabwe to find out how people's ritual beliefs and practices embodied in song and dance can be used to address the challenges posed by HIV/AIDS. Before him, Khabi Thulo[18] had merged indigenous ritual and modern theatre-making to come up with an inspiring HIV/AIDS performance entitled *They were silent*. Basimenya Mwalwanda[19] explored how the integration of process drama methodology and drama therapy can be used to deal with the traumatic experiences of people living with HIV/AIDS within a Malawian context. Ookeditse Phala[20] explored the adverse effects of stigma and discrimination in Botswana through a practice-based research HIV/AIDS performance called, *Lezzy my mirror*. Thokozani Kapiri[21] looked at how Nanzikambe Arts group in Malawi makes use of applied theatre performances to address risky traditional customs such as widow inheritance, cleansing ceremonies and circumcision rites.

*DFL* scholars have also focused on a diversity of themes in their practical projects. For instance, Grace Meadows[22] adapted Ariel Dorfman's play, *Speak Truth to Power* to address the xenophobic violence that took place in South Africa in May 2008. Bhekilizwe Ndlovu[23] (2009) explored the problem of homophobia in Zimbabwe using the play, *Trial of the senior citizen*. Tendai Mutukwa[24] focused on how process drama can be used as a medium for children's rights education in South African primary schools. Delphine Njewele[25] examined how process drama can be used as a learning medium in Tanzanian primary schools using the Children's Theatre Project as her case study. The readiness of students to broaden their horizons by moving beyond HIV/AIDS related themes indicates their capacity for adoption and adaptation of new structures of feeling. It also reflects their ability to situate their knowledge and understanding to changing learning contexts.

## 3. Challenges faced by the *DFL* programme

In spite of its successes in equipping students with the necessary theoretical and practical tools for engaging with problems confronting the SADC region and beyond, the *DFL* programme has not been without its own challenges.

There is a need for specialized training in practice-based research methodology, geared to meeting the requirements of applied theatre as an emerging discipline within the academy. Although students' research projects reflect a grasp of practical skills, the theoretical understanding of concepts and their application remains problematic. Honours and masters' students tend to struggle with research design and project implementation. In spite of doing 7-week workshops on research methodology, students still find it difficult to grapple with concepts involving practice-based research projects.

Although *DFL* meets the necessary university academic requirements for postgraduate programmes, one year of study is not adequate for students to thoroughly engage with their research projects and come up with rigorous reports. The academic training period needs to be extended to at least 18 months. It is not surprising that a number of students end up applying for permission to extend their period of study. The curriculum itself becomes too demanding as students have to compress all their coursework requirements within a short period of time.

Since students often find themselves working with vulnerable groups, they require more specialized training to deal with traumatized participants. It becomes counter-productive when students continue to apply one-off or parachute approaches to interventions. There is a need for students to foster long-term relationships with communities in order to realize the transformative potential of applied theatre.

Notwithstanding these and other challenges, however, *DFL* remains a unique academic training programme in Africa that continues to experience such phenomenal growth that it has now been accorded a separate departmental status offering degrees in Applied Drama and Theatre, including Drama Therapy at both honours and master's levels. The programme has produced over 70 postgraduate students. Most of these students have already been employed in various institutions, organizations and agencies. There is no doubt that the quality of training they received through *DFL* has equipped them with skills that are relevant to their professions.

## Case study 4: *Capacity building in and through applied theatre*, by Au Yi-Man

The smallest of the four projects, this case study documents an action research project in China comprising a single 'train-the-trainers' course comprising a total of 104 hours, mainly in 3-hour sessions with 24 NGO workers. This was explicitly designed to explore through theatre methods their needs and capacities for adopting TfD strategies and techniques. Some of these NGO workers are involved in contexts of dealing with HIV-AIDS, but from the start there was a wide diversity of organizations whose workers came for the training. As in the first case study, the writer was the principal trainer, and, in this case, the sole one.

## Background

Starting from the late 1970s, China has dramatically changed its economic structure by expanding the scope of markets and private ownership. The economic reforms have brought more social problems such as unemployment, inequality and increased pollution, but at the same time have greatly reduced the state's welfare commitment. This generates the need to expand the social sector to take on these functions. However, the general improvement in living standards, the time and space allowed for private and social lives are also another force which creates opportunities for NGOs to develop. There has been a rapid growth in civil society in China.

In the last 15 years, the number of NGOs has significantly expanded. Lack of capacity is one of the major constraints to their development. NGO is a new profession in China and there is no prior reference point about how to run a social organization. The increasing workforce in the field creates a demand for training. With this background, I have been conducting applied theatre training for NGO workers in mainland China since 2004. This approach to capacity building employs a pedagogy in which specialized drama and theatre techniques are located at the centre of the training programme. The positive responses from participants during the years of practice drove my curiosity to further explore the potential contribution that applied theatre training could make to capacity building for NGO workers. This became the focus of my PhD study which I commenced in 2009.

The journey started with practice-led research which allowed me to pursue the research through my own practice. As a practitioner-researcher, building from my past learning and teaching experience in applied theatre, I designed and conducted a training workshop with a group of 24 participants including full-time NGO workers, committed and casual NGO volunteers in southern China from March to May 2011. The training workshop was divided into three phases. Each phase comprised 8–10 sessions and each session lasted three and a half hours. I also carried out some post-project follow-up interviews, some months later. There were three different applied theatre approaches (Theatre of the Oppressed, Process Drama and Participatory Theatre) selected to share in each phase.

The research and training combined in the data I collected. My research involved setting up procedures which were not primarily part of the training tasks: interviews, observation notes, video and audio recordings, both in the training and in the post-project phase. Other data were set up primarily for the teaching and learning purposes of the training, such as individual journals, weekly feedback and phase-ending reflection forms, and an essay to end the course. These were aimed at assisting participants' reflection and documented what they had learnt, and also assisted me in reviewing the teaching. Other data were collected during the fieldwork, like workshop lesson plans; visual data such as photographic documentation, drawings, objects and images created in workshops; artefacts produced by participants such as scripts and their lesson plans. In addition, articles posted on participants' blogs, the emails and text messages sent by the participants during and after the training workshop were found to be relevant to the study.

17 out of the 24 participants, eleven women and six men, the full-time NGO workers or committed regular NGO volunteers, were analysed in this research. They worked in different areas of NGOs such as promoting rural education and voluntary work, developing civic society, protecting workers' rights, in services for people with mental illness and special needs, and working for youth and children. They came to the training workshop with different levels of applied theatre experience and I divided them into three categories, roughly corresponding to the first three levels of capacity building.

Category one comprised nine beginners who were at or pre-level one: with very limited experience or none in watching and participating in applied theatre. Although they had a positive impression of applied theatre, they had not attended any applied theatre before. They had no idea what they would face, how they should behave or the methods of teaching. Therefore, they spent quite a bit of time in the first phase of the project adapting to a kind of learning which required emotional engagement, physical participation and collaboration.

Category two comprised six with limited participating and facilitating experience; they had already experienced the setting and format of teaching of an applied theatre workshop. Therefore, they could pay more attention to observing the dramatic experience and making sense of its potency and learning the skills of facilitation.

In Category three were two who were in the early stages of level three: adoption. They had some practical experience in applied theatre and had previously attended workshops. They knew certain strategies and techniques and were able to design their own workshops though they were still in the process of understanding the applied theatre pedagogy fully.

## Applied theatre learning

The category difference showed up most in applied theatre learning from their different starting points in concepts, techniques, skills, rationale and pedagogy. Experience gained in previous learning showed up as a building block towards the next level of learning. There was considerably less difference among the categories in some of the other kinds of learning.

The category one participants moved from pre-level one towards level two, but were not really able to move to level three. Participants stepped forward and backward in the new learning process. At times, feeling comfortable, gaining personal confidence and managing to participate and use certain strategies or activities, they would feel greater learning confidence and understanding. However, at times their difficulty in understanding generated negative feelings to frustrate their confidence and make them feel incapable. Overall, the novel learning experience excited them and brought them confidence in the power of applied theatre methods and potential for their workplace. They changed their previous perception of applied theatre as mere performance; they gained some basic concepts of applied theatre as participatory, collaborative and change oriented.

In skills and techniques they mainly grasped the easy-to-manage single exercises, activities and drama conventions, and some basic facilitation, planning and drama skills through quite unstructured observation. They finished the course still in the process of sense-making, only able to generalize from a participant's perspective – observing their own personal changes.

The category two participants moved from level two towards and, in some cases, into level three. They also had personal struggles, mainly in self-evaluation. They did a lot of self-observation and at the same time were keen on observing how to facilitate and on the pedagogy. Their previous applied theatre experience gave them a basis to see the activities at a deeper level. When they found a new method difficult to learn, they did not lose self-confidence like the category one students; they found their own way to learn in the process. Although they did not feel accomplished in every method, they expressed increasing understanding and confidence in using applied theatre after the training workshop which helped them to move to level three: adoption. In skills and techniques they built on their previous knowledge; they absorbed new knowledge in applied theatre to add to their stock; and they learnt new possibilities for using the activities. Through purposeful observation they learnt facilitation and planning skills. New understanding of the pedagogy and its philosophy was for them the most explicit and appreciated kind of learning. They were attracted by aspects of the process like accepting and respecting each other, participative and inquiry-based learning, the active listening and the opening up of the senses that were involved. This kind of learning supported their developing role as facilitators.

The category three participants both moved from the beginning of level three to its heart, and there were signs that perhaps they might be able to move to level four. They were more self-directed and set up their own agenda for learning. They focused on the facilitation, pedagogy and structure of the training workshop. They also absorbed new knowledge from previously little known aspects of applied theatre. They had internalized the ability to reflect and comment on activities from a facilitator's perspective. They could make their own choice of areas for further development. After the workshop, they felt more autonomy in practice and confirmed their professional identity. Their specific learning was based on their own background, interest and experience into which they blended the concepts, techniques, skills, rationale and pedagogy. They did not just learn the operations but how to construct the concepts at the same time. One concentrated on learning the rationale and the facilitator's skills. Another emphasized building her own theory of applied theatre. They carried on their practice after the training workshop with the pedagogical confidence generated by personal experience and change as well as by seeing others change during the process. They both mentioned a belief in practice as a key to learning applied theatre.

The research shows the category two and three participants were able to practise independently and initiate collaboration, regardless of the nature of their jobs. The beginners were the only category that needed more external support such as immediate job relevancy, a platform to practice, or the availability of working partners, co-learners and/or mentors to motivate their ongoing practice.

## Other learnings

Apart from building capacity in using applied theatre, the participants across the categories also demonstrated other generic aspects of learning which were not so much influenced by their levels:

**Personal and social learning:** Most of the participants mentioned that their participation in different applied theatre activities gave them a chance to learn about themselves, leading to personal growth. The nature of embodied learning in applied theatre increased their expressive ability. They found enhancement of their social abilities such as the willingness to listen, and to be more empathic and sensitive. They found that the training had helped to improve their relationship with colleagues and clients at their workplace.

**Reflective learning:** It is the nature of applied theatre activities to encourage the capacity to see things from multiple perspectives, to create, to accept possibilities and to inquire. The workshop stimulated the participants' reflective thinking. In addition, the associated tasks and activities such as their journal, group discussions, immediate post-activity sharing and interviews set up in this workshop played important roles in developing their reflective capacity. Participants mentioned they could ask more 'whys' at work and had more sophisticated ideas after the training which had developed their critical thinking and analytical skills.

**Pedagogical learning:** The participants immersed themselves in the applied theatre workshop for 3 months. Most of them mentioned their appreciation of this way of learning which was experiential, participatory, interactive, dialogic, collaborative and exploratory. They also identified educational values of self-construction of knowledge, a people-centred approach, equal teacher-student relationships, the importance of respecting everyone's voice and ability and the emphasis on reflection and feeling. These led their change in pedagogical understanding. They found they had changed their attitudes and behaviour in their workplace, not just in respect of applied theatre.

## Moving from one level to another

The findings in this research show that the embodied experience of participating, the practical experience of facilitating and the intellectual experience of thinking, reflecting and generalizing on applied theatre pedagogy were the supporting factors which helped the learners move from one level to another. Therefore, the learners who had more prior experience in those three areas would be more advanced at managing and applying the methods. These are the differences among the three kinds of experience. The embodied experience is the first and fundamental element for beginners before they can move to the next level of learning. Although a beginner could generalize the pedagogy intellectually, s/he still could not well manage the practice without accumulating sufficient embodied experience. When learning continues, the practical experience is a critical force to bring the learners to another level. Intellectual learning can be gained from both embodied and practical experience. Reinforcing this, the data also show that the participants who had less opportunity to practise and/or further their learning in applied theatre after the training workshop were hindered from moving on to the next stage of learning.

Furthermore, the generic aspects of learning mentioned above not only directly enhanced the NGO workers' capacity in general but also closely connected with their ongoing applied theatre learning. It is impossible to learn applied theatre on a single occasion, and it is also hard for a person in a community to get systematic training. People who intend to learn applied theatre can usually attend various short-term workshops. Therefore, we can imagine that their piecemeal learning is fragmented and relies on self-organization. The capacities acquired from personal, reflective and pedagogical learning are the catalyst for supporting learners' professional development.

## Section 3: Travelling in the landscape

It is important to preserve a combination of humility and pride about the contribution that drama-based approaches can make within development work. They can help to open new possibilities for thinking and action, and generate liberatory spaces within the public imaginary. However, any artistic or pedagogical intervention used for the purpose of social change will be pitched against the ongoing material and social realities that shape people's everyday lives. Given this, neither the facilitator nor the programme should be evaluated solely in terms of immediate resultant behavioural shifts. Rather the programme and the facilitator should be appraised in terms of their contribution to the public imaginary. Facilitators are effective when, in association with the participants, the collective work that they lead opens the possibility of change and evokes the social courage that is the precursor to action.

This sage postscript from Helen Cahill needs to be borne constantly in mind when examining and trying to understand the complex, open and provisional nature of TfD and the deep contextual framing that always applies. Together with the title of her contribution, it politely but implicitly provides a post-modern warning about the limitations of a structuralist model of human behaviour, like the very one we proposed in Section 1 and are using throughout this chapter.

Another cautionary note is that all four case studies, careful and critical though they are, were undertaken and written by interested parties, themselves all at level five on our Axis 1, masters of their trade, and fully implicated in the set-up and management of their projects and the research.

Their clients however arrived in the capacity-building game at diverse points on the axis.

The Vietnamese women were mostly not yet even at the first level of *readiness* – being entirely new not only to any form of theatre work, but to their primary purpose, the teaching of sex and sexual health. In addition they showed reluctance to display or perform in public, and strong social taboos confining open discussion of sex. To deal with these, Cahill had first to encourage them into practical (in that way belying our neat model, by using the level two: experience to create the level one: readiness). Once those pre-level one barriers had been overcome, the subtle sequencing and structures of Cahill's capacity- and knowledge-building generated the participants' fluid oscillation between growing experience and growing readiness, and thence to a backward-and-forward oscillation from adoption to ownership that thoroughly disrupts our neat model. The gleams of real ownership in the ongoing work and glimpses of a future vision of mastery are soberly offset by Cahill's recognition of the contextual rocks and reefs that have to be navigated.

By contrast, the ambitious aims of the *DFL* programme demand nothing less than mastery. The postgraduate students who form the programme arrive mainly as fully trained theatre professionals. Some of them already have considerable on-the-ground experience in applied theatre, and ready-made contexts for applying their training and sharing this with the other students as part of their ongoing joint capacity building. They start already, mostly, at level three or four, pitching for full ownership and mastery. They have the benefits of a sustained approach that Cahill can only dream of, though it is noteworthy that Chinyowa still feels that some of them need even longer to get over the final hurdles, and in particular to develop the capacity for praxis-based research.

The PNG and Chinese participants were more disparate: both arriving in three discernible groups. In PNG these were formally identified by their prior training; the community educators and teacher educators were both split between levels one and two on arrival and they both made it comfortably through the level of adoption, with the teacher educators more confident about their ownership and the likelihood of their being able to utilize their new capacities. For all three groups – including the four co-trainers, who started at level three at least – the opportunity to develop into master-practitioners still seems barred to them at least logistically within their contexts, especially for the teacher educators, bound by the expectations of their systems, teachers and students of a transmissive and monological pedagogy. For some of them, as for the *DFL* students, the only answer lies in yet further study, and at a level that has to be overseas.

The most detailed observation is of the three loosely categorized Chinese groups for this project was set up specifically as a research project to study capacity building using this particular model and, fortuitously, included detailed longitudinal data. Yi-Man Au's research of these three groups reinforces the conclusions which the other case studies draw: that applied theatre training does build capacity and the ability to surmount the hurdles and move up through the levels. For her the key to each new level, for all three of her groups, was a combination of three factors:

- the embodied experience embedded in the training (as it was also crucial in all the other case studies);

- the time and ability to reflect, extrapolate and generalize from that, and apply it intellectually to their practice (for her students it was harder than for the South Africans and perhaps the PNG trainers, who came from a more openly discursive and potentially reflective educational environment);
- the direct influence and modelling power of the facilitator (something that surprised her considerably, and had to be factored – with unassuming reluctance – into her research).

This last factor, the quality of the leader's own teaching and modelling, is one that is implicit in all of the accounts, but with becoming modesty none of the leaders have made it explicit. My own familiarity with two of the contexts, and with all of the leaders, suggests to me that it is indeed a crucial factor in scaffolding the capacity to surmount the hurdles, at whatever level. Ironically a problem is that most research is carried out by high quality pedagogues and practitioners, thoroughly attuned to their contextual opportunities and crises, and the reports glow with success. However, Bamford's 2006 Global Compendium of Arts Education Research suggests[26] that poor-quality arts education may have no impact, or even a negative one, and James Thompson[27] in a TfD context warns of the real dangers of not understanding the relationship between the theatre provision and the context. Important evidence is slowly emerging to support both these assertions (e.g. Stinson).[28]

In terms of the knowledge categories, it is very clear that all the case studies built capacity in all of the categories, but with different emphases. In all four cases the scaffolding of the pragmatic knowledge and skills of theatre formed a suitable foundation for the development of other kinds of understanding and skills that were necessary for the participants. For the Vietnamese women, this was most importantly in the categories of personal and social knowledge. For the Chinese NGO trainers it was the ability to reflect on their practice, and the new pedagogical understanding of a dialogic and democratic pedagogy; both of these were unfamiliar territory, that those advanced groups who started with more prior knowledge of applied theatre were better able to incorporate in their improved practice. For *Life Drama*, Baldwin several times uses the unusual word 'excitement' to describe the participants' response to the new kinds of learning they were receiving – enthusiasm seemed to characterize this whole project. However, she also notes that they were daunted in part by the gap between the participatory and dialogic nature of the new applied theatre pedagogy and the dominant passive pedagogy in place in their own settings. She notes that without ongoing official support in addressing this disparity the trainees are unlikely to get over the final barrier to mastery. With more time at their disposal, and more advanced participants to start with, the lecturers leading the *DFL* programme are able to work with higher expectations – their participants already come with highly developed personal confidence and teamwork skills, as well as knowledge of and sometimes considerable experience in applied theatre. However, as Chinyowa points out, many of them struggle with the theory, and that also hampers their ability to design and implement projects – a crucial part of ownership and beyond. Some struggle to see beyond the quick fix – what Chinyowa terms a 'parachute approach'. Their ability to seek the long-term relationship with a community is inevitably hampered by their lack of an immediate common context – especially now that the programme has expanded from a single focus on HIV & AIDS prevention to a much broader range of developmental theatre aims that includes schools and curriculum. This is a disadvantage which the course leaders attempt to address by plentiful fieldwork, ensuring that the students all lead their own projects as part of the course – and as the examples attest, very challenging and sophisticated fieldwork.

Both the *Life Drama* and *Drama for Life* case studies reveal another kind of knowledge, omitted from our model, which is clearly an important factor and hurdle requirement at least for mastery: understanding of research and research design. Chinyowa observes that a 7-week workshop on research methods is not enough to counter the gaps in theoretical understanding that stand between these advanced students and mastery. Both programmes are trying to build higher degree expertise; both are looking beyond their shores for support and the highest level of expertise: practitioners and would-be scholars from the economically developing world have turned and continue to turn to the traditional centres of theatre knowledge, which are still currently from the Western tradition: to The United Kingdom, to the United States, to Canada, to Northern Europe – and to Australia in all these cases and for two of their leaders.

These cases, exciting and productive as they are, still embody some of the educational paradoxes which are part and parcel of TfD. Baldwin neatly identifies one: 'capacity-building cannot be dictated by the organisations seeking to build capacity – there is a need to consider the goals and motivations of individuals' – a truth also clearly borne out in Au's case study of the Chinese NGOs. The cultural parameters of each context demand a different web of capacities, something very difficult to build in a short-term 'capacity-building' course, and even in a much longer tertiary training, whether in a university or a drama academy. Those cultural parameters always demand a respect that the TfD worker may not have encountered before, such as particular gender taboos that inhibit the practical experience, or a complete unfamiliarity with and even disinclination towards reflective practice. Paradoxically, as Cahill points out, the very acquisition of the capacity-levels of adoption and ownership can inhibit the development of mastery, when the participants revert to their own traditions of transmissive pedagogy. The worldwide privileging of monological, disembodied and acquiescent, non-reflective pedagogy as orthodox practice is perhaps the hardest, most common and most brutal educational challenge facing practitioners in TfD, applied theatre and educational drama, whether they are teachers, facilitators or trainers seeking to develop or embed or at least work with the dialogical, embodied, critical and reflective pedagogy now standard practice in TfD and applied theatre. Each of these case studies shows a willing and at least partially successful attempt to wrestle with and defeat that monster.

# Isolation in Community Theatre

Marcia Pompeo Nogueira[1] and
Dimitri Camorlinga[2]

## Introduction

This chapter analyses an initiative undertaken to revert a delicate moment in theatre practice in the community of Ratones, a small village in the interior of Santa Catarina Island, in Southern Brazil, where we have been working with theatre since 1991. Various articles, published in Brazil and abroad, have spoken of this theatre project and point to its purposes, the methods employed and the creative processes developed, and attest to how much this practice has been an experimental laboratory of the possibilities for Community Theatre both for the theatre students who have worked there as interns or grantees, and for their co-ordinators.

Over the years of this theatre project, as indicated in the article 'Reflections on the impact of a long term theatre for community development project in Southern Brazil',[3] there were two main phases: the first of implementation, from 1991 to 1998 and the second of independent work, which began in 2002. The main difference between the two phases concerns to whom the project belongs:

From 2002 to the present we incorporated important new elements from TfD into the theatre project. The first was the passing of ownership over to the project participants. In the previous phase, we had been people from the university contributing to the community. We decided that the situation should be reversed and that they should be the project coordinators, not us.[4]

Various presentations were produced,[5] allowing the growth of the group in terms of its command of theatre language, at times emphasizing the education and identity of the participants and at other times highlighting ties with the community and the political and social role of theatre. The members of the groups only remained in the theatre group while they were in elementary and middle school. The passage to high school, mainly because there was no high school located in the village, marked a profound change in the lives of the youth from the community. It is a time when they begin to work and give up their studies, or go to high school in another neighbourhood. The type of employment to which many had access – in restaurants, stores or supermarkets – nearly always involves work on weekends. This phase, for most of the youths in the community, signified a premature entry into the adult world: work, study far from the community, marriage and even for some, children. Theatre was left behind; there was no more time for it.

The theatre group, because of this dynamic that was characteristic to low income populations, was constantly changing. Other than Natanael, who stayed at the theatre as co-ordinator and Rafael Buss Ferreira, who shared the co-ordination with Natanael for a few years, no one remained at the theatre after they finished middle school. This reveals a different path than that found in other community theatre groups, such as that of *Nós do Morro*[6] [We from the Hill], from the Morro do Vidigal neighbourhood in Rio de Janeiro; or the *Pombas Urbanas*,[7] [Urban Doves] in São Paulo, in which the formation of new groups is concomitant with the deepening of the theatre practice of the original group. In Ratones, there is no group of veterans, a group of adults who expresses the maturing of the group.

This is not to say that the theatre experience in Ratones has not been passed from one generation to the next. Perhaps through the conduct of the work or the exchange of experiences between the older and younger members of each group, I (Marcia) believe that there is a way of doing theatre that is characteristic of Ratones, based on a taste for improvising, and a collective creation process that emphasizes working with content that is relevant to the group and to the community. There are families in Ratones in which all the children have participated in the theatre group, each one at their own time, often passing the 'theater bug' to cousins and neighbours.

Another characteristic element of community theatre in Ratones is the location where the activities take place: the local public school. Even though it has undergone transformations over these 20 years, including structural restorations and a large increase in the number of students, the school has always been a safe haven for theatre. It is a space, as Helen Nicholson said, that is not a bit glamorous,[8] which indicates the precariousness of the teaching conditions, but a space in which theatre always found support, a rehearsal space.

## Theatre's ties with the community

The relationship between theatre and the community in Ratones has taken various forms. *País dos Urubus* (1991), the first play, was based on a mapping of the location, through 'work with paths,' that generated a map of the community constructed by means of the registration of the locations where the people in the group circulate in the community; and of the identification of the 'stories of lies and stories of truth' that take place on these paths in Ratones.

These proposals created the bases for our knowledge of the community and for inclusion, in the theatre, of the real and imaginary cultural universe of the group.

The *Outra História do Boi* (1995) was the play that brought the group closest to the community of Ratones. It created a parallel between a project to revive this traditional popular dramatic dance, the Boi de

Mamão, in the community, co-ordinated by Nado Gonçalves, and a theatre project that recreated aspects of this tradition and freely included other content proposed by the group that was supported in characters based on significant people in the community. The ties with the community became very strong in this production. It was a time of recognition of the theatre as part of the community, expressed in the appearance of the public and in its participation in the presentation, generated by the identification with the content presented.

In late 1998, our ties with the community expanded even more, during the process of creation of a mural, which was painted on the school in Ratones, and which was related to the production of *Desenterrando o Futuro,*[9] [Unearthing the Future] conducted by students from UDESC, based on a study about the perspective for the future for the youth of Ratones and the youth of the Landless Rural Workers Movement (MST). At the time, the youths from the community would meet under a large old figueira [fig] tree with many broad branches, but in need of care, with exposed roots and many weeds sapping the strength from the old tree. In this work, we identified the tree as a type of 'cultural center' because many youths from Ratones gathered around it.

> The figueira stands at the centre of Ratones community. It was where we first encountered the young people strumming guitars, singing and dancing. It was their youth centre. . . . It could be read to symbolise a place where a collective, gentle acoustic culture still exists, very different to the global culture which dominates their lives. . . . The figueira carried profound personal, democratic and political resonance.[10]

In this project, the image of the figueira was placed at the centre of a mural painted at the school, which was composed through questions such as: what are the *figueira*'s secrets? What has this *figueira* seen? And what will become of the *figueira*?

In the second phase of the theatre in Ratones, the tie with the histories of the community was present in *Deu até briga no 604 (2002)* [There Was Even a Fight on the 604], which portrayed a recurring feud in the history of Ratones, between the people from 'above' and the people from 'below', which culminated in a fight inside the local bus. It also portrayed the way that the community centre at the Catholic Church, built in a volunteer and communal work project by the residents, was taken over by new residents of the community, who were felt to have disrespected the local culture and to have limited the access of residents to the centre. These were very concrete themes that the group took to the stage with the goal of giving visibility to problems that the group identified in the community.

The *Quintal Esquecido* [The Forgotten Yard] (2004) was a study of the history of a community, which focused on toys and games of the past. It involved a rich encounter with the oldest residents of the community who presented life in the past, expressed in the way that people played, danced and got along with each other. This encounter worked with the community memory and brought together old and new residents to speak of this history, which was later incorporated into the spectacle.

After this production, the theatre work in Ratones began to have the support of the municipal Secretariat of Culture and of the NGO Carijós, which worked with environmental problems in Ratones and the surrounding region. In this period, Natanael worked in an independent manner, creating a series of theatrical productions in the community. It was a phase in which the ties of the theatre work with the university became more distant, but closer to other community institutions.

Despite this rich history of theatre, which involved a diversified interaction with the community, by 2012, theatre in Ratones appeared to have become fragile. The theatre group had about ten participants, from 7 to 15 years old, all very strong girls who spoke loudly and very much liked to perform. According to Dimitri, it was a lively but inconsistent group. 'They seemed unsatisfied, they often did not show up, and some of them talked about leaving the group.'[11] We also perceived that the girls, although their practice presented elements of the history of theatre in their community – in the love for improvisation and a great facility for acting – did not have much information about this history of theatre in Ratones. Natanael was their main reference, but he also wanted to give up co-ordination of the theatre. He no longer had funding from the municipal secretariat of culture or the NGO Carijós. He was unmotivated. He was now studying in the School of Education and his interests were becoming distant from the theatre. He wanted to be replaced.

## Reflecting on the problems

The group that proposed to confront this problem is the Group for the Training of Facilitators in Community Theatre (Fofa), a research and extension group composed of professors and students in the undergraduate and master's programs at the Center of Arts of the State University of Santa Catarina and people from the communities, including community leaders, trade union cultural activists, and members of the theatre groups from the four partner communities (Canto da Lagoa, Barra da Lagoa, Tapera and Ratones), including Natanael. What makes Fofa different from other university groups that work in communities is the participation of people from the communities in all phases of the project, from planning to evaluation of the results of each group's action. At the weekly group meetings, the participants study themes of common interest, take part in workshops about methodologies or different aspects of theatre made in community contexts and organize annual events, like the intensive theatre workshop,[12] and international theatre seminars in the community.[13] Each year we have chosen one of the partner communities to be the site of joint activities with all the Fofa members. This joint project always involves a theoretical-methodological study, which contributes to the education of all those involved, and indirectly, to the communities where they work.

Because of the problems identified in Ratones, in 2012, after consultation with the group and with support from Natanael, we chose Ratones for the work with Fofa. To contextualize our project, Dimitri, who was already taking over co-ordination of the group of girls at Ratones,[14] brought data about their motivation for the project.

Fofa made the diagnosis that the group in Ratones was starved of energy because of its isolation in the school space and the lack of contact with the community. It recommended that the history of the theatre in this community be revived, as a route towards the revitalization of the theatre practice. We had a desire to make it clear to the community that it has a history of theatre; to motivate former members of the group to do theatre again; and to bring new people to the theatre to contribute to the strengthening of the current group. The way that Fofa chose to revitalize this history and motivate the residents of Ratones to participate was to have a festival. The festival, according to Juliano Borba,

> is understood as a concept that refers to a collective, symbolic, human predisposition to mark, in a ritual and festive manner, aspects of memory and of identity. Celebration is a practice linked to the collective sense of joy: to come together to produce, share and consume together their material and symbolic goods.[15]

The festival could be a remedy for the loss of energy. We decided to create the Ratones Theater Memory Festival. Juliano Borba[16] and Zeca Nose[17] organized Fofa's educational proposal, based on an approach used by the Argentine group Catalinas Sur. Based in the Boca neighbourhood of Buenos Aires, this group was created at the end of the military dictatorship in Argentina, from a school parents association that began to do theatre in their neighbourhood square.

> Since theater practice emerged in Argentina in the year 1983 with the illusion of the democratic recovery and after ten years of a military government that destroyed and prohibited all forms of artistic practice. The Catalinas Sur theater group was a pioneer in placing this theatrical form in practice . . . to conduct work of neighborhood, social and cultural reconstitution in the location of which it was a part . . . and the understanding of theater as a right for all individuals and not as a privilege of the few.[18]

As in Ratones, the theatre practice of the group Catalinas Sur was dedicated to cultural and social work that could democratize access to theatre. But unlike in Ratones, the Argentine work took place in a public square instead of a closed classroom. This difference attracted other people. By working in an open space, it reached people, involving neighbours[19] of all ages with the theatre work. This characteristic, according to Bidegain,[20] helped to overcome problems of integration faced by the collective, concerning differences in ages, political perspectives and beliefs, creating a meeting space in the community.

> In the totality of these groupings, the inter-generationality, the pluri-generationality is one of the characteristics that gives the greatest wealth to the phenomenon. In addition to establishing an activity that is available to everyone, they achieve something which is not possible in other social realms. In these enormous groups the diversity encompasses everyone. Three-year old children, adolescents, young people, adults, and the elderly cross generational borders without criteria for selection, social status, party affiliation, function, or profession because the primary idea of the poetic of community theater is that the art must form part of the life of the people, and that one can learn together with the other, even those from another generation.[21]

In our studies about Catalina Sur we could perceive the role of the festival in the group's profile, both for those existing in the community and those that are linked to their theatre work. By emphasizing the traditional manifestations of popular culture, or through the emphasis on song, the aesthetic of the group, which had some 300 members, highlighted the role of the festival in the community theatre. We were able to get an idea of this approach during a training session that took place in an Oficina Intensiva [Intensive Workshop] of 2011, with Andrea Salvemini, who was musical director of the group Catalinas Sur. She said that she finds it easier to work with many people, of all ages, than to work with small groups, given that in a chorus, those who don't have great pitch, who would have difficulty singing a solo, are easily guided by the collective. In her experience, the words of the songs, created from parodies of popular songs, become the dramatic basis of the play. The scenes take place through the choruses with different voices, which take on shape, constructing the drama.

Zeca Nose brought to our training session the experience he had in a workshop with Adhemar Bianchi[22] in Barcelona, at which people without theatrical experience were involved in the process, presenting their stories through song and interpretation, very often in the format of the chorus, which gained theatrical body through subtle direction, assumed by Adhemar Bianchi. The work took place in a square and those who came over to watch what was happening were involved in the work and came to take part in the scene. Another curiosity of the group Catalinas Sur is the strategy of the *choripan*, the grilling of sausages at the group's festivals and presentations to attract neighbours through the aroma, bringing them into the vicinity of the theatrical production.

## Articulating memory and rediscovering the community

To incorporate Fofa's plan for the revitalization of the group, and to adapt the methodology studied to the context of Ratones, a path was being articulated through three actions. One involved the invitations to the casts of the different productions presented in Ratones to participate in the encounters of the current group, bringing a strong element from each play to be experimented with. As a complement, we wanted to find spaces other than the school for rehearsals, to make the theatre practice more visible.

Another action was the reconstitution of the presentation of the *Boi de Mamão* in Ratones, made by the group Arreda Boi, from Barra da Lagoa, through the project *Escola de Boi de Mamão: Prática pedagógica da brincadeira do boi de mamão*.[23] This work was organized by Nado Gonçalves, a member of Fofa who had worked in Ratones for many years, especially in the process of mounting *A Outra História do Boi*, when he began an investigation about the Boi de Mamão in the community. His work had a deep contact with the old singers and musicians and culminated in 1994 with the revival of the dramatic dance in the community. Nado's return to Ratones also involved a process of interviews with old residents of Ratones, who were involved with the Boi de Mamão.[24] The idea was to find a new group to 'play' with the *boi* (a puppet ox) in Ratones.

The third action, which united the two others, was the Memory Festival. The planning of this action involved all the members of Fofa. Each person brought a contribution and the synthesis of all of them was placed totally in practice, each detail planned – popular dances, community singing, Boi de Mamão, exhibits of photos and designs of the theatre process over the years in Ratones, theatrical skits created by the current theatre group in Ratones, a procession by the community with the animals from the boi de mamão as well as grilled sausages were all incorporated. To maintain the rhythm that would create a certain 'custom' in the community, seeking to bring together more participants, we planned three consecutive festivals, the repercussion of each one generating more interest, so that other people would participate in the following festivals.

The process of personally inviting the participants in the earlier theatre groups to participate in the encounters of the current group had already become an activity that led us to interact with the community. All the members of the current group participated in extending the invitations and we always took old photos that were admired by the former members, always stimulating conversation about the memories.

It was intriguing to walk through the community. Even for Natanael, a resident of Ratones, many things were new. He was surprised with the changes in the neighbourhood: 'Wow, how it's changed! How it's grown,' he said. 'There was only one house here and now its full of houses.' Even living there, he no longer knew the community as he did when he spent all day there. Today, working and studying outside the neighbourhood, he began to lose contact.

The first house visited by Dimitri, together with the girls, was that of Lincon, a former member of the group who had participated in the spectacle *A Outra História do Boi*, who lived relatively close to the school. Dimitri reported:

> After a meeting at the school with the girls, we went to his house, and arriving there we found him painting a wall, while his father and brother painted a boat. I began to say something about the theater group, realizing that he was already excited to see all the children that had come together to meet him. As soon as the issue was raised, the reaction of the three was unanimous. They began to speak at the same time and got excited about the memory of the time in which they participated in the group, and they soon joined in telling about the events that led to the spectacle 'Deu até Briga no 604.' The commentaries were that it was truly difficult for the people to be able to understand each other, and that the spectacle was perhaps the only way that the community had to openly discuss the issue.[25]

Situations like this made us hopeful as we continued the process of reviving the memory of theatre in Ratones. The invitations triggered positive reactions. People especially liked seeing the photos of the creative processes and the montages, but few appeared at the meetings in the school room, the location where the girl's weekly meetings took place.

In the search for a new environment, we undertook a rehearsal at the fig tree. We expected to find other young people there who could come back to the theatre or the *boi de mamão*. According to a proposal decided on by Fofa, at the fig tree we would be able to find others who were interested in participating in the group and even propose a moment for a snack with everyone, thus creating the possibility that the former participants would come to a more informal environment, where the activities took place more spontaneously. Nevertheless, during the first rehearsal at the fig tree, the group was alone. The tree receives much better care: a small wall was protecting its roots, but the young people no longer meet in its shade. There were only two girls playing at the tree. We thought of inviting them for a snack, but the girls from the theatre didn't like the other girls. The girls in the group had brought food but didn't want to share with those who hadn't brought anything. Our open rehearsal did not bring in anyone.

We left there concerned. For me it was also a shock to realize that I no longer knew the community. The fig tree, which was the heart of the community and the meeting place for young people, no longer had this role. Could there be other places where the young people met?

We were thus concerned that perhaps it would not be possible to have the festivals at the fig tree, and we thought of the possibility of finding alternative spaces. But the options that arose were always tied to an institution that limited the hours their space was available and the type of activity. The school, one of these places, already had a specific project for Saturdays, with a co-ordinator and set hours, which were not very flexible. The Residents Association of Ratones (AMORA) had a relatively new space with a sports court and a small meeting space, which was restricted to officially established activities, and had limited hours and not many openings for a festival. It was also farther from the area where most of the participants and former participants of the group lived.

We questioned whether the space was the problem or the fact that the residents of Ratones no longer got together as in the past. We insisted on the encounters at the fig tree, after the rehearsals. We therefore continued, insisting on the parallel meetings to prepare activities for the festival, such as a parody of the classic Brazilian song Asa Branca, in the spirit of the work of Catalinas Sur. The text created by the girls for the song spoke of the relationship between those who enter and those who leave Ratones, the theatre that is found there, the longing of those who are forced to leave, and the family relations that are very strong in this environment. Formation of Facilitators in Community Theatre (FOFA) also prepared for the festival by rehearsing the song created by the girls in the theatre group, and based on it, invented a group dynamic for community participation.

The festivals exceeded our expectations. In general, all of the elements that we expected were present at the festivals; food, popular dances, singing, the procession, the photo exhibit and the *Boi de Mamão*, everything helped to construct the festival, which little by little gained the strength that we expected, attracting the 'old' and current participants of the theatre in Ratones in an environment that is common to everyone, which in fact was part of a true celebration. Each activity attracted more people and people of all ages. The procession with the puppets from the *Boi de Mamão* was the first to 'awaken' the residents of Ratones. Everyone reacted with surprise and enchantment. The dynamics that were inspired by the music, with the support of Zeca Nose and the ideas borrowed from Catalinas Sur, involved all of those present, regardless of age, in an interaction that related two large choruses that not only sang, but also interpreted what the music presented. A proposal was even made to create a new part of the song, this time speaking of the negative aspects of the community, in an attempt to find an antagonist in this theatrical-musical relationship, but no one ventured to speak poorly of Ratones.

We realized, during the three festivals, that different people were present at each one, including former participants and the community in general, and many people participated intensely in the three festivals, and this participation in most cases was very active, whether in the theatrical dynamics, in the song that the group of girls composed, or even when observing the photos that portrayed the theatre of Ratones in other times.

Unlike what happened at Catalinas Sur, the grilled sausage did not attract as many people as we expected, and this was probably because it was not something promoted by the community, but by the group that helped to organize the festivals, FOFA. It did not interfere with the activities, but it did not have the expected repercussions.

We realized, at these festive moments, that the fig tree still has great potential for community gatherings. At least the community liked the festivals, which on those days, fulfilled their role of expressing the community.

# Final thoughts

Trying to assess this process, it is possible to say that it was successful in terms of the involvement of the community members in the activities. The festivals proved to be effective in terms of gathering people from all ages, different from the previous group activities, which were limited in terms of the age group that was involved in the activities. It brought joy, engagement with each other and recognition of the theatrical history in the community.

However, the aim of motivating former members of the group to do theatre again failed completely. The theatre group remained the same after the festival and the symptoms of isolation increased after the Fofa intervention.

The idea of finding another group to renew the *Boi de Mamão* in Ratones also failed. *Arreda Boi* members managed to make a new set of giant puppets to be given to what they expected would be the new *Boi de Mamão* group, in Ratones. At the end they were given to the head teacher, imagining that he could do in the school what we did not manage to achieve.

Analysing these results we can identify other problems that are beyond our power to change; a bigger 'disease' that affects several communities the world over: neoliberal capitalism.

The moment of finishing middle school is hard because, apart from religion, the school is the only collective space in the community. Leaving the school is not just a time that young people leave the theatre group. It is when the imposition of the economic system is made clear. It is when their time for playing together, for having a collective time enjoying themselves and organizing their view about the community and of the world is 'stolen'. The level of work demand is so high that it consumes all creative energy.

In this sense, the practice under the *figueira* tree happened because it was related to an event. It would not have worked without the high level of energy that the *Fofa* group brought to it, calling people to go out, to get together, to dance, sing and have fun. While they were there they showed that the community's nature was the same, as they still love to dance, to perform and to be together.

Does this mean that community theatre is not possible in the current neoliberal world? From our point of view, the desire of the community to have a cultural and artistic space, in order to be able to play, to create collectively is in opposition to the pressure of the neoliberal capitalist strategies to increase their profit as much as possible by exploitation of the working classes. This tension can generate several community and personal 'diseases'. Community theatre can contribute to reduce these tensions.

It seems that Ratones, like many other low income communities, is experiencing an unbalanced situation; while selling their labour, little is left for a creative production. For other communities, however, the demand for a creative space, to have voice, speaks louder and they fight for small spaces of freedom. That can be found in several communities and I would say that at the moment, in Brazil, they are increasing as it is possible to find a growing number of community theatre practices. Maybe theatre in Ratones needs to die in order to be missed, and then to return again.

# The Game of Identities: Intercultural Theatre in the Peruvian Amazon[1]

Rodrigo Benza Guerra

*I have never attempted to disguise my 'foreignness', the quirks and particularities of my own cultural identity which has been shaped through my own background, religion, location, education, travel. Rather, I have tried to work through my difference in order to confront other cultural identities in India with the implicit belief that we are connected through citizenship and, more deeply, through the memories, wounds and possibilities of a shared history.*[2]

When implementing theatre projects in communities, we usually focus on the benefits these can bring to the participants or communities, such as giving voice, teaching new languages, developing self-esteem, strengthening the organization, etc. Meanwhile, what happens with the facilitators or teachers who are not part of the community but coordinate this theatre work? What are the motivations of these facilitators? What do they learn?

These questions, and others, emerged in the process of my MA research, from my discoveries and questions. Originally, I aimed to explore how, through theatre, young indigenous students at an intercultural university in the Peruvian Amazon could reflect on their own intercultural identity. By intercultural identity I meant that identity that is formed from elements of different cultures.

My interest in working on identity has two main starting points. The first one is the observation that many indigenous people, especially those who live in the city, experience an identity crisis. In 2006 and

2007, I coordinated two intercultural theatre experiences with young indigenous persons and mestizos[3] in the city of Pucallpa, in which theatre and visual arts workshops were conducted and plays were created and performed in indigenous communities and in the city.[4] Thanks to these projects I was able to see that many young indigenous people who live in the city experience a 'belonging' problem since, on the one hand, the community is no longer their space, and at the same time the mainly mestizo urban society does not accept them as citizens with full rights. In the words of teacher Lener Guimaraes, from the Shipibo – Konibo culture[5]: 'I think we, the Amazonian cultures, are . . . in a time in which we have reached a place where we can't sail, go backwards or forward. . . . We have nowhere to go. What we need to do now is identify the course to clearly identify who we are.'[6]

The second starting point is my own life experience, because, to paraphrase Richard Schechner 'who I am, is not irrelevant'.[7]

I am a white man, born in the city of Lima, from the upper middle class, part of the dominant culture of my country, who studied in a private university, who grew up in a socialist family, who began to relate to the Amazon and indigenous people at the age of 17, who loves to travel, who feels more comfortable in a neighbourhood pub than in a fancy restaurant. I'm a theatre person who searches, through his artistic practice, to build bridges between different groups of society; to produce, through theatre, knowledge, recognition and learning within groups and from 'the other', the different.

Constantly, especially when travelling outside Lima, people ask me where am I from. 'Peru', I answer. 'You do not look Peruvian.' This still happens, but when I was younger the fact of not being recognized as Peruvian, mainly because I'm white, used to make me feel quite uncomfortable. I think this is the reason for my interest in interculturality as a way to find my own identity and my own belonging.

These two reasons, added to the reading of authors such as Amartya Sen[8] and Amin Maalouf,[9] led me to want to research how theatrical practice could generate an appropriate space to reflect, define and reshape identity in the context of the confluence of different cultures.

My intention was that, during the theatre workshop, the participants could identify the different elements that constitute their identity and the cultural origin of these elements, that is, if they are originally from their native culture or from Western culture. Then they would be capable of reelaborating their own identities through the theatrical exploration of these elements, deciding which of them are important to define who they are.

The research fieldwork would consist of a theatre workshop and the possible creation of a theatrical spectacle with indigenous students of the Intercultural National Amazonian University (Universidad Nacional Intercultural de la Amazonía, UNIA) located in the city of Pucallpa in the Peruvian Amazon. Before arriving at UNIA, I began to question all the principles on which I had based my research project. Which are these characteristics and values of Western culture? Which are the values of the indigenous people who, despite their differences, share common features? Which elements of Western culture could be appropriated by different cultures without losing their essence? What elements of indigenous cultures could be changed? Is it necessary to define a culture of belonging? How to know which features are derived from the indigenous culture and which acquired in contact with the Western world? And finally, I began to question these questions since they followed static conceptions of culture and identity.

At the same time, I was experiencing an unusual insecurity and anxiety about the implementation of the workshop. I felt that it was necessary to achieve the goals of the experiment because it was part of an ongoing research. But then I realized that if my focus was on achieving results, I could sacrifice the natural development of the workshop. What was more important, the research or the workshop?

During the first weeks of the workshop, I started to interview some participants and realized that to get to know them, to research their identities, I didn't need theatre. But did I want to research identity? Theatre? Theatre as a means to develop identity? These queries about working on identity with indigenous students were present from the beginning of the experience, as in these excerpts from my field diary:

August 15 (first day of the workshop)

I was thinking I needed to forget the research during the workshop to allow issues to arise. If it's really important for the participants, the subject of identity will emerge naturally. I realized that I was actually proposing a social study using the theatre and not a study on theatre. I also realized I was not interested in studying that. What interests me is the use of theatre to generate our own stories and enquiries: to produce spaces of freedom and creation – alternative spaces. I feel that instead of focusing on the issue of identity, I should focus on the evaluation of the ongoing workshop and let it flow naturally.

August 18

I have the impression that with them it is not so necessary to discuss identity. Is it? I don't know. Each time I get more convinced of the importance of working these issues with those who discriminate, those who are in positions of power, those who have a development vision based exclusively on the economy.

August 31

My initial interviews are not very useful for theatre research because they do not talk about the practical experience and I'm not getting to know the participants through theatre. It could be useful to know more about the participants' reality, and perhaps pick up possible topics for the scenes. But if I had been doing research that had nothing to do with theatre, I would have gotten the same information.

Then I found Rustom Bharucha who is an Indian researcher of the world and social phenomena, through theatre. His point of view is: 'I could not have addressed the overlapping narratives of globalization, communalism and culturalism without the concrete insights that I have gained about these phenomena through the immediacies of theatre.'[10] This working principle helped me understand that the different aspects (theatre, participants, society), involved in a theatrical work that seeks to generate a dialogical experience in the participants, cannot be separated. In fact, they are totally connected. Therefore, to understand

and develop a theatrical practice, it is important to understand the world of the participants and the social phenomena in which they (we) are inserted. At the same time, these phenomena can be better understood through the theatrical work.

On the other hand, following Phillip Taylor who says that when making an evaluation of applied theatre, it is not imperative to prove a preconceived hypothesis, but rather to allow the data gathered from the experience itself to generate the hypothesis,[11] I quickly decided to temporarily leave aside the concern about researching intercultural identity and focus on the workshop process that was already designed to work with identity issues. Later on I would see what to do with the survey data.

We started a workshop based on games for team building, generation of a climate of trust, and imagination development.[12] This was done through storytelling (fiction and non-fiction) brought by the participants themselves, and improvising and creating scenes as a response to different stimuli. For example, we created scenes depicting moments of their everyday life, from objects, or representing their ideas of what interculturality is.

In addition, the concept for all the scenic work was built around the creation of masks. The idea of working with masks comes from the interest in the subject of identity. The proposal was that each participant would create a mask of a symbolic self-portrait[13] that later would become a character. All the creative process would be mediated by the mask.

I wanted to work from masks for three main reasons. The first is that masks are universal. They are present in rituals and games around the world. The second is that the mask allows the actor to feel protected to do things that he/she may not feel comfortable to do with the face uncovered. The third reason is that I wanted to depart from a naturalistic representation.[14]

We built the masks and were able to do their map of life but unfortunately we could not do the scenic work with masks because we had to close the workshop due to the drop in the number of participants. I had planned an intense 2 months' workshop in which deep reflections and identity formation conflicts of these indigenous students could arise. But 3 weeks from the beginning of the workshop, we had to shut it down. What to do? Go away? Make a new call? Find another group to work elsewhere? In the midst of this crisis, my wife, whom I had left alone in the cold and rainy winter of Florianópolis, asked me: 'why do you go back to work in the Amazon?' This question, asked basically as a complaint, became, sometimes consciously and at other times unconsciously, the goal of my research.

I had given preference to indigenous students for the first workshop, although some participants were mestizos. This resulted in some mestizo students who could have participated not approaching me. We decided to solve this problem and, with the help of some of the participants, made a new call. In this new period some of the students of the first workshop continued and new students from different ethnic groups, including mestizos, joined us.[15] This variety of participants allowed the theatre workshop to become a forum for exchange and intercultural exploration for the students themselves.

In this second workshop we kept working with stories, games and improvisation from topics of interest for the participants who were gradually focusing on their experiences as students of an intercultural university and culminated in the public presentation in the auditorium of the University of the piece *¿Y tú?* (And you?), created by the 13 students.

As all the creative work emerged from the experiences of the participants, many elements of their collective and personal identities were naturally presented through the fictional work. Chris Johnston states that drama has a celebratory character in which dreams can be externalized, recognizing that below the surface, we all have aspirations and fantasies that do not find ways to be expressed in everyday life.[16] Censorship and fear of making oneself ridiculous, as well as the awkwardness of showing yourself vulnerable are huge. Often things that are part of us and had not been thought about but we weren't able to externalize, arise through works of fiction. According to Helen Nicholson, blurring the boundaries between reality and fiction generates a safe space to allow theatre processes' participants to transform their experiences in metaphors or to find meeting points that are presented theatrically. In this juxtaposition, new understandings can emerge.[17]

Fiction has this power to generate a distance in which, as stated by Tim Prentki and Jan Selman, the unsayable can be said thanks to the power of symbol and metaphor. 'Theatre allows us to enter difficult and dangerous territory, whether emotionally, socially or politically.'[18] According to Taylor this 'distant frame of reference' allows us to deal with painful scenes through the use of analogy, and parallels with real life can be made through 'indirect observation'.[19]

Some of the dynamics used in the workshops favoured the exploration of individual identities, for example, when creating the masks or working with games such as turning into an animal or plant. However, even in situations that are close to the participants' everyday life, we can identify fictional elements in the sense proposed by Barbara Hardy for whom the narrative is 'a primary act of the mind transferred into art from life'.[20] Thus, all the stories, including the most fantastic, have life as a starting point and at the same time, when telling a story, even a real one, it already has an atmosphere of fiction. I tell what I remember of what happened from a particular point of view, choosing the most important moments and emphasizing certain situations.

## Masks

The process of creating the masks was guided by the visual artist Jorge Caparó (Capa)[21] and began, as was said, from a symbolic self-portrait. When the masks were ready, the participants created their map of life,[22] which consisted of choosing a name for the mask and writing or drawing on three separate sheets the answers to the following questions about the mask:

1. Where is it from?
2. Who is it today and what are its dreams?
3. How will its future be?

On the maps interesting and complex characters emerged. For example, the name of one of the masks was *Bukea* and his map of life had the following texts:

Page 1: Bukea lives in the forest

Page 2: Bukea is a nocturnal animal. He lives where there are large trees, useful for wood. Father of the Forest. Protects the environment.

Page 3: His ongoing dream is to identify problems to solve them, and wants to be alone, with no fuss or enemies.

Page 4: Now he is the master of the woods. He's dangerous. He has no wings and walks on the air. WHO WILL HE BE IN THE FUTURE? Master of the forest. He will protect the forest, the air and the ravines, from contamination.

The participant who made *Bukea* was the youngest of the Awajun ethnic group. He was very quiet (not fluent in Spanish), but participated with enthusiasm and responsibility in the workshops.

Another mask was called *El Jaguar*. His life map matched text with drawings:

Page 1: Comes from the forest – it's cold – is swampy – is mountain – likes the river.

Page 2: Likes to start a family – will be a generous person – loves to sing – will be a teacher – wants to live in peace – will be leader of his people.

Page 3: He will be a wise animal that will protect the animals of the forest – Will use its force to face the danger of contamination – will be kind to other living beings – will be a rights defender – wants to be a doctor of pedagogy – will be a surgeon.

The participant who created the mask was one of the most active and, after living with him for 2 months, I realized that his kindness and generosity are accompanied by a deep, contained aggressiveness. The Awajun is a traditionally warrior ethnic group and despite being quiet in everyday life, they can also be very aggressive.

In general, the characteristics of the masks were related to the participant's characteristics. For example, the dream of the mask *El músico* (the musician) was to be a great musician, but he was afraid of the public. The participant who created it loved music and always carried his *quena* (Andean flute). Another participant, who is a nurse and worked on AIDS prevention in Shipibo – Konibo communities, created a character that was a tree that healed men in harmony with nature.

One element that emerged in three of the maps of life was the devil, or demons, and the desire to scare people.

## Transformation into animal or plant

In the Amazon, the contact with nature allows participants to have very specific references and models of animals and plants, so they could perform a very accurate transformation. For this game we went to a garden and, despite the problems (like ants), the following conversation revealed some very interesting things.

Two of the participants became *pelejos* (sloths) because they identified themselves with its slowness. One of them added that his survival gets more and more difficult because there's less food. Another participant became a mango tree because its fruits are good for people. She identified with the tree because she is a mother. Another one became a Capirona[23] because it is a big and strong tree. Another one was a dog because he looks after the women when they go to the field.

The representations, especially of the animals, were fairly clear and in general it was easy to identify the animal into which they had transformed. During the conversation after the game, everyone could mention specific characteristics of the animal or plant which he or she became and generally were related to concerns or aspects of their own life.

## Turn into sound

Another important game was to turn into sound. Eyes closed, the participants had to try to listen to all the sounds around, choose one and start to imitate it; look for a body for the sound and finally create a character from that sound. Elias became a tractor: 'When I heard the noise of the engine, I got upset because I was not used to it and I wanted to be in a free quiet space, and being here I felt I had no food, nor enough room to be calm.'[24] Alver turned into a bird:

> After focusing, you choose what kind of animal you are. So, right now, in this sunny afternoon, the bird feels tired, and then sits on a tree that has shadow and begins to sing. Looks for food. So we decided to go elsewhere to look for more food because we are out of it.[25]

Franguine focused on a cricket:

> I focused on the sound of a cricket, which is a sound that comes out, something special: trs, trs. He does that because he is feeling lonely, because he doesn't have a partner to answer him. He feels that he is the only one there under the sunlight, and sometimes feels sad. . . . This also made me reflect because often as persons, if we cannot count on our mates, if they have no interest in dialogue with us, . . . certainly he feels it. I imitated the sound of the cricket and at the same time I became a cricket.[26]

This game was very productive because of the wealth of the participants' experience. In the case of Elias and Alver the issue of the lack of food, which is present in their daily lives, is very significant. Franguine brings the theme of loneliness and sadness, which is also part of their daily life.

Some aspects of cultural identity, mainly of indigenous students, also came up. Here it is important to emphasize that our identity is formed by multiple dynamic elements that we absorb along our lives, while others disappear, become protagonist or remain in the background. According to Amin Maalouf, 'all the experiences and significances we give to different aspects of our life (religion, language, labour activity, etc.), establish our identity, but it changes in time, in relation to our own experiences'.[27] Therefore, some elements of our identity are flexible and variable, and are adapted and formed through the dialogue with others.

To the workshops' participants, both the formation of identities and the choice of the elements to be shown are directly related to their context and also to different forms of discrimination. In scenes created from improvisation, there were many situations of discrimination, mainly from mestizos towards the indigenous, including situations within the classroom and by teachers.

I realized that the strategy used by the indigenous participants to survive both in the city and in the communities is adaptation. In the city they adopt the ways and values of the mestizos, as in the case of Robert:

> What I use: pants, shoes, everything . . . is from the mestizos. So I always say: on the surface I am a mestizo. Why? Because of the way I dress. But inside I am Awajun, because of my language. . . . When I'm in a city, I do not live as an Awajun. If there is a group of mestizos where I live, I have to live also as a mestizo. . . . But when I go to my community, I eat my own culture's food, speak my language, and participate in all the communal activities, like *minga*,[28] for example.[29]

The teacher Haydeé, who attended the first workshop, confirms this: 'From the moment in which [the indigenous student] is in the urban area, studies and works there, he doesn't feel part of that world [of his home world], until the moment when he returns to his village, his home.'[30]

Despite the way they adapt to live in the city, the indigenous participants of the workshops had great affection and respect for their own customs and culture. Some of them even see the possibility of becoming teachers as a way to be able to convey in school, ancestral customs of their culture. This cultural value was perceived by Jimmy, a mestizo engineering student: 'Most of them truly like to be from where they are, they are not ashamed to communicate their origin.'[31] But at the same time, all participants indicate that they have colleagues who deny their indigenous origin because of shame.

According to the Peruvian anthropologist Luis Mujica :

Each person who claims to be part of a community can participate – and indeed participates – in worldviews, customs, rules of behaviour, artistic and culinary tastes, beliefs and ways of living. All of these elements change in time and within the social relations established.[32]

Now, when we talk about cultural identity, as shown in the previous examples, we can say that it is shaped in opposition to the other groups with which we are in contact.[33] 'Identity always exists in relation to another. That is, identity and otherness are linked in a dialectical relationship.'[34] The relationship with the other, with those who are different, is central to the formation and ongoing transformation of identities. It is in this contact that interculturality makes sense.

Before this project at UNIA, I had developed two previous intercultural theatre experiences, also in the city of Pucallpa, with young indigenous and mestizos. Those experiences focused on the contact between different people and producing knowledge through theatre. Initially, the experience in UNIA intended to deal with identity, and therefore, was conceived more as a space of self-awareness than interrelation. However, the process itself led naturally to recover that space for a fruitful exchange in which all of us could dialogue and confront our identities.

My first approach to intercultural theatre was through practical experiences that sought to create a space of understanding between people of different cultures through theatre work. However, when looking for theoretical background I found that the most extended forms of intercultural theatre are limited to experiences in which a text created in a different culture is used, different cultural aesthetics are blended or are experiences in which artists from different cultures participate, each bringing their own cultural expressions. This vision is focused on the show and seeks to generate an exotic aesthetic composed of different cultural elements.

According to Patrice Pavis 'we cannot speak of intercultural theatre as an established genre or a clearly defined category, at most as a style or practice of theatrical play open to diverse cultural sources.'[35] Pavis adds that this theatre has a 'concern on confrontation, exchange or a hybridization of different cultures.'[36]

To Eugene van Erven the mainstream stance on intercultural theatre is focused on the creation of great exotic shows, but he identifies with a grassroots perspective:

> Barring the odd reference to grass-roots theatre, inter-cultural perfor-
> mance studies tend to concentrate on the meta-cultural abstract
> productions of an international avant-garde operating in prestigious
> metropolitan venues and the world's major grand festival axis running
> from Avignon via Edinburgh to Adelaide and Los Angeles.[37]

There are, then, different positions on the meaning of intercultural theatre and I would like to make it clear that my position diverges from the practices that seek to generate great performances using exotic aesthetics of different cultures. The intercultural theatre I relate to is the one generated by the encounter of people of different cultures establishing dialogue through art. This process, according to Bharucha, is not limited to the understanding of other cultures, but the interaction between them through specific theatre disciplines and languages.[38] To this end, Schechner's definition of the integrative intercultural performance is useful:

> The integrative[intercultural performance] is based on the assumption
> that people from different cultures can not only work together
> successfully but can also harmonize different aesthetic, social and

belief systems, creating fusions or hybrids that are whole and unified. This is not a question of one culture or performance genre absorbing or overwhelming others . . . but of evolving something new from a basis of mutual respect and reciprocity.[39]

The intercultural theatre to which I refer is directly connected to the principle of intracultural work developed by Bharucha in which he seeks to 'create new possibilities of interaction and exchange within and across the wealth of "living" traditions from vastly different time frames and cultural contexts',[40] through theatre. Bharucha is more interested in the contact of cultural groups that interact in the same region within the national boundaries, than in experiments that seek to find the distant exotic to develop new aesthetics.[41]

Therefore, the goal of intercultural theatre would be to generate questionings through the contact with and knowledge of the other, of the different, in the theatrical experience, producing new narratives in this encounter. Intercultural theatre, like any theatre, seeks to entertain, but at the same time, seeks to produce interculturality.

To find a definition of interculturality is complex, but I like the elements of the intercultural concept presented by Alessandra Dibos: its unfinished nature, its critical focus on power structures, its historical consciousness, its dialogic disposition, and its openness and solidarity.[42] The interaction among these elements in different degrees enables intercultural situations to develop from its unfinished character, but always in dialogue and solidarity, taking into account the particular circumstances in which the relationship takes place. Moreover, according to Xavier Etxeberria, 'dialogue is the key word for interculturality'.[43] Therefore, it could be said that the main goal of intercultural theatre is to produce dialogue between people from different cultures through the theatrical experience.

There is a strong link between the principles of interculturality and those developed by Paulo Freire in his search to expand a dialogical education. This link was essential to understand how this intercultural theatre experience was more related to me and my own identity than

I thought. One of the principles of this type of education – which is particularly relevant to this work – is the change of all involved in the educational process. According to Freire, liberating education is 'a situation in which both teachers and students should learn'.[44] Therefore, the dialogical educator learns and experiences transformation, in contact, in dialogue with the students, as much as those in contact with the educator. This is fundamental for Freire's pedagogical principle: 'The more I investigate the people's thinking with them, the more we educate ourselves together. The more we educate ourselves, the more we continue investigating'.[45] However, we must be aware that there are many ways of teaching. According to Freire, people teach in a silent way, 'by their example, by their condition'.[46] Hence teachers should be fully open to receive this knowledge that doesn't belong to anyone, neither to the teacher nor to the students. The 'object to be known' is what guides the learning process. Teachers and students educate each other through dialogue.[47]

It is through dialogue that we form and permanently transform our identities. According to Freire 'dialogue is part of human nature'.[48] What makes us human is the ability to relate, to communicate and interact. But there can't be dialogue if there is no one else to dialogue with. So it is thanks to the existence of the other with whom we dialogue that we exist as humans. As stated by Mikhail Bakhtin: 'it is only through communication, in the interaction of man with man, that the "man within the man" is revealed to others or to himself'.[49] Therefore, it is through dialogue that we become subjects. It is in the interaction with others that we form and negotiate our identity and, at the same time, the other becomes subject thanks to their interaction with us.

To really make dialogue, particularly in an intercultural context, first we need to know ourselves, be aware of our cultural codes,[50] and secondly, recognize that it is in contact with the other, the one who is different from us, that we form our identities. This is why we must be willing to change our assumptions, and be open to 'recognize ourselves' to 're-construct our identities'[51] in a dialogic relation.

Intercultural theatre is a gathering of individuals from different cultures that, through creation and dialogue, elaborate alternative and authentic narratives.[52] In this experience no one is more important than the other and all the relationships, including the teacher-artist, should be through a horizontal dialogue.

Based on the fact that our identity is being shaped by multiple aspects that coexist and are in permanent modification, the encounter of individuals produces changes in all involved, including the teacher-artist or the team that is leading the experience. First we need to clarify that, in the context of the workshop, the teacher-artist is playing the role of leadership, of coordination, but this role is not intrinsic to the person. He is playing this role because he or she has a number of characteristics, such as knowledge of theatrical technique, that puts him or her in that position in this specific context. In any other context, in another situation, a participant can be the leader and the teacher becomes a participant. This follows the dialogic principle that everyone has knowledge that should be cherished.

During the experience in UNIA, one day we went looking for materials to build toys. On that day indigenous participants took full leadership. They knew how to walk through the forest, they knew how to seek materials. They had much more ability than me to see all that was happening around. At one point they told me to be careful not to lay a hand on the trunk of a tree. 'Why?' I asked. Because the bite of this ant hurts a lot, they responded. I had not seen that there were ants on the tree and could not know that the bite of this ant was particularly painful.

This is a simple or even exotic example of the possibility of exchanging the leadership roles. Consciously or unconsciously, the participants taught me many things about how to make dialogue, how to listen, about my own attitudes and contradictions, and about intercultural education. This mutual learning is the essence of dialogic processes.

A moment in which this equivalence could be worked was during a rehearsal when I went away and left them working on their own. At that moment, I had no control of the situation and left because I was tired, frustrated and feeling useless. However, the fact that I had gone delivered a message: you do not need the teacher to work and learn. The next day those who went to the meeting showed two very enlightening scenes (a parody of the workshop and a scene about corruption in hiring teachers).

As I stated earlier, my situation in Peru places me in a position of power. I am a member of the dominant culture of the country. However, the fact that I belong to this culture, of being white,[53] means that I'm not recognized as Peruvian and this was a motivation to research identity. How did the fact that I belong to the dominant culture affect the process? How was I perceived by the participants? I never spoke with them about the subject, so I have no way of knowing how it influenced our relationship. However, I can say that the fact of belonging to this group is quite comfortable because it opens doors and allows me to cycle through very different places. This is an advantage that can be leveraged for personal gain or to benefit the classes of power, but can also be used to generate and seek opportunities for dialogue and questioning power structures. It is also a comfortable position because, unlike the indigenous students, I can be myself always. I do not have to dress differently or speak another language. I have no social pressure to deny or hide my origin.

How does this relate to the experience?
At first I prioritized indigenous students over the mestizos. Why exclude mestizos? What did I pursue in the contact with the indigenous people that I thought (think) I could not receive from the mestizos? Is the fact that mestizos live in the city and, to some extent, have incorporated aspects of the dominant society from where I come and that I criticize, makes me feel less attracted to them? I discover a prejudice here: the mestizo as invader and as a shallow person. I perceive the indigenous as people who can teach me about different worlds, ways of thinking, of living, different values.

I try to have a dialogical attitude in my life and in my relationships. This attitude is fundamental in my role as a theatre teacher and director, which is very important to my identity. I find in intercultural theatre a learning path of confrontation and provocation, a learning path in my eagerness to become increasingly dialogical.

I do not seek to work in remote communities, but in meeting spaces, in this case an Amazonian city as a space in which different ways of life are confronted. Homi K. Bhabha says that rather than thinking of original narratives, it is important to think in terms of

> articulation of cultural differences. These 'in-between places' provide the ground for the development of strategies of subjectivation – individual or collective – that give start to new signs of identity and innovative places of collaboration and contestation, in the act of defining the idea of society.[54]

I'm interested in the space of encounter, of dialogue, of conflict – in the interaction of people, the learning from and with the different, in the exchange.

I wanted to work with young indigenous identity. Now I'm glad that this wasn't the focus and that the workshops became a place of encounter between indigenous people and mestizos. I have a romantic idea of the indigenous way of life and I have, deep inside, a preservationist instinct. This is not because I want the indigenous way of living to always remain the same, but because I believe that their lifestyle is not something of the past, but contemporary. I believe we have much to learn from indigenous people, especially in relation to community life and their relationship with nature. I am totally against those who perceive them as a hindrance to development. In this sense, I think we are urged to develop meeting spaces among different people, between those who have different values. We are urged to learn from each other, knowing that we can learn from each other, that there are other ways of seeing the world, that the different can be similar, that things can be built from the diversity and that this is a value not a barrier.

Theatre is a privileged space for these meetings and there is where its power lies: in providing ourselves and others with a new understanding while living and creating together. This allows us to begin to understand the dynamics of identities that make up every individual, instead of relating to the stereotypes of the other. Intercultural theatre would be a space in which participants as well as teachers, audience and actors, no matter their characteristics – origin, culture, social status, physical or mental disability, skin colour, gender or age – can recover in dialogue their condition as individuals.

A few days ago, I met a young Australian who was interested in going to Peru, to work with theatre in a community. 'I want to go somewhere – she told me – I'm needed.' 'No one needs you or needs me – I said – You better look for a place in which you want to learn new things. A place that can teach you.'

Why do I go back to work in the Amazon?

I go back because I learn about it, about its people and with them (both native and mestizo), about its complexities and its contradictions. I learn about myself, about my complexities and my contradictions.

I learn that I am the heir of a cultural tradition, that I'm part of the dominant society of my country. I learn that I'm a city boy.

I learn about power relations, about poverty, about discrimination, about interculturality, about opportunities. I learn about acquired discourses and baseless acts.

I learn about theatre as a means and as an end; about theatre as a space for dialogue and interculturality. I learn to play, to eat from the same dish, to navigate across the same river.

I learn that the noble savage doesn't exist; that the indigenous is not good just for being indigenous, and white, my white, is not a colonizer just for being white.

I learn that conflict is not bad, but is an important part of life. I learn about tolerance and intolerance. I learn to give, to receive, to shut my mouth.

I learn to dialogue.

# 6

# Imizamo Yethu – 'our efforts' to Engage Through Theatre

Veronica Baxter,
University of Cape Town, South Africa

*It is almost forty years since Iris Murdoch mounted a strong and influential argument for placing beauty at the heart of any project whose central question is 'How can we make ourselves better?'*[1]

It is often misunderstood what exactly theatre can do in a community, and never more so when that community is deprived of basic services that much of the world takes for granted. The theatre offers no material help – it cannot provide water, sanitation or safe shelter to the poor. To offer an engagement in theatre serves to raise expectations in those with whom you work, in particular if you come from a historically privileged race or class, and academic institution. An engagement over 6 months with the community of *Imizamo Yethu* (translated as 'our efforts') in 2012 and work with adolescents on the health implications of TB vaccination trials in the Boland during 2013 serve to illustrate these practical tensions in theatre work conducted in difficult political and socio-economic conditions. This chapter will compare and contrast these two applied theatre projects with a long-standing community arts project in Clanwilliam, in order to tease out some ideas around the importance of developing community and individual resilience, and the contribution of beauty and comedy in community-based work.

*Imizamo Yethu* is a sprawling township/squatter settlement near the pristine shores of Cape Town's Cape Point, set up against the Constantia

Nek mountain and closest to the mostly well-to-do Hout Bay. Part of the preparation to work in *Imizamo Yethu* (also known as Mandela Park) was observing a workshop[2] run with young men (and one woman) from the community, all of whom were from neighbouring countries, Zimbabwe, Namibia and Mozambique. Their tales were of a divided township, with very little integration between South Africans (mostly migrants from the Eastern Cape Province) and other nationalities. The township was deemed to have a 50/50 split between 'locals' and 'migrants', a very low rate of employment and a large youthful population. The choice of the participants in this workshop was by a fieldworker for the organization People Against Suffering, Oppression and Poverty (PASSOP).[3] Because he was a fieldworker for PASSOP, his concerns were for immigrants who were in process of applying for asylum or residency, and the complications faced by them under the South African Home Affairs department. This affected the subject matter of the eventual research work, in that from the beginning it became about community integration or the lack thereof. One of the aspects touched upon was the lack of provision of school education in English for the children of immigrants.

The workshop was remarkable also for the mapping of the community on a large piece of newsprint, where the site of each *shebeen* (informal pub) could be pinpointed, as well as the nationality of its clients. There was a great deal of discussion around why these *shebeens* were specific to nationality, the tensions that arose out of dating across nationalities and the 'ownership' generally perceived by men of women. There was discussion around the memory of the 2008 attacks on non-South Africans in the community, and some arguments put forward that these tensions remained high. The issue around so-called xenophobia and asylum seekers became the focus of two MA UCT students,[4] which will be briefly discussed in order to provide further context.

*Imizamo Yethu* only came officially into being in February 1991, when approximately 20 hectares were given over for settlement, site and service, by the regional council. Significantly, this area was originally given to 2,500 predominantly Xhosa-speaking South Africans. This was the first 'black' settlement area in the Hout Bay area that soon became a popular choice for migrants (local and cross-border) especially after the democratic transition in 1994. Settlement was motivated by economic opportunities in fishing, construction, domestic work as well as the tax-free, low-cost housing in room or shack. However by 2006 there were 20,000 people living on less than 20 hectares of land, sharing a dozen public toilets and communal taps, and living under makeshift shacks,[5] and the local council called it a health disaster.

The settlement is a political football between the ruling and opposition parties. The City of Cape Town was run by the African National Congress (ANC) as the provincial administration until April 2009. Since 2009, the Democratic Alliance (DA) – the parliamentary opposition party – has controlled the Western Cape, and according to DA spokesperson, Mmusi Mmaimane, conditions in *Imizamo Yethu* have improved, including 'new schools, hospitals, youth and community centres, drug rehab centres and libraries'.[6]

Rumour has it that there are now approximately 36,000 residents in the area.[7] Many of these new residents are the result of more than a quarter of a million people migrating away from the Eastern Cape between 2006 and 2011.[8] South Africa's President Jacob Zuma visited the area in mid-2013 and commented 'I came to see for myself and I have been shocked to see my people live in these conditions. Not even animals should be forced to live like this'.[9]

No matter the political persuasion of the observer, the conditions in *Imizamo Yethu* are appalling; the infrastructure for the initial stands cannot cope with the size of the current population as regards safe housing and basic sanitation. There are few toilets in the area, and according to one interview source, shack residents carry their faecal waste in plastic shopping bags to where they can dispose of it. *Imizamo Yethu* has limited services for electricity, sewerage and communications. Open fires, gas and paraffin heating are used for cooking and heating, causing a great deal of anxiety about safety.[10] It is literally a tinder box, with runaway fires destroying shacks and killing shack dwellers.

Electric cables lie exposed, and telephone wires are haphazardly strung across shanty roofs and informal shops.

The small group of theatre practitioners from the University of Cape Town proceeded to work with members of this community during the second half of 2012. One student, Shannon Hughes, worked with a group of local youths who belonged to a club focused on social development. She was intent on introducing a critical vocabulary through theatre, working with the youth in describing the community of *Imizamo Yethu* – in the hope of allowing xenophobic tensions to be discussed in a non-threatening environment. Her work was specifically process-oriented, but in order to create a community event, her group devised a short performance about a day in their lives in *Imizamo Yethu*, assisted by Mdu Kweyama, a physical theatre choreographer. Another student, Pedzisai Maedza, interviewed asylum seekers from other African countries and devised a piece of theatre with three actors/asylum seekers receiving harsh treatment at the hands of the Home Affairs officials, juxtaposed with former President Thabo Mbeki's 'I am an African' speech.[11] Mbeki's speech poetically traces his origins to all the immigrants as well as the indigenous people of southern Africa, and challenges the contemporary African:

> I have seen our country torn asunder as these, all of whom are my people, engaged one another in a titanic battle, the one redress a wrong that had been caused by one to another and the other, to defend the indefensible. . . . I have seen concrete expression of the denial of the dignity of a human being emanating from the conscious, systemic and systematic oppressive and repressive activities of other human beings.

Maedza was experimenting with verbatim interviews as a means to create theatre of testimony in a documentary style. Both these work-in-progress projects had a small showing to an invited community in a brief event at the end of 2012 in a local hall that also serves as a church, hospice centre, meetings venue, a feeding scheme, curio shop and artists' workshop. They performed under difficult conditions while an adjacent meeting room was used for band practice. While performance was not the overall objective of either of the projects, there was an evident disjuncture between the aesthetics of the two performance items devised by the UCT students, and the local aesthetic as shown afterwards in short comic sketches and choral performances. This disjuncture is indicative of an old divide between town and township, where the forms employed by 'town' (or here university-trained) practitioners do not cohere with the comic sketches showing 'township' archetypes and situations, and the beautiful choral work. While the divide has narrowed in the past two decades, nevertheless these performances showed that even meeting the expectations of performance can be difficult in an urban Cape Town.

Perhaps the most profound of these differences lay in the broad comic feel to the youth group's own performances, devised independently of our assistance, that focused on situations familiar to soap opera audiences, including establishing paternity, and marital infidelity. Dressed in negligees and hound tooth jackets, characters hid secret lovers and made ribald physical jokes about male potency. The youth group's other great accomplishment was to perform a selection of beautiful choruses, in traditional African gospel style. The group was evidently comfortable with their own 'vernacular' of performance, and shone in these sketches and as a choir, while their audiences were most appreciative of their skills. This was in contrast to the reception that both the student-directed works had received, which could be said to have bewildered their audience.

During this time with the youth group and asylum seekers, bewilderment was part of my own experience in working with children from *Imizamo Yethu*. Our initial tour around the settlement had included a visit to the library,[12] next to a set of offices where community groups and churches meet, and where post is sorted and kept. Any arrival at the library and offices is greeted by many children and dogs from the neighbourhood. The library was well worn, with quite a large selection of children's books, but little for adolescents, and close to nothing for adults. Children's tables and chairs characterized most of the library, and a female security guard, who kept order and an eye on the books and equipment.

The librarian in charge urged us to work with the children who do not have many distractions, especially during winter months. Therefore, assisted by a student, Samkelisiwe Mabaso, the library became the meeting point for drama work with children between 8 and 12 years old – although undoubtedly on many occasions we accepted children younger and older. We started off trying to tell stories with active participation inside the library, but it proved too noisy for other volunteers working with adolescents on school projects. Working outside did not seem feasible because keeping the attention of the children was difficult. Our path was smoothed by a very willing library staff member, who swept one of the offices for our use. Despite this, the aged carpet was thick with sand, and the room was small. The children were reluctant to sit on the floor but nevertheless we went ahead and began our classes. Using a series of African stories told in English, we tried to engage this group which averaged about 15 participants over the August–November period, intending to showcase some work with the other two projects happening in IY.

At first the group seemed impossible to work with – the group inside the office was shifting constantly, with mostly the boys leaving (and returning) to kick about in the sand and building rubble outside. Several children would go outside with the express purpose of looking in at us, climb trees outside the windows of the office in order to peer in, shouting sometimes for attention. There were constant fights that needed to be suppressed, sweet girls tugging at us for attention, and dust. Occasionally in between the chaos we achieved a few moments of real story re-enactment, like pulling the elephant out of the crocodile's mouth, stretching the trunk forever.

An attempt to explore possible tensions within the community through the eyes of the children revolved around the story of a community erecting a wall down the middle, cutting the one side off from fresh water, and the other off from fishing in the sea. Great mime efforts were made to make an imaginary wall, and two groups celebrated greatly on either side of the wall, until they realized they were thirsty and hungry. There were moments of actual deliberation until they came up with the idea of asking the other side of the wall for help, then made a hole through which the respective goods could be exchanged, and eventually breaking down the wall. There were moments when the drama held, and tensions were explored – but by and large the group were eager to solve problems with magical thinking. However, there was much to be understood from their depiction of the adult activities at parties, especially in a community where *shebeens* outnumber all other facilities.

Initially the work was focused on trying to explore and reveal the community's tensions, hoping that the children would develop a critical vocabulary and reflection through our story enactment. There were a few factors that prevented this, not least being that this kind of abstraction is not possible with younger children, and including the behaviour of the children, and the gradual realization that almost every child was Xhosa-speaking in our group (hence no xenophobic tensions). Because we were working with young children, very little English was spoken. Neither of us spoke good Xhosa, but we resolved to manage with the help of the older children. On further investigation it emerged that the *Imizamo Yethu* library was used by South African children, whereas the 'foreign' children would go to the Hout Bay library with their older siblings and parents because there was free internet access there, and far better facilities. It meant that our initial plan to investigate integration of different groups among the children was not possible.

It was often quite difficult work. As I observed the chaotic activities I took into consideration that the children may have been at school for the whole morning, and needed to let off steam. At the same time I was concerned with questioning how many of the children actually went to school at all, or had any structure to their everyday lives. I was aware of differences of economic status (and possibly parenting attention) between the children, and speculated greatly on the relationship between socio-economic deprivation and their behaviour. What was evident was that the children needed attention, affection and an imaginative break from the surrounding poverty. The dramatic workshops were not working, leaving us both weary and frustrated. A breakthrough came in the form of drawings and 'colouring in' – and not drama. I prepared a lesson with a story about a rhinoceros (3 October 2012). I decided to make a set of simple outline pictures of rhinos and a translation of key words into Xhosa, and a summary of an anti-poaching story. We told the story, which was a fairly basic narrative with strong conservation themes. Some of the children acted out the rhino lumbering around the veld, while others were more excited to be the game ranger with a gun. All the way through the story, the children were eyeing the pieces of pristine paper with images of the rhino called Themba (hope), and a picture of a ranger protecting her. At the end of the class we handed out the pictures, and the class was ecstatic. They all clamoured for a picture – to do with it whatever they wanted. It was theirs – they could take it home, 'colour in', or stick it on their wall. It seemed as if it was their own, as nothing before had been.

It seemed as if we had stumbled through a tunnel to the light. It was a very limited breakthrough, and it seems incomprehensible that owning a copy of a simple diagram could make a difference to children in 2012. From this point on, it seemed that the story we told was relatively peripheral to the activity of the children receiving something to 'colour in', which they could also take home.

We moved back into the library, working around children-sized tables and chairs, and lost a few rowdier members of the group. We gained some members who were perhaps attracted by the new calmer way of working. We would tell or read a story while the children coloured in pictures that I had brought. We would use only our voices and seated physical characterization to communicate, because the space was small. If there was a word that was key to the understanding of the story, one of the older children would be dispatched to fetch the English-Xhosa dictionary, reinforcing language learning for us all. Sam and I would colour in alongside, and some of the children would copy our colour schemes.

I had bought several children's books about Cape Peninsula animals, like endangered African penguins and Cape Peninsula baboons, continuing the conservation theme started with the rhino story. Stories were told, and we exchanged sweet hugs, children snuggled up to us, and seemed to hang on every word. There was calmness about the group most of the time, and slowly they started to take trouble with their drawings instead of cursory scribbles, and listened to the stories. It felt like improvement. At the end of each session they would take their drawings and colouring home with them, and it felt as if this was done with pride.

The stories were still told, but the activities were not drama 'on the floor' with full embodiment, but vocal characterization and gesture. It suited me to have this quieter, less active space – and I have a sense that for the children it provided a small moment of calm. In our last session on the 21 November 2012 we focused on Christmas because they were all from Christian families; a story was read, we discussed whether the children went away or stayed, whether they celebrated Christmas with food or gifts, while we all coloured in two different 'cards'. Many of the children chose to leave their Christmas cards strung up as decoration in the library, over the season.

What was clear was that there were not many children who would be away visiting relatives, eating Xmas roast, nor expecting much 'joy to the world'. Their Christmas cards may have been a fragile connection to a fragment of beauty in stark contrast to their surroundings.

**Figure 1** Christmas cards in the *Imizamo Yethu* library.

In this context, a little bit of drama and colouring in pictures from stories seems of little help in the real world, and it certainly wasn't applied drama. However the children showed obvious pride in their pictures, and took them home carefully. Influenced at the time by reading Joe Winston's articles on moral education, beauty and drama,[13] and having worked on the Clanwilliam Arts Project (discussed below) for the first time, this small act made me think about the role of beauty in applied drama and theatre.

Much of theatre work in South Africa over the past forty years has embraced the 'poor theatre' aesthetic, originally derived from experimentation with Peter Brook[14] and Grotowski's[15] idea of the holy actor in the 'empty' space, stripped bare of non-essentials like stage set and costumes. South African theatre directors, including Athol Fugard, Matsemela Manaka and Barney Simon, embraced the idea that the physical actor in an empty space was all that was needed to make theatre. This aesthetic choice resulted in some of South Africa's iconic theatre pieces, like *The Island* (first performed, 1973) and *Woza Albert!* (first performed, 1981). The 'poor theatre' aesthetic was embraced by many in South Africa as a direct result of the success of this type of work and was in keeping with community contexts where people were literally poor, therefore also serving as direct contrast to the extravagance of work made in formal and 'white' theatres, where government subsidies allowed for lavish spectacles in dance, theatre and opera. The aesthetic style to some extent became synonymous with theatre for social justice, and the choice of making 'poor' theatre allied to the cause of literally poor people of South Africa.

The constraints of 'poor theatre' arguably became a default aesthetic that dominated South African theatre, and, while serving the development of an extraordinary athleticism and physical theatre, has potentially stifled other aesthetic options, especially in community contexts. The actor-on-a-bare-stage aesthetic has also privileged what Anuradha Kapur[16] recently referred to as a masculine, Western aesthetic, in her discussion of contemporary feminist performance in India. In contrast to 'poor theatre', she showed photographs of productions with vivid-coloured, lavish sets and costumes, with attention to design of space and actor augmented by lights and sound effects that almost overwhelmed the senses. The effect of these performances is to engulf the senses in visceral beauty, and not only beauty as virtue in doing social good. Perhaps the effect of 'poor theatre' as a default position in much of South African community-based theatre has served to stifle creativity, spectacle and beauty – alienating the very people who most need the optimism of beauty in their lives.

Mark Fleishman writes about the importance of affect and beauty in the annual Clanwilliam Arts Project which takes place in the small town of Clanwilliam, 3 hours drive to the north of Cape Town. For 14 years he and Magnet Theatre's Jennie Reznek have worked with University of Cape Town colleagues and students, Magnet Theatre trainees and Jazzart Dance Company to bring a ten day-long workshop in the creative arts to the community of Clanwilliam. Each year the performance tells one of the stories from an archive of the /Xam (a clan of the San people) as told by //Kabbo to anthropologists, William Bleek and Lucy Lloyd, in 1873.[17]

Fleishman writes that the project is necessarily utopian in trying to re-insert /Xam stories in the community of Clanwilliam, through a week's workshops in storytelling, dance, drama, music and visual arts. Giant lanterns and small tripod lanterns are made and processed on the final evening, followed by a performance event. The work is intensive, and everyone becomes exhausted by the end of the week. However in my limited experience, helping with Clanwilliam over the past two years, all exhaustion is eradicated by the astounding beauty of several hundred children singing songs, the growing collection of lanterns and large puppet figures, and the exuberance of the final performance, outdoors at the hosting school. Giant paper lanterns of the animals in the story lead a procession through the 'coloured' township,[18] eventually assembling an audience of between three and four thousand people to watch. The performance includes a cast of the CommNet Company, students and trainees, at least 40 children, as actors, musicians, dancers, fire dancers, shadow

**Figure 2** Clanwilliam Arts Project 2013.

puppets' voices and manipulators. The performance culminates in a fireworks display.

Fleishman[19] cites James Thompson[20] in demonstrating his point that the act of making beautiful performance is releasing 'radical potential', arguing that

> When the young people of Clanwilliam are given the opportunity to create something by working together, something that they recognise to be beautiful, they want to share this recognition of beauty and their achievement of the beautiful with other participants and other members of the community. (172)

Philosopher Alain De Botton (2013) tweeted that '[W]hen we call a work of art "beautiful," we sense in it values to which we aspire but from which we have been exiled'.[21] While the children's 'colouring in' hardly qualifies as works of art, they nevertheless may have represented a moment in time and a potential for a life lived differently. Tim Prentki[22] argues that applied theatre is 'concerned with supporting change and transformation'. The exceptional work in Clanwilliam, and the small example of children's 'colouring in', raises the idea that social justice is not the only effect that applied theatre can strive for in seeking transformation – and indeed that the *affect* created by beautiful moments contributes towards developing resilience among community members.

Fleishman[23] suggests that in particular,

> faced with a world of 'superfluous evil' and overwhelming need, in which violence, impoverishment, inequality, injustice, silencing, and a lack of aspiration or opportunity for most predominates, we need . . . an aesthetic conception that is able to recognize both the beautiful and the sublime as parts of one idea of beauty.

Resilience has become a buzzword in development circles, generally perceived as the ability to recover from adversity, or a certain mental toughness that protects people and communities in hard times. Could a case be made for beauty (as both comforting and challenging) as part of resilience training? Positive psychologists emphasize the role of resilience in building well-being, and offer courses in resilience training[24] where various other affective attributes form part of the overall aims. These include a focus on optimism, gratitude and empathy, where one of the key indicators of well-being is doing something pleasurable for its own sake. Thompson[25] suggests that when practitioners ask 'participants to create something they understand to be beautiful [this] engages them in a quest that has powerful and potentially positive results'.

The idea of beauty in the arts has been off the table for so long that there is likely to be a collective shudder in the academy, because notions of beauty have been co-opted by capital, commodified and are linked to many other competitive, socially vapid pursuits. It seems frivolous to introduce beauty because of the pain and suffering in our society, which must be seen and heard so that we can bear witness. How can we talk of beauty when infants are raped and murdered, people are brutally attacked daily? Thompson[26] argues that

> Far from being valueless, beauty in being positioned within (or against) a site of suffering can be partly involved in heightening our awareness of it.

I would argue along these lines for placing beauty back into the activity of applied theatre, because beautiful things or moments offer transformative potential and hope and in 'creating a climate or ethos of working, which has structured within it possibilities of community change'.[27] Here I do not mean the pursuit of beauty in the neo-liberal capitalist, commodified sense, but rather beauty as an affective virtue, perhaps in the same way that Lauren Berlant suggests that we substitute 'habituated indifference with a *spreading pleasure*' in search of an alternative ethics of living.[28]

When it came to working with the South African Tuberculosis Vaccination initiative (SATVI)[29] in 2013 on an educational theatre piece about TB and vaccination trials, it was relatively easy to translate these ideas into practice. In order to be persuasive and educational, and so as not to overwhelm people with gloomy statistics, it is also necessary to consider creating beautiful and comic theatre. Designed for adolescent audiences at high schools around Worcester, (South Africa), the piece was based on research in the Boland (an inland part of the Western Cape Province) into the high tuberculosis (TB) infection rates, particularly among the 'coloured' community, and the research objective to find a new vaccination effective for older youths. The area has a high rate of TB (1,400 per 100,000 based on routine TB statistics),[30] and while the inoculation for new-born children is effective for about 10 years, the infection rate for older people is high. Naturally this intersects with infection rates for HIV and people living with AIDS, as well as both these diseases intersecting with poverty and lower rates of education. The performance was developed from a comic book that had been in circulation to adolescents from 2010, developed by SATVI, based at the University of Cape Town and in the Boland town of Worcester. The comic book's storyline followed the decision of a young mother, Karina, to enrol her infant daughter into a vaccination study, and encouraging her family and community to join her. The storyline focuses strongly on a young male adolescent, 'Tupac', who has a bad cough but is reluctant to be tested for TB. His test is clear but it is in this process that he and his family learn about the vaccination trials, and the effectiveness of the current BCG (Bacillus Calmette–Guérin) vaccination given at birth. Whenever there is this much specific fact to communicate and the objective is advocacy, there is a risk that the theatre produced will be dull and preach.

For our project we trained and devised theatre with a group of adolescent school pupils and their drama teacher, Ms Natasha Africa. Our objective was to not only create a piece of theatre that would inform audiences about the prevalence of TB, mention signs, symptoms and protection, but also encourage audiences to participate in vaccination trials. We also envisaged that by involving the school pupils, we would be creating peer educators for TB awareness, through their involvement with the theatre.

A particularly gifted student designer, Matthew Burn, created a pop art style set of portable flats and detailed costumes for the production. These served to lift the production out of the ordinary, and the costumes also contributed to the pupils' enthusiasm for the project. We worked in Afrikaans to create a script that capitalized on the humour of the original comic, the local vernacular, and songs that were memorable for their tunes and words. Together we crafted a piece of theatre that has toured to over 10,000 high school pupils in the Boland in 2013, with resounding success.[31] The audiences were enthralled by the visual and aural spectacle, found the piece very amusing and in follow-up focus group discussions suggested that it was memorable for the songs, and the vividness of the presentation: in short it was beautiful.

Joe Winston[32] explores the relationship between beauty and virtue, and cites the writer, Iris Murdoch, who suggests that an education in the arts is also about 'beauty' which trains us in the love of virtue. How is beauty at all helpful and does it present any radical potential in transforming the lives of children, adolescents and adults? Common sense, derived from television and magazines, suggests that beauty is most associated with the rich and famous, or at best with more elitist practices in the arts. This is a 'common sense' that needs to be resisted in applied theatre practice. The projects outlined here are snapshots of

**Figure 3** Karina se Keuse 2013.

projects that have other aspects to them, but seem to point towards the idea that moments of beauty can make a difference, create an aspiration for doing good or even a moment with renewed courage to continue on life's path. These projects serve to introduce the connections between resilience, optimism and beauty in an applied theatre practice that attempts to develop, in the words of Emma Goldman,[33] 'everybody's right to beautiful radiant things'.

# Theatre in Crisis: Moments of Beauty in Applied Theatre

## Peter O'Connor

Much of New Zealand is known for volcanic activity and New Zealanders often affectionately refer to their homeland as the 'Shaky Isles'. One area previously thought to be relatively immune from the threat of quakes was the city of Christchurch, and the surrounding Canterbury region. Christchurch City, with a population of 400,000, was known as the Garden City. It liked to fashion and promote itself as an idyllic England, transplanted into the South Pacific. Its tranquil city centre, with lazy Avon River, meanders through gardens planted with English Oaks and hosts of daffodils. In the spring it used to draw thousands of Japanese tourists who would wed in a mock 'olde worlde' England that has only ever existed on postcards, and in Hollywood movies. Its picturesque setting on the rich Canterbury plains within striking distance of the Southern Alp mountain range also hid a grinding poverty in its Eastern suburbs. In these suburbs the sins of the neo-liberal revolution that created the modern New Zealand, with the fastest growing gap between rich and poor in the world, was on full display. The debilitating poverty, high rates of unemployment, domestic violence and high crime were the markers of a nation that has embraced a particularly virulent form of neoliberalism since the 1980s.

It was the part of the city I knew well, far removed from the English inspired cathedral and the plusher, richer, landed parts of the city, populated by the proud descendants of the 'first ships'. Many residents of the Eastern suburbs were more recent arrivals: Pacific Island families who had come to New Zealand with the promise of work and a better life from the 1970s, refugee migrant communities from the Horn of Africa, or the original indigenous Maori community who had arrived long before the 'first ships'.

I had worked throughout this part of the city throughout 2009 and 2010, running a nationally funded TIE programme on family violence and child abuse. In the schools we worked in, through the winter months, children arrived in dirty and torn clothes, often without shoes, confirming in their very being the manner in which New Zealand has become a nation of two peoples; those with too much and those with barely enough.

Early in the morning of 4 September 2010, the city of Christchurch, and the surrounding Canterbury region, was hit by an earthquake measuring 7.1 on the Richter scale, causing widespread damage to buildings and infrastructure. Liquefaction and flooding made moving around the city difficult. Damage caused by the quake was estimated at billions of dollars. Thousands of people spent days living in emergency shelters created inside local schools and sports centres. As the city began the slow process of rebuilding, an almost constant stream of unsettling aftershocks rattled the buildings, the people of the city and the surrounding countryside.

On 22 February, I was supposed to be in Christchurch attending meetings about the work that was being planned for the resumption of the family violence work. I had however transferred out of the applied theatre company I had helped establish and was instead working full time for the university. Stephen Dallow, the National Programme Director for the company, had flown down that morning from Auckland and was working on his own in a series of meetings. At 12.48 he sent me a text message saying things were going well. I rang him and he said he was moving away from a building in order to get better cell coverage. I heard him say the word 'quake' before the phone went dead. By the time I got to the car 5 minutes later, the news was reporting that a 6.4 magnitude earthquake had struck, and the inner city of Christchurch was particularly badly hit. Stephen, in answering his phone, had moved away from a building that claimed 161 lives. He contacted me 4 hours later as he made his way out of a city still rocking and bucking under his feet. 185 people died that day, and billions of dollars of damage was caused. Besides the badly damaged inner city, as if a spiteful god had struck, the already poorest residential parts of Christchurch were the hardest hit. A first world city had undeveloped in a matter of seconds and was facing many of the issues facing developing nations.

The experience of the earthquake was felt very differently across the city. The richer areas were not as badly affected – not necessarily meaning houses weren't badly damaged or that many people in these areas did not suffer significant personal, human and economic costs. Many residents of this part of the city had options unavailable to people hit by disaster, in the poorer parts of Christchurch and in many other parts of the world. These people were able to pack up and go elsewhere, either nationally or internationally, short term or long term. Of course the poorest, who were the most badly affected, rarely had this opportunity. They were there for the duration.

## Initial efforts

The first few days after the quake, the media talked about the return to school as signalling a return to normality for the city. However, teachers were not trained, and schools were not in any way prepared, to handle thousands of children returning to schools – not only in a post-traumatic period but, because of the continuing aftershocks, in a period of ongoing trauma. I knew for those teachers the first days back would be hard work. They were expected to be the healers, those who would return life to some sort of normality for thousands of children, even if their own lives were shattered.

Teachers received little formal advice about what they should do when they returned to the classroom alongside the children. The Minister of Education at the time, Anne Tolley, suggested literacy and numeracy would need to remain at the forefront of classrooms, and that teachers of senior levels would need to work hard in order to assist students to catch up with any missed assessments for NZQA. Her only other response to the plight of teachers in Christchurch was to ensure 170 of them lost their jobs at the end of 2011 due to falling attendance rolls.

I knew teachers would be struggling with a range of questions as schools reopened. Should they talk about the earthquake? If they were to talk about the quakes, for how long should they? And how often? Was it appropriate to use the arts somehow to work with the stories of the disaster? Was there a way to use the arts to shift the narratives, in order to find ways of engaging children with school and learning, in such uncertain times?

Two days after the quake I connected with Ginny Thorner who runs a charitable trust in Christchurch called *Learning through the Arts*. Ginny's home had been badly damaged in the quake, and she was living with her children and husband in someone else's home.

In the two days immediately before the September quake I had workshopped with a group of teachers from around the city an old teachers' resource I had written about killing monsters,[1] and Ginny had helped me organize other teacher courses over many years. She was well connected in the Christchurch arts and education communities. I asked if she thought it would be a good idea if I came down and worked with teachers to help them in their return to their classrooms. Ginny said she was happy to help where she could in letting teachers know about the workshops. I said I wanted to work directly in schools with children, to model an approach and then to run a separate workshop for them.

Ginny organized a school for me to work in, where there would be three separate classes for teachers to watch me work with. She put the word out on social media and invited teachers to the workshop. The vast majority of the nearly 100 teachers were people I had previously worked with. It was arranged I would go to Christchurch in the first days that schools returned.

# Pulling it together quickly

Responding to a natural disaster with an applied theatre programme is made difficult by a range of issues I imagine are common to applied theatre companies working in developing countries around the world.

Flights in and out of Christchurch were filled with emergency workers and people leaving and re-entering the city, and flight schedules were also likely to be changed at the last minute as aftershocks rattled the city. Accommodation was of course tricky, but we managed to find a room through a friend of Ginny's who booked a place for us. My Head of School's brother lives in Christchurch and wanted to help and so rode around the city on a bicycle finding a venue for the teacher workshop. This, and seeking the little amount of funding I needed to get to Christchurch, took up all of my time over the 10 days between the earthquake and my flight to Christchurch. It meant that up until the day before we left, I hadn't really planned what I would do when I got there.

A colleague, Juliet Cottrell, had told me about a drama she was working on with children, involving the repair of a torn cloth of dreams. I found further resources written by two other colleagues in Australia, a process drama resource about dream makers.[2] I only had time to read the first line of the story, the line that would sit at the heart of the resource:

> A girl wakes up in the morning and when she gets up, she trips and tears her cloth of dreams.

I only had time to pull together a rough plan of what I might do in Christchurch, with just this small fragment. I was intent on showcasing work that was not about children coming back to school and retelling their stories, but instead creating a fictional context for them to work through the issues that sit behind natural disasters. The sudden and inexplicable tearing of a cloth of dreams seemed to provide a framework for working metaphorically with the issues. I was also intent on creating a dramatic encounter that empowered the children to see themselves as people with agency – people who were not simply the passive victims of the earth's whims. Not that they could change what was happening to them, but how they might be able to see ways to have some control over their response. The sketchy plan I had was to enroll the children as people who might help the little girl in the story. I packed a few blank pieces of curtain material and a box of crayons, thinking I would somehow involve the children in creating new dream cloths in order to return the dreams to the little girl. I planned to take on a teacher in role, as a dream maker, looking for experts in repairing damaged dream cloths. There was only time to plan a few questions that could be asked in order to attempt to provide a rich aesthetic experience for the children.

I flew to Christchurch from Auckland 12 days after the initial quake, with Molly Mullen – a PHD student in applied theatre at the University of Auckland, and a group of dance students lead by Dr Nicholas Rowe, also from the University of Auckland, who had experience of working in trauma sites, including the Gaza Strip. As we took our seats on the plane, it became very clear we were among only a handful of people not in uniform. Any hope of rescuing people from the rubble had passed, and the men and women who had been involved in the search and recovery efforts immediately after the quake were returning for their second furlough with the unenviable task of recovering bodies from the rubble. At that point, I felt overawed and completely inadequate. I was intensely aware of the critiques of limitations regarding the arts I had made myself[3] and how the arts don't literally save lives. I reached into my cabin bag and opened a book I had been given the day before. These words of Freire offered a comfort and a resolve:

> The privileged routinely look for solutions in the wrong places and then when they cannot find the solutions they feel despair, and become convinced that broader change isn't possible and therefore not worth aspiring to or acting towards.[4]

Within an hour of landing we were in our first classroom. As the 20 children arrived with the 15 teachers who were to watch me teach, a small aftershock reminded me of what the work was about.

I told the first line of the story. I asked the group of 5–8-year-olds what kind of story they thought this was. They told me it was a sad story, because when you lose your dreams they might disappear forever. I explained how when I usually tell a story, I have pictures to show as well. I asked if they would mind showing me what they thought the little girl might look like when she finds her cloth torn. The children created still images (or tableaux) from this moment of the story. There were children standing over their pretend cloth with their fists closed, angrily staring at the torn cloth. There were others looking sad and lost, while some stood with a questioning look on their faces. I wondered what the little girl might be thinking, and I used the drama convention of tapping in for thoughts. I clicked over the children's heads so we could hear the little girl's thinking:

'Why did this happen to me?'

'Will my dreams ever come back?'

'This is the saddest day in my life.'

I asked the children if they would like to help the little girl in the story. There was a loud chorus of 'Yes, we can help her'.

I asked if we could pretend I was a dream maker, and if they could be people who helped dream makers. The idea seemed to go down well, so we rubbed our hands together to then warm where on our bodies we kept our imagination. I watched most children put their hands on their heads, but others put hands over their hearts. One little boy put his hands on his legs because he said he liked dancing.

I told the newly recruited dream makers about the little girl, and how sad, worried, and even angry she was at having torn her dream cloth. I asked if they knew, as dream makers, what we might do to help. One little girl mentioned how we could make the girl in the story a dream cloth to borrow until she got hers fixed. Another child suggested putting their own dreams on the cloth for the little girl to use until she got hers back.

I told them how, as a dream maker, I had spare blank cloth. I asked if they could add their own dreams to the cloth. The children climbed across the fabric and busily began using the wax crayons to draw their dreams. A little girl who had lost family in the quake sat and carefully drew herself flying on a unicorn over 'The Land of Everything that is Good'. Her classroom teacher sat and drew a huge oak tree. The roots were long and deep. I asked her about her drawing after the lesson. She explained how she was in the downtown area during the earthquake and had headed to Hagley Park because she felt it would be safer there with the huge trees providing shelter. When she got to Hagley Park the giant, 100-year-old oaks were upended with their roots facing the heavens. She said she wanted to draw the roots back where they belonged.

When we were finished making our new cloth, we stood back to admire our work. One child said, 'It is beautiful, it will work just fine for her'.

We sat and pondered about what we needed to do next.

'Remember we said we'd fix her cloth', said one child. 'But how?' I wondered aloud.

'We get magic thread and fix the tear that way'.

'Do you know how to make magic thread?' I asked.

'Of course, you need all sorts of things'.

'Do you think you could write down what things we need?'

In pairs, the children gathered around while I handed out small pieces of paper for them to write ingredients for a thread strong enough to repair broken dreams. When they had finished writing I asked how we might put all the ingredients together. One child said;

'You'll need a cloud bowl'

'Oh, do you have one?'

'Of course, it's over there' pointing to an empty part of the room.

As we walked over to the bowl, she said, 'Of course it needs to be a big bowl to hold these ingredients'.

We spent some time making sure the bowl was cloud shaped, and we stood around its edges, shoulder-to-shoulder, to help us see the shape of it easier.

I asked for the first ingredient.

One boy said,

'Three bales of belief'.

'Is belief heavy or light?' I asked.

'Heavy'.

Three thousand aftershocks; I thought, of course belief is heavy.

'Right then, we had better roll it in' and we all bent over, and pushed, and shoved, and heaved the belief into the bowl.

Three cups of love, the hugs from your mum and dad, and two pinches of night-time giggles were all added to the cloud bowl.

Finally, I asked, 'Is there anything else we need?'

A seven-year-old girl offered,

'Yes, a teaspoon of light from the darkest tunnel'.

'And how do we add that to the bowl?' I asked.

'You sprinkle it in'. She stood on her tiptoes and held her pretend teaspoon in front of her, and as she added it to the cloud bowl she said;

'See, the light goes through everything'.

We all looked, and I nodded and said, 'Yes, you're right'.

With our magic thread made, we bent over a sleeping Molly and wrapped her in the cloth we made. We stood back and admired our work in making a sad girl happier.

I taught another two classes that day, watched by teachers who had their own heartaches and grief to deal with.

The next day we worked with 70 teachers from across the city. I now had a teaching plan to share with them, based on what I had done the day before. We worked in a bar at a golf course close to the airport. Tourists were playing in the glorious sunshine when only 5 kilometres down the road bodies were still being pulled from the rubble. The incongruity was almost unbearable. We made our own dream cloths and talked about how the lessons might be adapted and built on when they returned to schools over the coming days. As we prepared to fly back to Auckland that night, the news of the devastating quake and tsunami in Japan had broken. Once again our flight was full of uniformed men and women. They were headed to Auckland to catch international flights to Japan. I was overcome by their bravery, and I wept on the plane, at the thought of the scale of their heroism.

## The development of a hero narrative

Hero narratives have bedevilled applied theatre for many years.[5] However, these have been replaced increasingly by a questioning of the claims of its most fervent advocates.

Many of us can recognize how too often applied theatre has 'been positioned as the new Amway, the new medicine man's brand of cure all, the panacea for lifting literacy, numeracy, stopping truancy, empowering poor communities to remain poor, enabling the disabled, a magical potion for curing all the ills of the world'.[6]

However, Prentki and Preston[7] argue that although only a recent term within academic discourse, the origins of applied theatre can be traced to the 'soil of progressive, radical people's movements in various places around the world'. The left-wing, progressive politics of these movements have shaped and guided the pedagogic, ethical, and aesthetic intents of applied theatre practice. Prendergast and Saxton argue, 'this is theatre as activism, enfolded in the safety of entertainment'.[8] For Nicholson[9] applied theatre engages with the notions of active citizenship, and the possibilities of democracy.

However, I would argue that in recent years the desire within the academy to resist the hero narrative has created a timidity of intention, and a growing cynicism about the potential of applied theatre. It has reduced academic discourse to such a level that Michael Balfour argues the most we can hope for is a 'theatre of little changes'.[10] I too have argued elsewhere that applied theatre can be naively complicit with an agenda for social change which can all too easily be subverted or used against itself by state funders.[11] Yet beyond the academy, the response to the Teaspoon of Light narrative suggests a strong desire for celebrating the potential of applied theatre remains. It suggests we might still dream of bigger things than little changes.

The Teaspoon of Light work quickly developed into a hero narrative. The night of the first workshop, I sent an email to my Dean at The University of Auckland and also to friends in applied theatre across the globe. It described the workshop and my response to it. The Dean sent it around the university, and friends forwarded it on so I received acclamation for the work from many different places. A few weeks later, once I had returned to Auckland, I gave a talk that was pod cast and placed on YouTube. Within weeks, thousands had downloaded the video clip of the talk. Within a year the several YouTube clips had been watched over 10,000 times, and I was emailed by people in Mississippi, Queensland, and Finland, saying the clip was being used to talk about the power of the arts in education, to undergraduate classes. I have been invited to tell the story in Australia, the United States, Singapore, Hong Kong, Ireland and throughout New Zealand.

So, despite my own angst about hero narratives, the Teaspoon of Light has developed its own narrative, one which suggests the arts are transformative. However, I have always been conscious that the work in Christchurch was motivated by a desire not to change the world, but rather to find meaningful ways for teachers to engage children within their classrooms when returning to school following a natural disaster. Everyday life for the thousands of children was not changed by this work. There was no transformation. The children I worked with still had to endure thousands of aftershocks and have helplessly watched their parents deal with the demeaning bureaucratic nonsense that always follows disaster. They may have been transported by the work, as Nicholson suggests, into a place beyond the world in which they routinely exist.[12] However, the work has changed little for the lives of children in the quake zones.

What I have increasingly recognized, however, is that the teaspoon of light reminds educators and applied theatre workers of what is still possible within the classroom, and in applied theatre settings. At a time when the world which, regardless of natural disasters, seems to be at a point of continual crisis, the narrative reminds educators and theatre makers that there is another way of working; that there are other possibilities. It reminds educators that literacy and numeracy are not the only goal of education. I often notice the tears flowing freely as I retell the events of this day, and I ask people afterwards why the story makes them weep. I am told of how the story reminds people of why they initially engaged with the arts, in education, in applied theatre. They see in the story not so much a hero narrative as a justification for their own engagement with the arts. I understand too, from their comments, that we work in applied theatre not because of the evidence that what we do makes a difference, but often despite the evidence. We work as an article of faith about the power and potential of the arts to create those moments so that:

> At times, when I confess, I'm startled by beauty, by sudden insight, by a glimpse of my soul. Everything comes together and apart in one brilliant, elusive flash. I sense the wonderment of feeling human.[13]

Applied theatre, I might boldly suggest, is not justified in the post-natural disaster context by what it might do to change the lives of people involved. The purpose of the work might be simply in its ability to startle us back into feeling that wonderment of feeling alive, of creating beauty amidst the ugliness of the disaster. Perhaps the tears flow in the retelling of the story because we are moved by the naiveté of belief in beauty and hope that children might still hold onto in moments of great darkness. Measurements of effectiveness, of change brought about by the work might be useful for funders (although in 30 years of practice, I have always found the power of narrative far more convincing for funders than numbers). But the Teaspoon of Light reminds us the power of the theatre is inside the moment, in that fleeting presence of make believe, that arrives and disappears when we can barely apprehend it. These moments require no justification beyond themselves.

I have wondered too what meaning might come from the description of the light from the little girl, and why it relates so strongly to people. She explains the light must come from within the darkest tunnel, not at the end. How a young child might know the strongest of lights needed to repair broken dreams comes from the darkest of places has often perplexed people. However, the single truth about applied theatre with young people is that it might engage them in knowledge that might most aptly be described as emotional wisdom.[14] Emotional wisdom suggests that children have a capacity beyond emotional intelligence, one based in a deep-seated knowledge of the world which might best be aroused through the arts.

The metaphor of the Teaspoon of Light speaks beyond the original application when people involved in the arts for change consider their own work. I have worked in applied theatre for over 30 years, attempting to make changes to how the world is structured so that ordinary people might benefit. When a little girl suggested that just a small teaspoon of light is enough to make the final difference, I feel vindicated; that it might be worth persevering. I sense others recognize the power of this metaphor for their own work as well. This is entirely a romantic notion of applied theatre, and yet it strikes me it speaks deeply to practitioners in the applied theatre world. In a conversation with Jonothan Neelands, he told me of an occasion when he was challenged at a conference with what was clearly an accusation 'You're merely a romantic modernist'. Jonothan said his reply took the appellation as a compliment and rejoined, 'What other choice do we have?'[15]

In the great reasonable discourse of the academy, we might resist the grand narrative of possibility inherent in applied theatre, but perhaps, the story of the teaspoon of light reminds us that it is exactly the romantic possibility that draws so many of us to the art form. The possibility, that if our work is sprinkled carefully, we might achieve the goals we still ardently seek, but are too reasonable to articulate, rings true for those who engage with this hero narrative.

The hero narrative might therefore be useful, if it doesn't celebrate an individual. In this case, for example, it is very clear this is quite a simple and basic theatrical process requiring not a great deal of skill from the facilitator. It claims nothing beyond itself other than in the telling. It doesn't claim to have changed the world for people, but it does in its startling simplicity remind people how applied theatre has the potential to create light in the darkness, to shift the experience of participants, and in the moment create a sense of what it might mean to rise above and beyond the world.

## Who has the right to help?

When the children were asked if they will help the little girl in the story, they responded with eagerness and it seems a genuine desire to make a positive difference to the story. There is no 'Well, if she has damaged her dream cloth, it's up to her to find a way to fix it herself. Who are we to think we have the solutions to her problems?' There is no 'Perhaps we should wait until the little girl or her family invite us to help her, after all it is her dream cloth, not ours'. There is no 'Well, we don't want to create a culture of dependency, by helping. She might become reliant on outside help and that ultimately doesn't help her at all'. There is no 'People need to live their own lives, who are we to say torn dream cloths aren't culturally appropriate?' There is no 'We might think we have the answers to their problems, but perhaps intervening will only make matters worse'. Instead, the children respond naively, openly and with integrity to the issues inside the drama. I suggest that their response was from a deep concern for someone who had suffered, like they had. Not exactly the same, as the children I worked with didn't literally have torn dream cloths, but they understood at a felt level what it might mean to lose something of this importance from your life.

## The outsider

Perhaps it isn't surprising that criticism of the work was based on questioning my right to be involved in Christchurch, without being invited into the area. I was from the North Island. I hadn't lived through the earthquakes. I didn't know what had happened. My motivation for coming to Christchurch was suspected. The criticism stung very deeply, and at a personal level, because it challenged the intentionality of the work, and therefore my own integrity. As the hero narrative developed, it also did me little favours in managing the criticism.

This made me reconsider and wrestle with the notions of who gives, and what gives, the right to work in applied theatre within a community. This has been a vexed question in both applied theatre and theatre for development for many years.[16]

Syed Ahmed's denunciation of theatre for development, where he wished for a world without its existence, was based on a recognition that:

> development has emerged as a self-perpetuating industry serving the needs of globalisation which is only imperialism in a 'civilised' guise. Underneath all subterfuges of development and theatre for development, if one listens carefully, the haunting question is 'development for whom?'[17]

He rightly questions the motivations of applied theatre companies with development agendas perpetuating rapacious capitalism. Ahmed recognizes indigenous theatre companies also have problematics, but clearly he sees intervention from the outside needs to be treated with suspicion.

Briar O'Connor[18] in considering an applied theatre project in New Zealand discusses how notions of the local can be both an enabling and disabling discourse. She notes that calls for local or insider control over projects can be reduced within the New Zealand tribal context, to areas that define sub-tribes, to areas no bigger than small valleys. Members of the wider tribe from outside the valley can still be considered outsiders with no rights to 'intervene'. There are not the resources within these very small communities to manage the multiplying effects of colonization, and the devastation of 30 recent years of neoliberalism, which has compounded the poverty of marginalized indigenous Maori groups. Yet the romanticized notion that local solutions to local problems, that only indigenous people are appropriate to work with indigenous people, pervades thinking about education and social work practice in New Zealand.[19]

It means that even though I had worked in Christchurch for many years, had family and many friends who lived in Christchurch, and I had nearly lost one of my dearest friends and colleagues when I heard his cry of 'quake' as it hit, I wasn't welcomed by some – and simply because I was an outsider. I could have attempted to justify my engagement on the basis of this shared experience. It simply wouldn't have been enough. I could claim that I could work in the Eastern suburbs because I too had grown up in impoverished and ghettoized circumstances. Yet this seems to me, to miss the point entirely.

If we work from a position that applied theatre is merely a theatre of little changes, and we limit ourselves by applying strict rules as to who might have the right to work inside and with what marginalized groups, we run the risk of paralysing ourselves into inertia. We can buy ourselves into a neo-liberal argument, leaving the poor and the abused to their own devices. We can use it as an excuse for inaction. We can, as I have done in the past, condemn the action of outsiders as akin to missionaries or messengers, both undesirable and useless[20] or naively complicit[21] in the wider agendas of globalized capitalism. Or we can despair in the tangled webs and murky terrain of applied theatre[22] so that we are trapped into inaction.

I have worked recently with a team of geo-technical engineers from Auckland, a number of them awarded significant national honours from the government for their concerted efforts in Christchurch over a number of years. They spoke of the criticism they too received, as an Auckland company working in the disaster relief. Their motivations and their results were questioned in a way that did not deter them from continuing with their work.

Nor did the criticism of Teaspoon of Light deter me from continuing. I continued to work in Christchurch for the next 3 years. The work developed into multiple phases, funded through the New Zealand Commission of UNESCO, and the Mental Health Foundation of New Zealand. A Teaspoon of Light Theatre Company was established which was to work with thousands of children in the Eastern suburbs. The workshop team leaders enrolled the children as members of their Teaspoon of Light Dream Recovery Unlimited. They are handed a torn dream cloth and through a morning they repair the cloth through a range of arts processes, including embodying the dreams and bringing them back to life through a dance/movement sequence. The Teaspoon of Light Company was made up of local artists and teachers, who at this phase of the recovery were able to move beyond caring for their own survival needs, into working with others. This work extended the original phase of the work in a way that I have felt has given greater credibility to the initial drama. The original work could be dismissed as one off intervention, but a 3-year commitment to the city and the teaspoon of light process has moved it into a position so that the inside/ outside argument becomes irrelevant.

Although Ahmed might argue for the end of theatre for development, he certainly doesn't argue for the end of theatre. Instead he demands a 'plain and simple theatre . . . that allows debate, dialogue, reflexivity, dreaming the impossible and the flight to infinity.'[23] It is vitally important to consider the intentionality of applied theatre work. It is vital to consider the implications and unintended outcomes of our work. It is vital to engage in robust critical debate about work that illuminates the problematics of what we do. It is vital we do not perpetuate romanticized notions of the power and potential of applied theatre, and the sense that it can only do good when this is clearly not the case. But perhaps we need also to keep our work vital. Alive to making mistakes, alive to acting on impulse, acting as the children in the initial Teaspoon of Light programme did; without recourse to over intellectualizing, but from a belief that however small their contribution might be, dream cloths might be restored.

# Exploring Theatre as a Pedagogy for 'Developing Citizens' in an English Primary School

## Alison Lloyd Williams

This case study concerns a Theatre for Development (TfD) project I led in an English primary school, which invited pupils to create and share performance work about themselves and their communities with school pupils in Uganda.[1] My analysis of this project brings together ideas about education, development and citizenship in relation to theories about childhood and performance to reassess the notion of the 'developing citizen' and the role of the school in citizenship development. I make a case for a pedagogy of Theatre for Development in education, configuring schools as key sites for development within their communities and children as active participants in that development.

My use of the term Theatre for Development in relation to this research project is specific and intentional. I aim to reclaim the notion of 'development' in relation to citizenship education by bringing it back into conversation with applied performance processes through a Freirean praxis of 'developing citizens'. This approach challenges the limited notions of development contained in policy around childhood and citizenship education, constructing children as fellow 'active' citizens, engaged alongside adults in an ongoing process of development. Indeed, I argue that TfD, with its praxis of social change, invites us to rethink ideas of development in relation to citizenship. As such, it presents one of the best forums for children to learn how to become active citizens. This suggests the possibility of using TfD with children to create a more active role for schools in the community in citizenship education and development. Starting from the premise that we are *all* developing citizens opens up new models of subjectivity and spaces for change.

## Theorizing childhood and citizenship development

Contemporary understandings of citizenship go beyond the notion of citizenship as a status. As theorists such as Andrea Cornwall and Vera Schatten P. Coelho suggest, issues of democracy and participation have moved to the centre of the global policy agenda since the end of the twentieth century,[2] shifting the emphasis to the substantive nature of citizenship, or citizenship as a practice. This highlights a key point about agency in relationship to citizenship: it is no longer just a matter of citizens having rights but how they exercise them. It is useful here to draw upon educationalists Audrey Osler and Hugh Starkey's suggestion of a third strand of citizenship, beyond those of status and practice to that of 'feeling',[3] what they call 'a sense of belonging'.[4] This affective dimension of citizenship is connected to the concept of active citizenship in a democracy – that citizens can, by their actions, shape the society in which they have a stake. Active citizenship is about having the capacity to *claim* one's citizenship status, translating rights and responsibilities into actions that call to account both the horizontal relationships between citizens and also vertical ones between citizens and those elected to power. As Cornwall and Coelho put it, 'For people to be able to exercise their political agency, they need to first recognise themselves as citizens rather than see themselves as beneficiaries or clients'.[5]

This understanding of active citizenship has implications for ideas about citizenship development and education for citizenship, particularly for children who are not yet eligible to vote. Like citizenship, childhood is a socially constructed concept and tied to notions of identity. Also like citizenship, childhood has become a focus of political discussion in recent years. A number of commentators agree broadly with Chris Jenks's suggestion that late modernity's response to the uncertainties of the age has been to 're-adop[t] the child'.[6] Michael Wyness discusses, for example, contemporary culture's renewed 'desire for certainty', arguing that childhood has become the focus for a form of 'moral rescue'.[7] I suggest that the heart of this project is the rhetorical configuration of the child as a 'developing citizen', whereby childhood development has become attached to a broader vision of social development. As education has become a key site of investment, children have become appropriated as policy vehicles to bring about a better future for all of us.

Jenks argues that development is the 'primary metaphor through which childhood is made intelligible'.[8] He describes the influence of the twentieth-century developmental psychologist Piaget in shaping the contemporary (western) understanding of childhood as a journey towards adulthood. This construction of children as 'becoming' creates what sociologist Susie Weller calls an 'adult/child binary' which has implications for citizenship, defining children by their state of incompleteness and denying them a sense of agency except in relation to attending to their own development.[9] It valorizes 'progress' and 'growth', metaphors which, as Jenks points out, resonate with the 'culture of modernity' but which, in relationship to citizenship, suggest that the concept is finite.[10] Adulthood becomes a destination at which point, by implication, development ceases and citizenship is attained. This developmental model remains a powerful one in contemporary discussions of children. Jenks argues that, while feminism and post-colonialism have helped to deconstruct discursive categories such as gender and race, the 'ideology of development in relation to childhood has remained relatively intact'.[11]

Paulo Freire's liberatory approach to education is fundamentally about issues of citizenship development in ways that are helpful in challenging this ideology. His notion of conscientization posits a self-reflective subject who is able to locate herself in relation to questions of knowledge and power that lie at the heart of our development as citizens, in order to take action in the world. Freire defines this self-reflection as a sense of presence:

> Our being in the world is far more than just 'being'. It is a 'presence', a 'presence' that is relational to the world and to others. . . . A 'presence' that can reflect upon itself, that knows itself as a presence, that can intervene, can transform, can speak of what it does, but that can also take stock of, compare, evaluate, give value to, decide, break with, and dream.[12]

As Freire suggests, there is an inherent sense of possibility to this presence – an awareness that anything could yet happen and that the subject has a role to play in creating those possibilities. This is the difference between a form of education that creates active as opposed to passive students/citizens, or the sense of the individual as a 're-creator', as Freire calls it, rather than just a 'spectator' of knowledge.[13]

Freire's pedagogy of 'developing citizens' is centred on the notion of 'praxis' – that iterative process of action and reflection which, he claims, is uniquely human. Indeed, Freire argues that '[o]nly human beings *are* praxis', explicitly assigning the capacity for progress to the human condition.[14] For Freire, our ongoing state of development is central to his educational vision. At the same time, he connects the subject's state of perpetual 'unfinishedness' to that of social reality which is also always mutating and this underlines his point that these two processes of development work in conversation with each other.[15] Freire notes that the '[w]orld and human beings do not exist apart from each other' but in 'constant dialectical relationship'.[16] In this sense, he recognizes that citizen and society shape and are shaped by each other. The reflexive praxis of conscientization that lies at the heart of Freire's critical pedagogy aims to create what I would define as 'active (developing) citizens', who recognize and seek to understand that dialectical relationship between themselves and the world, and are able to act on that understanding by participating in change-making at an individual and collective level.

Freire's pedagogy suggests a more dynamic understanding of development that becomes particularly clear when mapped onto current theorizing about childhood. Recent work by academics in Childhood Studies has challenged the dominant 'development' model of childhood as a state of 'becoming', which inherently defines children as deficient and thus non-actors. Instead, theorists have sought to present the child as a social 'being', 'who is actively constructing his or her own 'childhood', as sociologist Emma Uprichard puts it.[17] However, Uprichard draws on theories of temporality to move on from the dichotomization of being and becoming to argue that children are both 'beings and becomings', stressing the importance of considering both of these aspects together.[18]

The construction of (children's) subjectivity that Uprichard puts forward resonates very strongly with Freire's notion of 'presence': that heightened sense of being in the world, capable of reflecting on the past but also looking forward and imagining new possibilities for the future. For Freire, we are indeed at once and always both 'being' and 'becoming' and the reflexive duality of this process is at the heart of his pedagogy of change. In terms of citizenship development, it also points to that affective dimension that Osler and Starkey suggest is 'interlinked' with citizenship as a status and a practice.[19] *Feeling* like a citizen and *doing* citizenship are connected to *being* a citizen and indeed contribute towards changing the experience of what being a citizen actually is. The effect of this analysis is to open up possibilities for citizenship, rather than close them down. Freire's idea of praxis, then, reminds us that citizenship development is a process in which we are *all* engaged *throughout* our lives, thus dismantling rigid binaries of adult/child, citizen/non-citizen, developed/developing and being/ becoming. It thereby attributes the capacity for agency to children, as fellow active citizens, developing alongside adults, and points to the need for an education that recognizes that capacity and provides opportunities for their active participation.

Helen Nicholson has discussed the value of theatre in revealing how people 'perform *as* citizens in different local, regional and global contexts, highlighting how the work can usefully bring different experiences and forms of knowledge about citizenship into dialogue.[20] She notes that the intersubjectivity of performance provides the opportunity for people to reflect on their own and others' practices as a way of 'theorising citizenship'.[21] The body is the site of citizenship development, where action takes place. Like the other discursive categories discussed here, it is, as Nicholson suggests, 'a site of struggle'.[22] As an embodied practice, TfD can become a means, then, for children to engage directly with the struggle around the politics of their representation as developing citizens and analyse questions of agency in relation to their own performances of citizenship. Testing the boundaries of their identity formulation through the creative and imaginative play of theatre processes points to the possibility of new notions and practices of citizenship development, both for the children themselves and for their audiences. In that sense, TfD can provide not only a 'deconstructive' but also a 'reconstructive' role for citizenship, as arts educator Beverly Naidus puts it.[23]

The concept of performativity is helpful in theorizing TfD as a practice centred on the dynamic of both 'being' and 'becoming'. On the one hand, TfD processes invite children to explore their performances of citizenship via the materiality of their lived experience, or their present state of citizenship 'being'. At the same time, however, the creative and aesthetic nature of theatre provides a means of imagining the future, pointing to the possibility of acting differently and thus our state of citizenship 'becoming'. Thus TfD is not only a space to explore our sense of *who we are*, questioning ideological concepts in relation to our own material practices, but it can also be a space to experiment with *who we can become*. This is the basis of my understanding of TfD's contribution in helping children to develop as active citizens: premised on the sense of 'presence' that Freire advocates, it invites participants to engage in a praxis of action and reflection in order to bring about change. This openness of the performance space is very exciting. Anything is possible through the fiction of the stage, and new ways of developing can be explored through the focus on the endless possibilities of performing differently.

The work of educationalist Henry Giroux is useful to this discussion, as he has specifically advocated a more critical role for schools in terms of active citizenship development. Giroux builds on Freire's ideas of a critical pedagogy in relation to the contemporary need to reinvigorate citizenship education in schools. He describes citizenship as a 'site of struggle' over 'forms of knowledge, social practices, and values' associated with particular times and places.[24] Given that citizenship, like democracy, is a 'socially constructed historical practice', we need to recognize that it needs to be 'problematized' and 'reconstructed' for each generation.[25] Herein, according to Giroux, lies the role for schools as public spaces for such a process of problematization and reconstruction. Giroux suggests that schools can become sites for a grounded project of 'critical citizenship',[26] which explores students' own accounts and experiences as a means of calling dominant ideologies, including those around the school itself, to account.[27]

This approach invites students to engage directly with the analysis and reproduction of citizenship. It demands, according to Giroux, a new definition of active citizenship, one that goes beyond critique to a 'pedagogy of possibility'.[28] In this sense, Giroux is pointing to the need to go beyond balancing real experiences against ideological notions of citizenship to the idea of engaging young people in imagining new possibilities for citizenship. I propose that my model of TfD can be a means to activate Giroux's notion of a 'pedagogy of possibility' in schools, promoting the role of students and educators as 'active participants' in public discussion about citizenship and helping schools to become public sites of citizenship development.[29]

## The project: TfD as a pedagogy for developing citizens

The group I worked with was the year five class of 24 children aged 9–10 from a primary school in the north-west of England. Also involved was the class teacher and school music teacher. I visited the school twice over the course of a year in 2010–11, travelling to their partner school in Uganda in between. At each stage, I worked with the group over a period of about 8 weeks. The sessions took place in a workshop setting, using a range of theatre and other creative and participatory methods such as discussion, art and writing. Each stage ended with a final performance that was given at the school for teachers, pupils and parents.

The school link with Uganda had been going for about a year when I started this project and had mainly involved letter exchanges. However, baseline assessments I conducted at the beginning of the research revealed the children held mainly stereotypical views of Uganda and Ugandans that were shaped by the western lens of television or charity campaigns. In response to a question about how they would describe their partner school, answers included descriptions such as 'dirty', 'unkempt', 'dusty', 'not very stable' or simply, 'They are not as fortunate as us'. These negative impressions kept reappearing in discussions in which the children described Uganda as a country lacking in clean water and decent healthcare and housing.

However, it was striking that alongside the negative descriptions in these initial questionnaires were other, more positive, impressions, such as the idea that the school was 'friendly' and 'happy' and that it was good to have the link. This highlighted for me what was already an emerging tension in the children's apprehension of Africa in that the initial contact with 'real' people and places in Uganda had begun to challenge received knowledge about the continent. The story emerging about the Ugandan school showed people getting on with their lives and not defined by poverty, something that was clearly at odds with dominant narrative, what Nigerian author Chimamanda Ngozi Adichie calls the dangerous 'single story' that speaks of the power of those to narrate the lives of others.[30] Challenging the single story would become a key theme to our project.

The first part of the project focused on getting the children to reflect on their own community in order to present themselves to their partner school through their initial performance. An early activity the children did was to recreate their local village within the workshop space and give me and their teacher a 'guided tour'. Various items were made available such as rolls of material, ribbon and pipe cleaners, paper and pens, and the children were free to use these however they wished, along with anything else they could find. The pupils worked in small groups to create different areas of their village that they identified as important such as the school, the shops, the river and the church. Their response to the task was creative and imaginative: bodies were used to create bridges, animals and fish; locations, such as the interior of classrooms, were produced in meticulous detail. Children demonstrated actions they regularly undertook – from skateboarding to taking a dog for a walk – as well as playing other members of their community such as teachers, shopkeepers and doctors. In this way, the activity revealed the children's understanding of how their actions intersected with those of adults and other children, something we would continue to explore in further work.

We followed this activity with an exploration of the concept of children's rights, as we began to look at the needs that are common to us all, particularly the worldwide community of children. I first asked the pupils to come up with their own ideas for children's rights and compared these with the 1990 United Nations Convention on the Rights of the Child before moving on to explore the responsibilities that come with these rights. I was keen to unravel some of the complexities here, as well as ensure that the children understood that responsibilities were vertical as well as horizontal. In the discussion that followed, some children made sophisticated connections, pointing out, for example, that enjoying the right to follow a faith means respecting the right of others to follow a different faith, even if it seems, as one of them put it, 'funny'. Another child commented that this also means the government is responsible for allowing people to follow the faith of their choice and shouldn't tell them what religion to follow. In one activity, I asked the children to work in pairs, one person creating actions that showed a child exercising a right and the other showing a responsibility that went with that right. Some actions showed the children taking responsibility themselves, such as turning off a tap or a light to conserve water or power, revealing something perhaps of the way that British children are socialized into environmentalism. Other sequences clearly showed adults intervening, such as supervising education or play. What was clear was that the children could identify the role adults needed to play to support children in various different social spaces.

Following on from this exercise, the pupils created scenes in groups that demonstrated problems associated with the different areas they had shown me in the guided tour. Here, the role-playing moved to a new level as, through the exploration of different possible solutions, we began to unpick the various rights and responsibilities of the individuals in these different communities. One scene about school showed two boys seated (inevitably) at the back of the class, causing disruption which the teacher couldn't see because she was standing with her back to them, sorting out something on her computer. The impact of the naughty boys' behaviour was made clear: one girl rolled her eyes impatiently, physically turned away and brought her book closer to her face, as if to block out the boys' presence. The other boy in the scene was presented as a more obvious victim, as the other two threw things at him and pulled faces when he turned round. Unlike the girl, the boy was left looking visibly upset and incapable of continuing with his work.

During the ensuing forum both groups unpicked the importance of the right to education that was being violated here by the behaviour of the victims' peers. They then tried out different solutions to the problem being presented, which in both cases included various approaches to getting the teacher's help, often through the assistance of the 'witness' who could help and support the victim to come forward or simply take it upon him/herself to report what had happened. The children improvised with a pupil playing the role of the teacher and we talked afterwards about the different levels of responsibility here: from the teacher who had responsibility for the class's welfare, for setting an example of what is expected of the children's behaviour and for responding to children's concerns, to the pupils' responsibility to report things.

While this may seem like the forum was constructed towards a rather obvious outcome, it's important not to underestimate the importance of the process. The scene modelled what for many children was the ideal scenario: turning to adults when help was needed and adults acting on that call for help. This created a dynamic in which the children were equally active with the adult in producing the space, suggesting their capacity as citizens to contribute towards change. As such, it pointed to one of the ways the work could help to 'theorise' children's agency, as sociologist Alan Prout proposes, by exploring *how* children engage with adults in their community.[31]

These explorations developed into the first performance piece of the project. We put together a 15-minute assembly, focused around four small-group scenes on different aspects of the community that we had explored: the school, church, play-park and river. Around these, we scripted a commentary-style conversation between the teacher and two pupil narrators about the work the group had been doing. All the children were on stage throughout the performance and played a variety of roles. The assembly highlighted the themes of community and children's rights, which had been new to the class at the start of the project and which were likely to be new to many of the children in the audience.

Each location in the community was introduced via a stylized action sequence based on ideas generated in the community 'tour' exercise, accompanied by soundscapes the children associated with these various places. The action sequences then developed into short scenes that explored particular rights in practice in the different spaces of the community: education, faith, play and healthy environment respectively. These scenes showed ways the children saw their rights being supported or infringed, demonstrating who they felt was responsible for protecting these rights and some of the steps children can take when they see rights being violated. For example, the school scene showed an adaptation of the forum work we had done on school bullying. Here, one of the pupil narrators drew the teacher's attention to the naughty children's behaviour and talked about the responsibility of teachers to ensure a safe classroom, as well as the onus on pupils to do their best in order to make the most of school. Through these forum scenes, the children set out a vision of a world in which adults and children worked together, as fellow citizens, towards the development of their community. This was reinforced by the fact that the class teacher performed alongside the pupils in the piece, thereby modelling the participatory ideal in our work and demonstrating the learning process as a shared endeavour. Interestingly, while she was very nervous about taking part in the performance, the teacher said the process made her feel 'part of the community' of the class and both she and the pupils enjoyed her involvement.

The second phase of the project and the final performance evolved very differently. Given the children's pre-conceived ideas about Uganda at the beginning, it was important that the work I brought back was used to explore these perceptions. I was conscious that I returned to the school just as the annual Comic Relief telethon was airing and I wanted the children to start questioning the 'single story' of Africa in British culture. I showed the children a video clip from a previous Comic Relief campaign in which TV presenters, Ant and Dec, visit Kenya.[32] This piece maintains a strong and hierarchical sense of separate spaces, reinforced by the way the celebrities are placed within the 'other' space and weep on camera at what they see. While the reality of poverty is doubtless there, what the presenters do not do is reflect on their position or analyse their own space in relation to that of the people around them. Indeed, it serves the interest of the fundraiser to draw clear distinctions between the spaces, rather than note where they overlap. Instead, while we are encouraged to sympathize, we are constantly reminded of the fact that these spaces are not our spaces.

After showing the Ant and Dec clip to the children, I asked them what image of Africa was being presented here. They had no trouble identifying the very negative portrait, comprising 'lots of' 'sick', 'poor' and 'miserable' people, 'people you want to help', living in 'small houses' in 'a place you wouldn't want to visit'. The children also recognized that this was a deliberately one-sided image designed to persuade the viewer to donate money and by this point they had an arsenal of alternative images that challenged this biased perspective. Some of their Ugandan friends' houses were not at all like those in the Ant and Dec documentary; they had also seen and heard about the abundance of fruit and vegetables that the Ugandans grow on their land and heard about how much the Ugandan children enjoyed their school. Balancing the reality of the relative poverty that does indeed exist in the lives of the Ugandan children against the fact that this is not their *only* defining reality had been a key challenge in this project but was a concept that the children were beginning to understand. Their final performance would focus on sharing that knowledge with other members of their school and local community.

Our starting point was the children's fascination with the similarities and differences between them and their Ugandan partners. They were amazed, for example, at the length of the school day for the Ugandans and the contribution the children made to the household in terms of chores, as well as intrigued by their shared love of Premier League football. These comparisons formed the framing device for the final performance piece, as we investigated how the two groups of children might spend their days. We workshopped a range of activities the English children engaged in such as computer-gaming, feeding pets or making the bed and then experimented with some of the actions that the Ugandan children did such as slashing grass, playing basketball and brick-making. I then counted through a 24-hour clock, as we explored what activities might be done at different times of day by different children in each location.

With the help of the music teacher, the children went on to devise a range of rhythmic patterns for different types of activity from a slow, quiet beat for sleeping to a loud and energetic sequence for playing and a steady beat for school lessons. This activity drew attention to the contrasting tempos of their different experiences. Certain activities such as schoolwork converged, while others clearly diverged. This process led the children to question some of their assumptions about each other and challenged the kinds of 'knowledge' they had about their own and each other's spaces. The material nature of inhabiting each other's world through the embodiment of their actions was inevitably performed at one remove but, I would argue, provided a critical distance from which to reflect on these actions and compare them with their own daily actions that they generally took for granted. In this sense, these activities opened up new possibilities for the children's own sense of identity, through the embodied exploration of the practices of others. At another level, some of the children observed how tiring it was to engage with the range of tasks the Ugandans did, on top of school, and developed a certain respect for their level of contribution.

In the final performance, we divided the stage in half with a 'human clock', operated by three pupils down the middle bearing a clock face, a drum and a cowbell. Two drummers sat on one side with half the class – they would represent the English pupils; on the other side sat two drummers and the other half of the class who represented the Ugandan pupils. What followed was a highly complex sound and movement sequence in which the clock marked various hours of the day. We used images on the split screen behind and action sequences on each side of the stage driven by the sometimes contrasting rhythms of the drummers which were themselves set to the pace of the central 'clock' drummer. For example, the first time we marked was 5 a.m., a typical time that Ugandan children start getting ready for school. The 'Ugandan' drummers played an abrupt rhythm to jerk the children awake and they performed a series of actions such as washing, having breakfast, brushing teeth, sweeping the bedroom and running to school. While this was happening, the English children remained 'asleep' on their side of the stage with a quiet sweeping sound from their drums. Sometimes, then, the sequences were different, although actions could also be echoed across the spaces. Thus, the getting up sequence in Britain also involved washing, eating, brushing teeth and running to school, while also including differences, such as smoothing the duvet and brushing hair. At other points, we created sequences that were the same on both sides, such as working in the classroom and chatting over lunch. At these points the drummers all beat out the same pattern, making the noise louder and more emphatic.

The piece itself began with a clear sense of separation between the two locations and the groups were presented as totally distinct and apparently unaware of each other, going about their daily routines within their own communities. However, as some of the children's practices began to merge and map onto each other, this sense of separation was challenged. Indeed, the piece sought to demonstrate the children's growing awareness of each other. For example, during the lunch sequence the two groups started to catch each other's eyes across the space and 'look' at what the others were eating. We used one word here – 'beans' – as we had discovered that this was a staple food in both locations. One child from the Ugandan side called across to someone from the English side, pointing to his plate and asking 'Beans?' The 'English' child nodded and confirmed 'Beans'. Both then looked at the audience in animated excitement at this discovery, gave a thumbs-up and shouted 'Beans!'

This idea of looking across spaces continued through the piece. For instance, in a classroom sequence we showed the problem of bullying in both locations, as it was an issue that both groups had shown each other during the first phase and had explored through 'foruming' exercises. During the final performance, the children recreated the problem as both groups had originally presented it, the Ugandan case showing the theft of a book and the English case involving two pupils laughing and pointing at another child. Both groups of children had come to similar conclusions through the forum, so here we showed a pupil from each location reaching out to the victim and deciding to seek adult support. For the English children, this sequence echoed the scene from their previous assembly. This time, however, they explicitly demonstrated how this problem spanned the two locations and how an awareness of each other's situation created a sense of solidarity which inspired them to act in their own space: the two pupils who acted as the aid to the victim looked across to each other and nodded in agreement before moving off to seek help.

This growing sense of solidarity culminated in a sequence that centred on play. At first, the two groups of pupils presented a series of actions in their own spaces that showed them enjoying some leisure time after school. Gradually, however, as the rhythms on each side merged and became louder, one or two of the children on each side started to interact, throwing or kicking an imaginary ball across the stage. Eventually, other children started joining in or began playing together the games that both groups had devised together during the project. Having kept rigidly to their own side of the stage until now, the children started moving freely across the whole space. Eventually, the whole group came together in a circle and 'exchanged' songs we had devised together through the project and which had been hugely popular with both groups.

This part of the performance seemed to symbolize much of what the project had achieved for the English children in terms of breaking down preconceptions about the space of Africa and finding points of solidarity with their Ugandan counterparts. The performance of the songs in the circle served as a powerful metaphor for the project itself, acknowledging some of the differences both within and between the two groups of children while also identifying the possibility of co-operation. The performance as a whole highlighted ways in which the various communities the children belonged to merged and diverged. This created a more multivalent sense of children's spaces which reconfigured the two groups and the relationship between them, breaking down the conceived spatial dynamics of 'here' and 'there' contained in notions of 'us' and 'them'.

Another key strand to the performance was the sense that the children were actively critiquing the single story of Africa through their actions on stage. The children now recognized that the image of Africa that is often presented in the media contradicted the one they had seen through the project and were keen to present their alternative vision to the audience. To do this, we added another layer to the final performance piece, punctuating the movement/drumming sequences with a series of pre-recorded 'TV news reports' that were shown on the screen behind. The pupils worked extremely hard with their teacher to do further research into various aspects of Uganda and create a series of 'alternative' news bulletins that explored Uganda's wildlife, food and sporting culture. I provided each news team with a stimulus research pack to get them started but each group took their report off in a different direction and had great fun scripting their pieces and finding their own costumes and props. The final pieces included, among others, a *Match of the Day* style report on the African Cup of Nations, a 'David Attenborough'-style piece on the gorilla and a holiday programme on what to see in Uganda.

What is obvious from these examples was that the children appropriated cultural media forms that they were familiar with – the nature documentary, sports punditry and so on – but reinterpreted these in inventive ways. As such, they subverted both the means, as well as the focus, of the representations and became the agents of production around knowledge of Uganda, while also beginning to learn a little about the role of media in these forms of cultural production. Tim Prentki has discussed the way that global technology contributes significantly to 'the coloniz[ation] of our minds today'.[33] He argues that 'our cultural space must be defamiliarized' in a Brechtian sense, requiring the audience to 'position' itself in relation to the 'sociopolitical contradictions that hegemony disguises'.[34] In a very small way, the work the children created defamiliarized familiar media norms and used them to highlight contradictions around the space of Africa. In that sense, it began to gesture towards transforming 'the familiar space' into 'the learning space'.[35]

It was important to engage the audience in discussion about the work we had created as a means of extending this 'learning space' and pursuing the issues further with them. Before the performance I issued each class in the school with a questionnaire to ask them what they knew about Africa or their link school in Uganda. Their responses from children of all ages, even those in Reception, were weighted towards negative rather than positive comments and drew heavily upon well-worn media images of poverty-stricken Africa that resonated with what we saw in the Ant and Dec film, including lack of food and water, drought, disease/death, poor housing ('huts'), having to 'walk miles' to school 'in bare feet' and so on. The message was spelt out most clearly from a member of Year 6 who summed it up as 'We are better off than them'.

After the performance, the youngest pupils went back to their classroom and had a feedback session with their class teachers, using a prompt sheet I had created with room for the teacher to jot down the pupils' responses. The older pupils remained in the hall with their teachers and other adults who had come to watch. I asked everyone a short series of questions and gave them time to talk to each other before hearing their responses. The pupils who had performed were also present for the discussion and responded to various questions and issues that arose. When asked what they had learnt about the partner school and, more broadly, about Uganda, the audience's responses were quite varied, including 'They like beans, just like us', 'They get up early', 'They eat different food', 'They don't have games consoles, i-pods and Nintendoes', 'They do the same sorts of things as us at school', 'There are only 380 gorillas left in the wild', 'They have to work a lot more'.

What is evident from the responses is the way some of the children in the audience, like those in the performance, began to view the Ugandan children in relation to *themselves*. The piece invited them to locate themselves in relation to the experiences being shown on stage and not necessarily in merely hierarchical terms such as 'We are better off than them'. The head teacher told me that in some ways she was surprised that the piece showed less of Uganda and so much about the pupils' own community but I can see now that the process of developing as citizens is as much about understanding your own location as it is understanding the location of others. She also commented on the participatory nature of the post-show discussion, noting that the children in the audience had picked up on things that she had missed during the performance. In particular, she liked the fact that the children were able to give their opinions immediately and she saw it as an example of enhancing 'pupil voice' within the school.

The children involved in the project spoke positively about their sense of connection between the groups: 'I will remember being fascinated by the connections between us', 'They have the same rights as us', 'they are more like us than I thought!', 'I will remember [names one of the Ugandan pupils] the most because he is exactly like me' and 'We taught each other things'. The class also spoke enthusiastically about their participation. During a small-group evaluation discussion, one boy said that he found rehearsing for the assembly the most exciting aspect of the project, not only because he enjoyed the creation of it, adding parts to it each time to 'make it better' but also because of the thrill of being involved with others: 'you know you are going to be a part of it and everyone's doing something in it'.

This pleasurable experience of working with others towards a common goal is critical to the issue of agency. It is part of that affective dimension of citizenship that Osler and Starkey discussed – that *feeling* of being a citizen that is implicit in Freire's notion of self-reflective 'presence'. The pupil's comments also resonate with Jonothan Neelands' discussion of the 'idea of the 'ensemble' as being 'the political heart of AT'.[36] In his discussion of the relationship between developing as 'artistic' and 'social' actors, Neelands points up how the performance space maps onto wider social spaces in providing participants the opportunity to practise working together, providing them with 'a second order identity as citizens struggling together, on a civic stage, to create and continuously challenge and modify ideas of the "common good"'.[37] What is clear from the boy's feedback is that this can be an exciting pedagogical process in terms of learning the possibilities of participation. As Nicholson puts it, 'learning to participate through theatre' is 'arguably, one of the most important elements of education'.[38]

I suggest that the performative platform of TfD validated the knowledge the children brought to this project, creating a space to demonstrate the capabilities of children by playing with the identity markers written on their bodies and challenging assumptions about the performance of childhood and children as developing citizens. At the same time, however, the work the children created presented the opportunity to open a discussion with the audience around the issues they raised, starting to identify ways in which they and their audience could do citizenship differently in future. As such, the work invited a re-examination of the relationship between schools and their communities and suggested a different role for schools as sites for 'developing citizens'. In pointing to the possibility of acting differently, TfD highlights not only the role children play in active citizenship but also the task facing all of us as developing citizens to transform the world in which we live.

# The Ludic Box: Playful Alternatives from Guatemala for the World

Doryan Bedoya and Eugene van Erven

As we write this, it is the second half of September 2013. The Guatemalan-Dutch collaboration that this essay explores formally ended when five young Guatemalans returned to their country on 25 June. They had been in the Netherlands since 22 May to work with five Dutch partners on a site-specific performance piece called *Verborgen Oorlog/Guerras Escondidas* [Hidden War'], which they performed six times in the grounds of the nineteenth-century fortress Nieuwersluis as part of a regional festival. The creative process that led to this production, however, had already started in the summer of 2012 and the Dutch-Guatemalan partnership that nourished it had been evolving for many years before that. What prompted this collaboration? How did it develop organizationally and artistically? What did it mean to those directly involved and to the larger cultural and development sectors in our respective countries?

These and a number of related questions we will seek to address by drawing on the perspectives of the two nominal authors of this text,[1] some recent British, Dutch and Latin American research on art in conflict and art in public space, the original playscript of *Hidden War*, a rough edit from a 50-minute documentary made by a young Catalan film maker that covers the last 7 months of the project, and the personal recollections from participants and the two artists who led the enterprise, Catalina García and Anouk de Bruijn. The result is a multi-layered, multi-vocal tale about art and development and transcontinental artistic partnerships. Guatemalan arts collective Caja Lúdica,

**Figure 4**  Utrecht Community Arts Lab (Photo: Peter Valckx).

Dutch youth theatre company De Rest, the Community Arts Lab Utrecht, and the reverse development scheme 'E-motive' of Oxfam Novib figure prominently within it.

Doryan Bedoya (b. 1961) is a Colombian native, who, in the year 2001, together with fellow Colombian Julia Escobar (b. 1967) and four local youngsters founded Caja Lúdica ['Ludic Box'] in Guatemala City. Bedoya is a poet and Escobar a theatre artist. Both are also experienced teachers and grass-roots cultural organizers. Before they moved to Central America, they were core members of Barrio Comparsa ['neighbourhood parade'] in Medellín. This organization was founded in 1990 in the Manrique Oriental neighbourhood by Luis Fernandez García and five of his friends. It was a time when large areas of that city were still heavily infested by drug-related criminal activities associated with the cartel of Pablo Escobar Gaviria, his competitors and his paramilitary opponents. In a recent weblog, Barrio Comparsa recalls:

> We began as an alternative for the lives of young people in Medellín, which back then was going through a period of increasing violence. Since then we have consolidated ourselves as a multiplication project for arts and culture. We do this through festive, carnivalesque forms

of expressions like parades, music and street performance. In our group we involve neighbourhood residents from Medellín who come together to celebrate life, joy, and fantasy.[2]

It would be exaggerated to claim that Barrio Comparsa single-handedly turned Medellín from one of the world's most dangerous cities into the comparatively safer place it is today. Yet, in the company's own words the 'Ludic Methodology' it developed and implemented over the past 23 years contains an explicit peace-oriented social change agenda:

We generate a new type of leadership based on stimulating human sensitivity, creativity, cultural management and facilitation, citizens' participation, community self-management, interculturality and introducing paradigms that break down lack of self-confidence, exclusion, fear and resistance to participation. We do this by involving the population and engaging them to become agents of large scale transformations that contribute to personal and collective growth and the consolidation of democracy and a culture of peaceful coexistence in the country.[3]

Barrio Comparsa was one among many other participatory grass-roots initiatives connected to the arts, health, education and religious sectors of Medellín and that was loosely co-ordinated and supported under a city-wide policy entitled *del miedo a la esperanza* ['from fear to hope']. In combination with a number of economic and political factors that lie beyond the scope of this chapter, these combined activities allegedly contributed to a relatively strong decline in the number of homicides in the city, including in the Manrique Oriental neighbourhood.[4] But a recent report also suggests that drug-related criminality continues to thrive in Medellín and that the worst violence may have simply shifted to other urban areas, particularly to downtown.[5] There seems little doubt, however, that over the years Barrio Comparsa has had a positive influence on the lives of countless young people in its own neighbourhood – and later in other parts of the city. And it is very evident that in 1999 its work inspired a group of Guatemalan delegates to World Youth Day in Medellín, because they invited Barrio Comparsa to their country to set up a similar enterprise.

In October 2000 Bedoya and Escobar travelled to Guatemala to participate in a grass-roots festival called *Octubre Azul* ['Blue October'], where they taught some of the techniques they used to create street parades back home in Medellín. Their work hit a spark. Prompted by two young Guatemalan artists, Julio Osorio and Renato Maselli, the two Colombians decided to stay.[6] Bedoya recalls how Caja Lúdica started its first Guatemalan activities under this new name:

> After we had identified some youngsters that could serve as a core group, we needed a space where we could consolidate ourselves as a collective. That's when we discovered the old abandoned post office. Together with 6 or 7 other groups we took over that space and within less than a month we opened up shop, offering free artistic activities for everyone. They came in droves, forming lines around the corner, just to try and get in. It drew the attention of the authorities, the mass media and the citizens in general, which resulted in official support for this initiative.[7]

The first activity Bedoya and Escobar organized attracted 200 youngsters. For 15 days they taught them the basics of stilt walking, mask making and how to design a colourful, musical, moveable spectacle, with which they subsequently entered the public space in downtown Guatemala City.[8]

## Intervening in public space

In a recent study, Jonathan Offereins,[9] who visited Guatemala in August 2012 as part of our exchange, links the work of Caja Lúdica and its Colombian antecedents to Latin American popular theatre, collective creation methods and post-colonial theory. He remarks that the post-colonial discourse tends to be dominated by Anglophone academics based at Western institutions who appear more interested in former French and British colonies in Asia and Africa than in Latin America. Because the latter continent has experienced a much earlier decolonization process (in the nineteenth century), it does not fit comfortably in the Anglo-Saxon post-colonial paradigm. As a result, South American thinkers have developed their own post-colonial discourse in which the relation between mestizos and indigenous populations, class struggles of various kinds, land ownerships and the influence of the United States play a prominent role.[10] A similar argument could be made for studies in art and development and art in conflict zones, categories to which Caja Lúdica's work could also be connected. In these fields, too, references to Latin American practices are the exception rather than the rule, despite the widely acknowledged influence of Boal and Freire. In *Performance in Place of War*, for example, the British authors explicitly apologize for not including 'powerful examples of work, particularly those in Spanish-speaking contexts' because they lack the necessary linguistic abilities. They equally honestly admit that their frame of reference is limited by having their home base in Manchester, which 'has slanted the research towards Africa and Asia and away from the Americas, and towards former British colonies more than the French and the Portuguese.'[11] Even so, by adding some Latin American inflections to their admittedly European inspired theories, the analyses in *Performance in Place of War* of arts practices in public place elsewhere in the world are also relevant to the work of Caja Lúdica in Guatemala and their recent exchange with the Netherlands.

Several Latin American sociological studies see public space on their continent as quite different from Europe.[12] Andara, an urban studies scholar based in Venezuela, traces the design and use of public space in his continent from the establishment of the first colonial cities (as Spanish military strongholds) to the present. Cleverly linking this development to the formation of élites and clientelism, he sees this as the essential source for much current social dysfunctionality in Latin American cities and nations. Ecuadorian researcher Ramírez Gallegos points to the effects of militarization (and its often violently enforced regulation of public space) during the various dictatorships that dominated Latin America between the 1960s and 1990s. Depending on one's political affiliation, for any Latino older than 30 personal relationships to public space are bound to be overshadowed by this recent history. Regrettably, Ramírez Gallegos sidesteps this delicate but pertinent issue. His notion of public space remains a rather abstract arena into which he sees new social agents and movements appear in the 1990s. He argues that these new forces have innovated political culture through rather undefined participatory experiments that provide an alternative to 'the privatising tendencies of politics and public space promoted by neoliberalism'.[13] Ramírez Gallegos is particularly critical of Latin American colleagues whom he believes too simplistically (and optimistically) apply Habermasian ideas about new voices entering discursive space in order to argue that the level of participatory democracy in his part of the world has improved. It is true, Ramírez Gallegos continues, that minorities, women and other excluded groups are now included in public discourse after many decades of being silenced. But he notices that the illiterate are still excluded. Basing himself on fieldwork in the north-eastern suburbs of Medellín, the author warns that all kinds of seemingly positive participatory processes at the neighbourhood level may have been compromised by paramilitary violence and other forms of intimidation (like the operations of territorial gangs) that continue to be a daily reality in many Latin American contexts.

If we keep the above South American considerations in mind, *Performance in Place of War* offers valuable insights into the relation between the arts and public space that also apply to Guatemala. The book critically describes a variety of practices, ranging generically from installations and parades to more intimate text- or movement-based performances – and geographically from the Balkans and Rwanda to Sri Lanka and the Middle East. The more ludic examples of invading public space they cite are obviously akin to the work of Caja Lúdica. But the authors' warning against 'making facile links between the practice of theatre and the assumption of an inevitable "humanizing" outcome' is equally relevant. After all, they insist, it is also 'humans that create war and commit atrocity against each other'.[14] The book is full of such sobering reminders that we need to constantly look for more nuance whenever we use terms such as 'human', 'beauty' and 'creativity' to justify the art work,[15] favour the authenticity of literal personal stories over more figurative approaches,[16] or assume that the 'more ethical practice is intrinsically about *bringing together* rather than *standing apart*'.[17]

In their chapter on arts practices in periods after warfare has ceased, the authors of *Performance in Place of War* turn to French cultural theorist Michel de Certeau[18] because of his interest in 'how imaginative and creative engagements in the everyday can create and invent new possibilities that are generated from the bottom up, outside of or beyond the control of legislative or administrative bodies'.[19] The carnivalesque parades of Caja Lúdica are good examples of what de Certeau would call 'spatial practice' and which Thompson and his team interpret as attempts to temporarily, gently, playfully take over mechanisms that control human, sensory and physical elements in a public place. Artistic interventions in such places, they believe, generates 'new possibilities and narrations of site, identity and nation'. They turn these places into spaces where people can 'live in ways that include more voices, challenge the disciplinary mechanisms of a place of war and expand the possibilities for everyday activity'.[20] High time, then, to look at how Caja Lúdica 'practises place' in the volatile context of Guatemala.

## The work of Caja Lúdica in Guatemala

Caja Lúdica's activities consist mostly of ritualistic and parade-like performances in public space, arts training for young people of all ages as well as for teachers – with a strong emphasis on peer-to-peer education – and local, national and international networking. Among this broad range of activities, the carnivalesque appearances in the open air are the most visible manifestation of what in effect is a constantly growing emancipatory arts movement. Julia Escobar gives an indication of how the organization and the reach of the group have expanded since they first began in 2001: 'Where we started with a core group of 4, which later became 10 people, we have now grown to

40 young (and some, like us, not so young anymore) men and women. We now work in 30 different localities all over Guatemala, reaching 2,500 participants.'[21] Today, the work of Caja Lúdica even spreads across national boundaries. The collective is a leading partner in various Central American collaborations and is a very active member in one of the world's largest arts networks, *La Red Latinoamericana de Arte para la transformación social* ['The Latin American Network for Art and Social Change'].

In Guatemala, Caja Lúdica's activities are particularly geared towards strengthening youth emancipation and how this relates to human rights and the position of the indigenous population. Based on a census held in 2002, the Guatemalan National Institute of Statistics (INE) estimates that 70 per cent of the total population of 14.3 million is younger than 30.[22] Edelberto Torres-Rivas, a respected Guatemalan social scientist, claims furthermore that of the 18.8 per cent of the Guatemalans who live in extreme poverty (i.e. earning 49 US dollar cents per day), 71 per cent is of Mayan origin and 54 per cent is younger than 15.[23] According to Escobar, 'In our country, these young people are very stigmatized and criminalized. That has been a constant struggle because they don't have spaces where they can get together or express themselves freely.'[24] Bedoya is certain this situation is related to the Civil War, a bloody conflict between the military and insurgents that lasted from 1965 until 1996 and which particularly affected Mayan populations in rural areas: 'The Report of the Commission for Historical Clarification[25] mentions that at least 60,000 people disappeared without trace. It talks of genocide and also how after the peace accords of 1996 no real process of justice and reconciliation has gotten underway, because of lack of political will.'[26]

Today, Bedoya and Escobar are no longer leading Caja Lúdica. In recent years, their task has been gradually taken over by a handful of Guatemalans who were among the first to join the group in 2002 and are now responsible for its outreach and training programmes. These include informal arts training for young people inside and outside schools in the poorer neighbourhoods of the capital and in some rural zones further afield, but also degree-granting courses for primary and secondary school teachers that qualify them to teach community arts.[27] It is a comprehensive approach based on peer-to-peer training for which the 'Action-Participation-Transformation' principle provides the central logic. An 'action' can be any kind of ritual, parade or performance in public space or even in a black box, according to Bedoya. 'Participation' means actively involving people in the development or presentation of these events but also in more informal arts activities at the grass roots. A large arsenal of games and deceptively simple technology forms the basis for this work. 'Transformation', finally, happens almost naturally after that, when art has become part of people's daily life and participants pass on the skills they have learnt to others in their own age group. 'It's about changing your own life and helping others to do the same', Bedoya concludes.[28]

The four members of Caja Lúdica who formed part of the Dutch exchange each in their own way confirm the effectiveness of the Ludic Methodology and its importance to young people in the light of the country's recent history and its continuing violence in the present. Allan Hack (18) is one of the company's most gifted stilt walkers and dancers. He was born in Livingston on the English- and Garifuna-speaking Caribbean coast of Guatemala.[29] After his parents had migrated to the United States, he moved to the capital to live with his grandmother. He encountered Caja Lúdica at age 8 when in 2003 he attended a dance workshop facilitated by Catalina García at an alternative community school in Ciudad Quetzal, a poor suburb to the north-west of the capital where he was living at the time. 'Today I am happy', he says, 'because I could be part of an artistic process that made me feel good about myself and allowed me to pass that seed on, to replicate it further, like a chain reaction'.[30] Graced with a gregarious personality and contagious enthusiasm Allan has become one of Caja Lúdica's more effective facilitators. He is too young to have experienced the Civil War directly, but as a dark-skinned young man he frequently experiences discrimination.[31] 'Today's war is more internal, more silent, more hidden', he knows.[32] Dalila Agustín, a young woman who is now enrolled in the

**Figure 5** Caja Lúdica.

advanced courses of Caja Lúdica, concurs: 'I am not talking necessarily about physical aggression, but rather about an oppression of thought. It locks you up in a ball and causes you not to feel free as a young person. That, too, oppresses your imagination.'[33]

It is easy to see how the festive outdoor manifestations of Caja Lúdica can be considered as celebrations of life in the face of death, fear and constrictions of personal freedom that abound in Guatemalan daily life. They are nourished by a wide range of arts activities geared towards liberating the imagination, familiarizing people with the more playful sides of the arts, teaching them techniques to make masks, costumes and musical instruments, and, in the process, helping them to lose their fear of expressing themselves. 'The different components of our methodology operate simultaneously in people', theorizes Bedoya:

> They mobilize cognitive, physical and spiritual dimensions, stimulating self-awareness and knowledge about others and nature. They also diminish fear and lack of self-confidence, helping people to evolve from being timid and isolated to becoming creative and expressive

participants in society. By working together with others, egotism changes into something more communal and then relationships based on solidarity, respect and love can begin to happen. The first territory which our methodology affects is the human body, which rapidly transforms. It lifts it up by recuperating posture and breathing, thus making it once again conscious of its energy. And once confidence and people's voices are strengthened, their gaze is lifted to the eye-level of other people who, like them, are fighting for a better world.[34]

Finding young kids through the many neighbourhood associations and other social organizations that have become part of their city-wide and national network, exposing them to the playful pleasures of the arts, involving them in public spectacles, continuing to train them in advanced programmes and supporting them as they begin to organize the first arts activities in their own communities: that is the essential logic behind Caja Lúdica. But would it also work in Holland?

## The exchange: A Dutch perspective

Eugene van Erven (b. 1955) is a theatre scholar and cultural organizer. He has only been to Guatemala once before. In the summer of 1978, he travelled overland by public transportation from Gainesville, Florida (where he was an exchange student at the time) through Mexico, finally entering Guatemala via the contested border with Belize. His connections with Latin America were later consolidated by trips to Central and South America in 1979 and 1980 and again, when he was working in the Dutch Caribbean, in 2005 and 2006. In November 2006, he co-organized a community arts festival in his hometown Utrecht. On Sunday morning 26 November, Julia Escobar, assisted by the young Guatemalan artist Victor Martínez, conducted a closing ceremony for this festival in the courtyard of the Utrecht School of the Arts, locally known as *Hogeschool voor de Kunsten Utrecht*, or HKU.[35] 'Many of the presentations we saw at that festival demonstrated a very serious practice and reflection of a level which we in Central America did not yet have', Escobar would recall 6 years later: 'That's why this encounter on another continent was an eye-opener for us. For us it was a starting point to begin an alliance which could help us and our partners in Holland to develop our work'.[36]

Escobar and Martínez had been invited on the recommendation of Jet Vos, the HKU's international placement co-ordinator who in the previous years had encouraged several students to go work with Caja Lúdica. One of them was Anouk de Bruijn (b. 1980), who had already gone to work in Guatemala for 4 months as a volunteer in 1999 and again for a year and a half in 2000 and 2001. Visiting the country once more in early 2003, a friend had taken her to one of Caja Lúdica's parades. There she met Catalina García (b. 1980), the daughter of the founder of Barrio Comparsa in Medellín who had just arrived in Guatemala City.[37] It was hardly surprising, therefore, that de Bruijn opted for a placement with this company during her third year in the theatre and education degree programme of the HKU in 2005. 'But I hardly worked with Catalina during that time', she recalls: 'my main contact was Samuel Ochoa. Once a week I taught a youth group in the neighbourhood where he lived. Lisbeth Reyes, who also participated in our exchange in 2013, lived there as well. And Mono I saw mostly in the offices of Caja Lúdica and on weekends when we went to the rural areas'.[38]

---

I grab Mono's hand. I feel fear in that hand. That's impossible. Mono knows the city so well. Mono is never afraid. 'Don't look back, just listen to what I say. In a minute we'll cross the street and will continue walking on the other side'. Those are his streetwise antennae speaking. 'Always know who is walking behind you. Never walk into an empty street, even if it is much shorter'. In Guatemala City I can always feel death. As if it is always watching us from a rooftop. I feel its gaze. I don't want to be asking myself all the time whether it will visit me today. I would go crazy if I did. But the question is unavoidable when you read the newspaper. And see the names of all those who have died that day.[39]

The festival that Escobar attended in Utrecht in 2006 was the first public appearance of a cultural enterprise called the Community Arts Lab Utrecht (CAL-U).[40] This was a subsidiary programme of the Treaty of Utrecht, a long-term arts and culture project financed by the local and regional government to draw attention to the historical peace treaty that was signed in this city in 1713. The modern-day Treaty was also commissioned to prepare a series of festivals and events during 2013 to commemorate the tricentennial of the original peace accords. Last June, the Community Arts Lab produced one of the festivals, a two-day event around the theme of art and reconciliation for which it asked Bedoya and Escobar to conduct a Mayan-inspired opening ritual. *Hidden War*, a play that was co-created by de Bruijn and García over a 12-month period, was given a prominent place in the programme.

Between 2006 and 2013, CAL-U partnered with Dutch community artists in the field not only to document and help them reflect on their work, but also to inspire them with the work of colleagues from elsewhere in the world.[41] As part of this work, the Lab became deeply involved in 'Living with Differences', an on-the-job coaching project for recently graduated artists who wanted to work in urban communities. Anouk de Bruijn, who had graduated from the Utrecht School of the Arts in 2006, was one of the four artists selected for this programme. Between 2007 and 2010 she created several participatory theatre productions. She proved to possess a particular talent for intimate site-specific work in combination with text-based scripts based on the personal stories of neighbourhood residents who also acted in the shows.[42] When at the end of 2010 the Treaty of Utrecht organization asked CAL-U to develop an international festival around the theme of community arts in conflict zones, the idea to renew the relationship between de Bruijn, CAL-U and Caja Lúdica immediately came up. After all, we had stayed in touch since 2006 through correspondence, a 7-month exchange of cultural work student Eefje Verherbrugge in 2009, and two extended visits to Holland of Caja Lúdica artists Billy and Samuel Ochoa between 2009 and 2011. This time, we wanted to explore each other's realities and ways of working much more intensively by taking joint responsibility for a theatrical co-production. Collaborating towards a common goal, on the floor in Guatemala and Holland, working through cultural and methodological differences, we believed that those who were directly involved would learn much more than by a mere exchange of ideas, a short methodology workshop, or one-off visits. And then, on 2 February 2011, the very same day that van Erven asked her to take the plan for a co-production with Caja Lúdica to a more concrete level, de Bruijn received word that Victor Aroldo Leiva Borrayo had been killed in Guatemala City at age 25. Better known as *Mono* ['monkey'] for his dancing ability and his outspoken and teasing nature, he had been one of the leading figures of Caja Lúdica. He was also the fifth member of the collective to have been killed since the company was founded. Mono's death prompted the Dutch partners in the exchange to find a way to translate that deeply felt motivation of the Guatemalans to generate participatory art in the face of life-threatening violence into a form that would inspire Dutch community arts.

## The economics of North-South exchange

In a chapter called 'Other Places', the authors of *Performance in Place of War* address arts projects in areas with high instances of civilian victims of urban violence which 'are not usually termed "war zones" and therefore rarely attract international attention or intervention'.[43] Drawing on the work of Indian globalization expert Arjun Appadurai[44] they point out that despite its many drawbacks, new information technology has also allowed small-scale forms of international solidarity to emerge.[45] Like the three projects Thompson and his team discuss, *Hidden War* simply would not have been possible without the latest developments in globalization. The authors might well have been referring to our own enterprise when they write: 'The projects here could be presented as attempts to "breathe and move". Each in its own way might be an example of the reconfiguration of space and time in a way that expands the possibilities for practice in everyday life and secures quality time and mutually beneficial encounters with each other'.[46] Building on the mutual trust established during our earlier live encounters in Guatemala and Utrecht, much of the crucial project design and organizational work was advanced through E-mail and Skype.

Given that the Dutch gross domestic product is roughly 22 times higher than Guatemala, it is hardly surprising that the financial balance of power between our two countries was uneven.[47] However, Caja Lúdica more than pulled its weight by investing staff hours and rehearsal facilities and providing local hospitality for the visits of Offereins and de Bruijn in August 2012 and of de Bruijn and Hernández in January 2013. CAL-U raised most of the funds with substantial amounts coming from the Treaty of Utrecht, the Netherlands Fund for Cultural Participation and the Oxfam-Novib subsidiary E-motive.[48] Because CAL-U knew it would cease to exist after the completion of the tricentennial celebrations of the Treaty at the end of 2013, it placed the production of *Hidden War* in the hands of youth theatre company De Rest. The artistic leaders of this young company, Renée Fleuren and Jasper Hogenboom, had themselves worked in Central America during their student years. Furthermore, they had expressed interest in experimenting with the Caja Lúdica methodology in their work with young people. It was particularly this methodological transplantation from Guatemala to the Netherlands that had attracted E-motive. Partially reversing the usual development paradigm, this programme, a special division of Oxfam Novib, wants to stimulate Dutch organizations to learn from colleagues in the developing world. Their emphasis lies on transferring knowledge from South to North and on strengthening public awareness in the Netherlands about the importance of international collaboration with partners in the South 'by presenting successful solutions from there, bringing innovation and inspiration'.[49]

The *Hidden War* collaboration officially began when de Bruijn went to Guatemala for a month in August 2012. She was accompanied by a young researcher, Jonathan Offereins, who was assigned to document the Ludic Methodology. Together with her Colombian-Guatemalan counterpart Catalina García, de Bruijn would lay the groundwork for a theatrical co-production that would contain typical aesthetic elements from Caja Lúdica (rituals, parades, visual arts, movement, poetry) as well as a characteristically Dutch personal story-based approach to community theatre.[50] The daily work of Caja Lúdica, but also more private experiences in Guatemala, would provide the contents for a script that de Bruijn would write and that she and García would eventually co-direct. In August 2012, the four Guatemalan participants were selected: Allan Hack (18), Lisbeth Reyes (25), Dalila Agustín (22) and Plinio Lepe (22). None of them had ever performed in text-based theatre before, let alone in a production partially based on details from their own lives.[51] Much the same could be said for the four Dutch participants whom de Bruijn managed to find in the autumn of 2012.

One of the issues that *Hidden War* wanted to address was the growing popularity among Dutch tertiary-level students to travel to Guatemala to learn Spanish in combination with volunteer work. Regarding the country as a cheap and exotic destination, many of them gravitate towards relatively safe tourist destinations like Antigua and Lake Atitlán and return to the Netherlands quite oblivious of the daily realities in Guatemala. By including the accounts of four young Dutch women who had recently completed placements in Guatemala and to juxtapose these with the stories of four young Guatemalans, García and de Bruijn hoped that their production would break through some of that naiveté.[52] But just like the actors, along the way they needed to confront some of their own preconceptions as well.

The first leg of the exchange in August 2012 was followed by a month-long visit of García to Holland in October and November. It was her first trip to Europe. She spent much of her time exploring ideas with de Bruijn for the performance they wished to make. They also meticulously analysed the interviews de Bruijn had conducted with Dutch students who had gone to Guatemala. During interactive workshops at an E-motive symposium, in the youth theatre school of De Rest and at the Utrecht School of the Arts (HKU), García planted seeds for the further implementation of Caja Lúdica's Ludic Method in Holland and for the later participation of 25 HKU students in an open-air parade that concluded the six performances of *Hidden War* in June 2013. García also met four of the ex-students that de Bruijn had interviewed. They were so impressed that on the spot they committed to performing in the show. Their names were Sandra Harink (a nurse), Marjolein Jegerings (an anthropologist), Karina van der Meijden (a primary school teacher) and Eefje Verherbrugge (a cultural development worker).

In February 2013, De Bruijn travelled once again to Guatemala. This time she went together with Angie Hernández, a Catalan film maker who has been assigned to create a documentary and film footage[53] that could be used in the show. Taking turns facilitating, de Bruijn and García worked with the four Guatemalan actors on collectively developing material for *Hidden War*. 'I watched them play games and improvise on themes like discrimination, machismo, violence, corruption, egotism, fear, and sexual harassment', Bedoya remembers.[54] But they also wrote texts together and visited Arabal and Livingston, the respective birth places of Plinio and Allan.[55] For the Guatemalans de Bruijn's personal story approach was a new and sometimes confrontational way of working. 'There was catharsis, weeping, and smiling', reports Bedoya; 'fears and traumas came out. Yet, everyone opened their heart', and, as Plinio explains, it was all worth it: 'I know this is going to be valuable to me, for my personal growth as a human being. It is a good way to process these experiences.'[56]

Immediately after her return to Holland de Bruijn composed a provisional script from all the interviews, improvisations, jointly developed ideas and her own personal impressions. She remembers the period immediately after sending the script to Guatemala as unsettling: 'I had assumed that Catalina would read the script together with the actors, but she was away in Colombia. I know how important this part of the process is, to check whether you have got the personal stories right and whether everyone is behind it. So I organised a Skype session with the four of them and then read it out for them, in Spanish.'[57] But it was not until after the Guatemalans had arrived in Utrecht at the end of May and had met the Dutch actors for the first time, that de Bruijn started feeling confident that the script would work.

The group worked mostly on weekends and sometimes in the evenings because of work or study obligations of the Dutch actors. Again, de Bruijn and García took turns directing, which led to occasional tensions. Jasper Hogenboom of De Rest, who provided dramaturgical advice, believes this was caused by cultural as well as personal differences:

> I thought that Catalina sometimes took charge too quickly and that Anouk then too easily resorted to being a passive interpreter between Dutch and Spanish. By our standards, the Guatemalans also took enormously long for the warm-ups: as long as an hour and a half in a three-hour session. And then, as is common in *creación colectiva*, they gave the actors a lot of room to spout ideas when we had so little time to mount the show. The Dutch, on the other hand, yearned for precise instructions and efficiency. When Anouk did just that, some of the Guatemalans complained that she did not respect the collective process enough. But in the end, the show was so powerful and satisfying for all concerned that these intercultural obstacles, which are unavoidable anyway, became easier to accept and forget.[58]

## *Hidden War*: The performance

The show had two starting points: one for locals at the gate of Fort Nieuwersluis and another for people from Utrecht, who were taken to the site on an American Bluebird schoolbus, a type frequently used in Guatemalan public transportation. Bus passengers were welcomed by two guides who, during the half-hour trip, shared facts about Guatemala and played a quiz.[59] After this physical and intercultural transportation, the audience walked through an exhibit on the human rights situation in Guatemala in one of the rooms of the fortress before being led into the small performance space.

The show begins in semi-darkness with a Mayan ritual of incense, candles and chants. Over the sound of a beating heart the eight performers, each in a different corner, take turns to introduce themselves. In poetic phrases they announce where they were born and what their connection to Guatemala is. Translations appear on a screen, together with the real identity papers of the actors.

In the second scene, the Dutch performers explore what danger means to them in Guatemala. It humorously reveals the naiveté of the exchange students, who do dangerous things so they can boast about it to friends at home. The play is full of such intercultural jokes, which at first are mostly at the expense of the Dutch exotic gaze. These are gradually stripped away and mixed with Guatemalan perspectives.

In the third scene, Lisbeth and Dalila narrate their stories – in poetic language that is simultaneously performed in Dutch by Sandra and Karina – about how their parents came to the capital from the countryside and constructed improvised houses from recycled plastic and wood. They talk about how in the city they became disconnected from nature and traditional Mayan ways and how, through their involvement with Caja Lúdica, they are now beginning to find some

**Figure 6** *Hidden War* (Photo: Peter Valckx).

of it back. At the end of this episode, Marjolein steps forward and presents statistical facts about the Civil War. Almost imperceptibly, Plinio's voice takes over while hers fades away. He tells how at age 13 he found out that his father had been forced to participate in a mass murder in his hometown Rabinal ('He bought his life and our freedom by killing innocent people')[60] and how his mother and her children decided to leave him and move to the capital. Meanwhile, photographs of the victims of this massacre are projected on the screen and the other performers grab pieces of clothing from a wooden coffin placed centre stage.

At first sight, the Dutch perspectives in *Hidden War* pale in comparison with the dark intensity of the Guatemalan side of things. But seeing the young Dutch women struggle through prejudices and fears (also among friends and family back home) to a growing understanding of themselves and Guatemalan realities is equally impressive. In the middle of the play, fragments of scenes are presented on stage of their confrontations with locals in the countryside, ill-fated taxi rides and fights with possessive boyfriends in the Netherlands. Like with Plinio earlier, the Dutch stories cross-fade with tales from the Caja Lúdica members in which Mono is also frequently included through short video clips. Thus, Lisbeth explains that her family does not approve of her involvement with Caja Lúdica and that she has to work in a sewing factory during the day ('from 8 to 5, standing all the time, 30 minutes break'). The performance continuously changes perspective and stories are fragmented, interwoven with other stories, and interspersed with projections, recorded or live sounds, objects moving through space, and physical movement. For example, Dalila tells her story about the Mara gangs in her neighbourhood while seated on a swing, going higher and higher, and she ends it with a song, accompanying herself on a guitar.

The emotional climax of the play is undoubtedly the final scene about Mono's death. It begins with Eefje going about her business in Holland: grocery shopping, having to make appointments with friends a week ahead (rather than dropping by spontaneously as she had done

**Figure 7** *Hidden War* (Photo: Peter Valckx).

in Guatemala), worrying about exams and then the shock of finding out, through Facebook, that Mono has been killed. Her story cross-fades with memories from Lisbeth ('the night he died I was dreaming of him in a yoga position') and an almost expressionistic stream of consciousness performed by Plinio. Close to tears, he produces a litany of fears ('of the risks Mono took, of losing him, of loving him too much, of falling ill without a proper health care system, of becoming macho, of being lonely, of no longer being able to smile, of becoming a destructive hurricane, of being trapped inside myself'). Eventually, his increasingly emotional words are drowned out by a slowly swelling soundscape produced by the other Guatemalan actors, which ends abruptly when they throw open the door and run outside. This is immediately followed by an epilogue in which the Dutch actors reluctantly let go of their romantic views of Guatemala (Sandra: 'In Guatemala I feel more alive'. 'Lisbeth: Really? Wanna trade places with me?'). Meanwhile, while the light inside fades and a *comparsa* outside becomes visible through the open door, Mono is projected on the wall, talking about how one should embrace fear, because 'if you don't fight it, you can't live'.[61]

**Figure 8** HKU students in self-created costumes and the Caja Lúdica artists (Photo: Peter Valckx).

Mono's final words, confusing and contradictory in the light of his murder, linger as the audience joins the bittersweet parade composed of the HKU students in self-created costumes and the Caja Lúdica artists with Allan towering high on stilts. The percussion and the gentle movements and interaction help the audience process what they have just witnessed. Surrounded by a colourful, dancing mob, many spontaneous conversations ensue. Annemarie van Drecht, the event's producer, would later say that several parents of exchange students told her that only now they understood what their children had been through. For Eefje, Anouk, Catalina and the four Guatemalan actors, the inclusion of Mono in the show was more than a memorial tribute to a good friend. The authors of *Performance in Place of War* employ the useful term 'difficult return' for situations like these, because they offer 'a form of memorialization where history is allowed to remain problematic and unresolved in the present. These practices are more likely to make provocative connections between past and present that demand critical interrogation of contemporary realities, rather than safely bracket off the past from the present'.[62]

Any conclusion to this chapter has to be provisional, because the exchange is still continuing. What we *can* say, in midflight, is that it has been full of learnings, many of which were joyful and others more painful. On either side of the equation we have become more conscious of the relativity of our own realities, knowing that across the ocean we now intimately know people who live in very different circumstances. 'We have enriched our imaginations and have created new frames of reference', writes Bedoya:

> All those who participated are now more aware than before that being born in the first world is not the same as being born in the third or in the fifth world. The inequality is enormous when it comes to education, science, employment and health. The project revealed the ineptitude, and the corruption of the political class in Guatemala. Everything that we learned during the construction of *Hidden War* touched the very fibre of our sensibilities. It produced sarcasm, anger, fear, discomfort, and impotence, all of which found expression in the work. These feelings were transmitted with sincerity and clearly affected the audiences that came to see it. It is a provocative, deeply moving piece that makes us think about the relationships that we build with others and with mother nature. It forces us to question the attitudes of human beings and to look at ourselves in the mirror. There we can see that our societies are very different but also very similar in our commitment to construct a harmonious planet, for the well-being of all.[63]

In Holland, Doryan Bedoya (who had never been to Europe before) experienced for the first time in his life what it was like to move through public space and feel totally safe. It is a freedom the Dutch take for granted, but at the same time seldom exercise. To prove the point, on 14 June, Doryan and his fellow Caja Lúdicans taught a group of Utrecht University students and their teachers the guilty pleasure of creating a parade and then invading public space without, heaven forbid, a permit. As another tangible result of the exchange, youth theatre company De Rest wants to use the techniques they have learnt from the Guatemalans to feed an embryonic network they have started up with municipal youth workers and several grass-roots groups. But with a much lower level of community organizing than in Latin America, that will be far from easy. It confirms that E-motive's one-way logic could use some stretching as well, because when Northern realities aren't taken seriously or understood well enough, before you know it the moral scale tips towards the South. Along the way, we managed to work our way through several delicate moments where such a thing might easily have happened, were it not for the trust we had built up over the years. At the heart of the project was an honest, balanced, genuinely collective artistic process that resulted in a beautifully constructed original piece of theatre that clearly moved the 278 people who saw it. Along the way, it seriously tested the worldview and sensibilities of both the Dutch and the Guatemalans. In Holland, many people, including Anouk de Bruijn and Theatre Company De Rest, will continue to work with what they have gained from the experience. And as we write this, Caja Lúdica is adapting *Hidden War* for local performances in their own country. They are convinced that the mix of Dutch and Guatemalan aesthetics and perspectives will appeal to Guatemalan audiences as well. But that will be another story.

# Afterword: What Next for Theatre for Development?

The contradiction that has dogged Theatre for Development (TfD) since its inception is that between social accommodation and social transformation. In either case the methods for developing the process may be similar but the intention, articulated by the community and supported by the facilitator, is different. The failure to address the contradiction or, worse still, to mask it in Freirean rhetoric has brought TfD to a crossroads. It can locate itself cosily among the plethora of practices which proclaim themselves as applied theatre and be distinguished not by its politics and poetics but only by its context. This is the position apparently ascribed to TfD by Monica Prendergast and Juliana Saxton in *The Locations of Applied Theatre*[1] when they assign to the TfD section case studies from Bangladesh, Uganda and Pakistan. TfD is something which happens 'over there' where the less fortunate 'other' needs help; in other words a version of the traditional, colonial paradigm where development is something done to others that they may become more like us. If the discipline makes a right turn and continues down the path of accommodation, it will become the exclusive property of governments (increasingly rarely in an era of permanent austerity) and NGOs and be wielded as a tool with which to support and encourage 'pro-social' behaviour. Although this may produce some incidental benefits for individuals such as improved confidence and social skills, in the main its consequence, perhaps unwittingly, will be to make systemic inequality and injustice tolerable. In so doing it will perform a similar function to Labour parties around the world which seek to mitigate the most blatant savagery of capitalism and, in doing so, prolong the life of the very system whose ills they are attempting to cure. The leftward turn where the path is much less defined, steep and strewn with awkward twists leads to a discipline that focuses on the developmental potential of the theatre process, applying itself to nothing more and nothing less than the right of each and every human being to live creatively and not to be disfigured by having to shape her body, her thoughts and her dreams to systems imposed for the profit of others. Not only is this a route of heartbreak and danger, it is also one without an end. In TfD there are no outcomes, no destinations but only the journey where the resolution of one contradiction is merely the prelude to the emergence of the next. In essence the choice is between a practice that is circumscribed by the surface structures of the present neo-liberal world and one that builds into its process a utopian dimension founded upon an analysis of the deep structures of living. This is what I take Brecht to mean when he wrote: 'Taught only by reality, can reality be changed'.[2]

According to one reading of TfD's history its great days and its big events are long gone. The people's theatre at Kamiriithu is a forgotten ruin. Philippine Educational Theater Association's (PETA) role in the People Power Movement is a matter of history. The great anti-apartheid plays have given way to an era of corruption and 'coconuts' (black on the outside, white within) in South Africa. Radical, large-scale performance inspired by the Cuban Revolution has been superseded by more modest, grass-roots community action. In the age of globalization TfD is changing its aspect but does that mean it has jettisoned its soul? The world in which it operates is characterized by an ever-growing inequality of material and social relations where the 1 per cent with access to capital and the means, therefore, of making money out of money, live on the backs of the 99 per cent. John McGrath's 7:84 political theatre company would today need to be renamed the 1:99. We have been living with capitalism for a long time but the different element today is that all human activity is measured in terms of monetary value. In this commodification process the individual, as a consumer, is valorized at the expense of the collective which is depicted as either a quaint throwback to the communism of yesteryear or a rabble of the dangerous other. The other features of contemporary globalization that impact directly upon TfD are the immense reach of private media organizations peddling the agendas of their owners and thereby manufacturing among publics consent to the very policies that victimize them, and the primacy of the virtual over the real in communications' interactions.

Is there any place for TfD in such a scenario? An aesthetics which enables counter-hegemonic strategies is a *sine qua non* for countering the effects of neoliberalism on critical consciousness. In the face of the ubiquity of the internet and satellite technology a live medium may be tempted to put up the shutters and retreat into an ever-diminishing territory. Instead TfD should look towards ways of working in tandem with the communicative possibilities opened up by digital technology by asking how the virtual can support those things which only exist in live spaces. The dissemination of the insights arising from TfD participants and audiences can be enhanced by the virtual to produce an engagement loop that feeds back into the next phase of the live process. As in most other areas a dialectical rather than a binary approach to the relationship between the virtual and the live is likely to be more productive. This applies also to the often falsely juxtaposed binary of the individual and the collective. A collective is only a collection of individuals even if they become greater than the sum of their parts through joint action. In other words the individual is necessary to produce the collective which in its turn reshapes the consciousness of the individual as a consequence of experiences which can only be created collectively. Only by asserting the creative power of collectivity can the destructive cult of individualism with its shrinking of the capacity for empathy and social mobilization be resisted. This is why making connections with existing people's organizations is essential for any effective, sustainable practice of TfD.

By eschewing domestication in its practical applications, I am proposing that TfD takes a lead in the re-interpretation of development. Instead of being a destination to which the unfortunate can aspire, as to the membership of an exclusive country club, it becomes a journey upon which anyone can embark provided that they are not labouring under the misapprehension that it ever comes to an end. The unfinished nature of the concept applies alike to the individual and to the nation or other macro-grouping. Within such a concept the particular contribution of TfD is the way in which it enables participants to establish connections between their lived experiences and the deep structures which are usually hidden from view by an all-pervasive hegemony designed to engender passivity through apparent lack of alternatives to the dominant mode of being. The most frequently stated aim for a TfD project is the raising of the consciousness of the target group of participants. If this is the sole or main aim, it has the effect of divorcing the two elements that comprise Freire's concept of 'conscientisation': critical consciousness in a dialectical relationship with social action. Without the second element participants are left, like Samuel Beckett's characters in *Waiting for Godot*, with no social function for their newly acquired state of raised consciousness:

> VLADIMIR: We are happy.
> ESTRAGON: We are happy. (*Silence.*) What do we do now, now that we are happy?[3]

So those undergoing the TfD process are entitled to ask: 'what do we do now, now that our consciousness has been raised?' In all probability this consciousness applies only to a specific issue (I now know that I should not chop down trees for firewood), rather than to the ways in which such issues are related to a broader pattern of resource depletion. Srampickal makes the point forcefully:

> Essentially, consciousness raising reaches its full extent only when people are enabled to analyse and find out the relations between various issues, how an event happening in their village falls in line with the national and worldwide system of oppression.[4]

The facilitator who may have been instrumental in helping to make the connections between local experience and the world now has to support the next phase in the process as the community determines what courses of action are available to it in the light of the new knowledge. These actions may involve further theatre processes for different audiences or may mean organizing beyond the theatrical space, or both. Whatever the precise trajectory chosen for action by the community, the facilitator's contribution is always to remind it of the power of the human resources of irony, paradox, contradiction and fooling. In redefining development I am also asking for a redefinition, or at least a re-emphasis, for TfD away from its earnest and worthy communication of messages for self-improvement, and towards a playful, beguiling engagement with those it seeks to shift from their entrenched, oppressive positions. The serious can quickly lead to the ideal which, in turn, leads to a plan to be imposed monologically to build a better world. My notion for TfD, born out so thrillingly in the case studies of this book, is not that it is a device for weaving the escapist fantasies of creating another world, but rather that it contributes constantly to the rehumanizing of this one – people-centred, more just, more imaginative, more playful.

There is no blueprint for the correct way of 'doing' TfD. There is cumulative experience and the unfinished intimations of praxis. There are flexible intentions, dodging and diving in and out of the constantly shifting, shape-changing dialogue between improvisation and context. There are core principles but even these are not immune from the unpredictability of novel circumstances. In proposing a new direction for TfD, not turning back on our tracks but rather taking a new one that runs obliquely up hill and off to the left, there are signposts and pathfinders in the tangled undergrowth of history. Among these are different approaches to the idea of resistance. In place of the revolutionary uprisings and head-on confrontations of former epochs, today resistance to neo-liberal domination comes in many forms and most of them contain elements of parody, irony and play as they seek out the contradictions in that monolithic block; cracking its solemn face into a smile and in that crack planting the seed where a different kind of flower might grow. One such approach is that of the Zapatista Army of National Liberation (EZLN) in Mexico under the guidance of the anonymous, balaclaved, self-styled figure of Subcomandante Marcos. Initially the movement appeared, armed, in Chiapas looking like another glorious but doomed revolutionary group to add to the long list thrown up by Central America. Echoes of Che Guevara were deliberately sounded by Marcos and the Mexican Government responded with predictable violence to what they supposed was a violent threat to their hegemony. But the EZLN's weapons turned out to be the shape-shifting armoury of the trickster. Under the slogan 'leading by obeying' they exemplify the role of the interventionist facilitator who acts on the wishes of the marginalized and oppressed by organizing interventions into the macro-world of politics in the name of those people. One memorable example of their tactics was the surrounding of an air force base and, from the encircling heights beyond the perimeter, bombarding the compound with paper aeroplanes on each one of which was written one of the demands made by those for whom the EZLN was 'fighting'. In his speech to the National Democratic Convention at Aguascalientes in 1994, Subcomandante Marcos underlined the difference between his notion of politics and that of the established order:

> Yes to the effort for democratic change that includes freedom and justice for the forgotten people, the majority of our country. Yes to the beginning of the end of this long, grotesque nightmare that is called the history of Mexico.
>
> Yes, the moment has come to say to everyone that we neither want, nor are we able, to occupy the place that some hope we will occupy, the place from which all opinions will come, all the answers, all the routes, all the truths. We are not going to do that.[5]

Marcos here proclaims himself kin to the foolish facilitator, dodging the traps of certainty and ideology, refusing to do other people's thinking for them. Instead of a clash of ideologies, Marcos is calling for the releasing of the potential of all Mexicans, not just those with access to wealth and power. This trait of playing with ideology rather than dictating one for others also characterizes the interventions of the anti-consumerist clown at the heart of that most consumerist of societies, the United States, the Reverend

Billy. Bill Talen, like Subcomandante Marcos, selected a persona which would simultaneously echo a well-known, popular type in their societies – televangelist in one case, revolutionary hero in the other – while simultaneously being an ironic or parodic version of that type. Much of the energy of Talen's interventions into the dark hearts of consumerism stem from his ability to become Reverend Billy rather than take on a character in the manner of conventional performance. Like TfD participants performing their own story, he is at once the actor of himself and himself. Even as 'himself' in conversation, Bill Talen's overlap with the Reverend Billy overflows into his discourse:

> Life, life! We believe in life and wonder! We all have that voice in the back of our brains that is marveling [sic] at life every second of every day. Because it is amazing, isn't it? Even the most cynical people have this question going on. So engaging that voice, letting that question – what is life? – get aired out once in a while, will make you jump and shout and do the damndest things. That's what we do in our church. We don't want that deity with the answers. We want that life with the questions. Amen?[6]

The Reverend Billy exploits the religious thrill, the force of being a congregation but then diverts the torrent away from blueprints for a right-wing ideology in this life and the life to come and substitutes a questioning, an exposing of the contradictions of a society which leaves us dying of consumption. In other words the Reverend Billy is a means of gaining access to powerful conservative discourses in US society in order to undo them from within, like Azdak as judge. Talen has also been involved in a phenomenon that is gathering momentum across the world, reflecting the increasing autonomy of the global metropolis, that of the comedian, performer, fool as mayoral candidate. As disillusion with national politics assumes epidemic proportions and the whole notion of the state comes under pressure, the city-state has re-emerged with folly becoming a vital ingredient in any civic future:

At the end of the mayoral campaign we came to the idea that the Bloombergs are in control. They are in control of the putative government, but there has to be a colorful shadow government informed by a cultural revolution of humor and music. Community-making is taking place under the nose of the redcoats. Consumerism puts distance between people. But that isolation is being defeated right now; it's crashing.[7]

There are connections to be made between aspects of the Reverend Billy project and the interventions of Bepe Grillo and his Five Star Movement on the stage of Italian national politics. In both cases a reconceptualizing of civic and national futures without recourse to traditional political structures is under way. The immediacy of performance, particularly comic performance, is being invoked as a potent communication with ordinary people that throws into relief the constant failure of the political establishment to find a language through which to talk to its electorates. On a grand scale figures like Reverend Billy and Bepe Grillo are archetypes of the foolish facilitator, enthusing their participants/followers/audiences with utopian visions and the audacity to dream of social change. Grillo's links to Italy's medieval past have been made explicit by Dario Fo who has, over many years, fashioned himself as a latter day *giullaro*; the storyteller, clown, wandering minstrel who employed his performance skills in the service of criticizing the powerful in church and state on behalf of the peasants.

Grillo rose to fame mixing comedy routines with references to political scandals in the towns he was playing in, a straight lift from his medieval peers. 'He is from the tradition of the wise storyteller, one who knows how to use surreal fantasy, who can turn situations around, who has the right word for the right moment, who can transfix people when he speaks, even in the rain and the snow', explains Fo

Even the internet-based forums where Grillo's followers argue over policy have their roots in the Middle Ages, argues Fo. He says: 'We had extremely democratic town councils in medieval Italy which knew the value of working together and every now and then, down the centuries, this spirit returns'.[8]

The Five Star movement may never take up positions within the formal political structures nor Grillo become prime minister and perhaps the fool should never aspire to do so lest she lose her function, but the intervention is nevertheless of a magnitude that demonstrates to an erstwhile neglected electorate that there are other, more democratic ways of organizing political life. Grillo is seeking out the play in the system to discover where it bends and where it breaks. In so doing he takes up the baton of TfD and shows that it can operate at macro as well as micro levels.

The system has to be shaken from its inertia not to fulfil some romantic revolutionary dream but because the contradictions within it are threatening the survival of the planet and all creatures upon it. Without embarking on a new book just when you hoped you had reached the end of this one, let two related contradictions suffice as examples. The capitalist system demands continuous economic, material growth. All regimes around the world are wedded, more or less, to a philosophy of growth. To stand still is to die. However, this philosophy ignores the fundamental reality of a planet whose resources are finite. Sooner or later the contradiction will have to bring forth a new, more sustainable way of living. If this situation were not dire enough, it is exacerbated by largely uncontrolled population growth. The lie that the capitalist system sells to the people is that ever more people can enjoy ever higher material standards of living. TfD as an art form dedicated to exposing and playing with contradiction is ideally suited to juggling with these concepts in order to produce the sociopolitical changes necessary for our survival.

At the end of his meticulous study *Collapse: How Societies Choose to Fail or Survive*, Jared Diamond forms this conclusion:

> For our society as a whole, the past societies that we have examined in this book suggest broader lessons. Two types of choices seem to me to have been crucial in tipping their outcomes towards success or

failure: long-term planning, and willingness to reconsider values. On reflection, we can also recognize the crucial role of these same two choices for the outcomes of our individual lives.

One of those choices has depended on the courage to practice long-term thinking, and to make bold, courageous, anticipatory decisions at a time when problems have become perceptible but before they have reached crisis proportions. . . . ,

The other crucial choice illuminated by the past involves the courage to make painful decisions about values. Which of the values that formerly served a society well can continue to be maintained under new changed circumstances? Which of those treasured values must instead be jettisoned and replaced by different approaches?[9]

The most effective, in Diamond's terms, 'successful' choices are those which are owned by all the members of a particular society. The old ways of representative democracy, degenerating into a system where the politicians represent only themselves and a small section of the business elite, shoring up the old institutions that privilege themselves, cannot deliver these choices. 'Different approaches' depend upon the participation of active citizens who practise direct democracy, drawing upon the power of their creativity and their criticality. In the critical, creative space delineated by TfD the contradictions at the heart of 'treasured values' can be exposed and possible alternatives rehearsed. At the very least, in the terms set for us by John Holloway, when we are making TfD we are not engaged in a capitalist mode of production:

> We make capitalism by creating and re-creating the social relations of capitalism: we must stop doing so, we must do something else, live different social relations. Revolution is simply that: to stop making capitalism and do something else instead.[10]

TfD is not a rehearsal for revolution; it is part of the process which produces revolution conceived not as a destination but as a process. It is a way of art which can stand outside the nexus of capital and therefore be, in itself, part of the social change towards other ways of becoming. It is, according to Holloway's concept, one of the ways by which capitalism can be 'cracked':

> Fight from the particular, fight from where we are, here and now. Create spaces or moments of otherness, spaces or moments that walk in the opposite direction, that do not fit in. Make holes in our own reiterative creating of capitalism. Create cracks and let them expand, let them multiply, let them resonate, let them flow together.[11]

The foolish facilitator or Joker working within a TfD process can be a means of opening up one such 'crack'.

If TfD wishes to lay claim to being a process that can enable the transformation of individuals, groups and the societies in which they intervene, its aspirations should be no less than these words. Theatre for Development will then point, at worst, the path to recovering a fairer, social democratic form of capitalism, at best, to a world beyond capitalism of equitable social relations.

# Notes

## Introduction

1  Yeats, W. B., 'He Wishes for the Cloths of Heaven', in *Collected Poems*. London: Macmillan, 1950, p. 81.

## Chapter 1

1  Taylor, Philip, *Applied Theatre*. Portsmouth NH: Heinemann, 2003; Thompson, James, *Applied Theatre: Bewilderment and Beyond*. Oxford: Peter Lang, 2003; Nicholson, Helen, *Applied Drama: The Gift of Theatre*. Basingstoke: Palgrave Macmillan, 2005; Prentki, Tim and Preston, Sheila (eds), *The Applied Theatre Reader*. London and New York: Routledge, 2009.

2  Eco, Umberto, *The Name of the Rose*. London: Picador, 1984.

3  Fo, Dario, *Accidental Death of an Anarchist*. London: Pluto Press, 1980.

4  http://www.bartleby.com/124/pres53.html [accessed 15 May 2013].

5  Ibid.

6  Ibid.

7  Sachs, Wolfgang, *The Development Dictionary*. London: Zed Books, 1995, p. 4.

8  http://www.un.org/en/documents/udhr [accessed 21 May 2013].

9  Ibid.

10  Jackson, Tony (ed.), *Learning through Theatre*. London and New York: Routledge, 1993, p. 1.

11  Ibid., p. 18.

12  Freire, Paulo, *Pedagogy of the Oppressed*. Harmondsworth: Penguin Books, 1972.

13  Prentki and Preston, op. cit., p. 9.

14  Vine in Jackson, op. cit., p. 112.

15  McLellan, David, *The Thought of Karl Marx*. London and Basingstoke: Macmillan, 1980, p. 152.

16  Ibid., p. 156.

17  Marx, Karl, *Selected Writings*. Oxford: Oxford University Press, 1977, p. 300.

18  Willett, John, *Brecht on Theatre*. London: Eyre Methuen, 1978, p. 248.

19  Ibid., p. 186.

20  Ibid., p. 79.

21  Weber, Betty and Heinen, Hubert (eds), *Bertolt Brecht*. Manchester: Manchester University Press, 1980, p. 35.

22  Willett, op. cit., p. 80.

23  Ibid., p. 79.

24  Freire, op. cit.

25  Brecht, Bertolt, *The Measures Taken and Other Lehrstücke*. London: Eyre Methuen, 1977, p. 34.

26  Boal, Augusto, *Theatre of the Oppressed*. London: Pluto Press, 1979.

27  Freire, op. cit.

28  Freire, Paulo, *Pedagogy of Freedom*. Lanham, MA: Rowman & Littlefield, 1998, p. 74.

29  Boal, op. cit., p. 141.

30  Etherton, Michael, *The Development of African Drama*. London: Hutchinson, 1982, p. 345.

31  Ibid., p. 345.

32  Kerr, David, *African Popular Theatre*. Oxford: James Currey, 1995, p. 161.

33  Ibid., p. 153.

34  Ibid., p. 160.

35  Ibid., p. 165.

36  Ibid., p. 149.

37  Ibid., p. 138.

38  Epskamp, Kees, *Theatre in Search of Social Change*. The Hague: Centre for the Study of Education in Developing Countries, 1989, p. 111.

39  Mda. Zakes, *When People Play People*. London: Zed Books, 1993.

40  Ibid., p. 173.

41  Ibid., p. 173.

42  Kerr, op. cit., p. 148.

43  Mlama, Penina, *Culture and Development*. Uppsala: Nordiska Afrikainstitutet, 1991, p. 91.

44  Ibid., p. 65.

45  Ibid., pp. 67–8.

46  Ibid., p. 93.

47  Kerr, op. cit., pp. 240–56.

48  Ngugi, wa Thiong'o, *Decolonising the Mind*. London: James Currey, 1986, pp. 34–62.

49  Etherton, op. cit., p. 354.

50  Legarda, Maribel in Adams and Goldbard, *Community, Culture and Globalization*. New York: The Rockefeller Foundation, 2002, p. 337.

51  Adams and Goldbard, op. cit., p. 337.

52  Fajardo, Brenda and Topacio, Socrates, *Basic Integrated Theater Arts Workshop*. Quezon City: Philippines Educational Theater Association, 1989, p. 2.

53  van Erven, Eugène, *The Playful Revolution*. Bloomington: Indiana University Press, 1992, pp. 19–28.

54  Spolin, Viola, *Improvisation for the Theater*. Evanston: North Western University Press, 1963.

55  Fajardo and Topacio, op. cit., p. 3.

56  Ibid., p. 7.

57  Ibid., p. 7.

58  Willett, op. cit., p.277.

59  van Erven, op. cit., p. 63.

60  Adams and Goldbard, op. cit., p. 340.

61  Ibid., p. 348.

62  Balanon, Faye, *Rated PG*. Quezon City: Philippine Educational Theater Association, 2012, pp. 11–12.

63  Srampickal, Jacob, *Voice to the Voiceless*. London: Hurst & Co., 1994, pp. 173–4.

64  Ibid., p. 180.

65  Ibid., p. 206.

66 Etherton, Michael in Boon, Richard and Plastow, Jane, *Theatre and Empowerment*. Cambridge: Cambridge University Press, 2004, p. 190.

67 Munier, Asif and Etherton, Michael, 'Child Rights Theatre for Development in rural Bangladesh: a case study'. *Research in Drama Education* 11, 2 (2006): 175–83.

68 Srampickal, op. cit., p. 220.

69 Ganguly, Sanjoy in Boon and Plastow, op. cit., p. 233.

70 Ibid., p. 245.

71 Ganguly, Sanjoy, *Jana Sanskriti*. London and New York: Routledge, 2010, p. 139.

72 Ganguly in Boon and Plastow, op. cit., p. 256.

73 Ganguly, op. cit., p. 139.

74 van Erven, op. cit., p. 156.

75 http://www.natyachetana.org/mission_vision.html [accessed 28 October 2013].

76 Crow, Brian with Banfield, *An Introduction to Post-Colonial Theatre*. Cambridge: Cambridge University Press, 1996, pp. 134–5.

77 Natya Chetana, *Looking Back to Ten years of Natya Chetana*. Bhubaneswar: Natya Chetana, 1996, p. 8.

78 Etherton in Boon and Plastow, op. cit., p. 192.

79 Ibid., p. 194.

80 Ibid., p. 203.

81 Ibid., p. 215.

82 Weiss, Judith, *Latin American Popular Theatre*. Albuquerque: University of New Mexico Press, 1993, p. 136.

83 Ibid., p. 136.

84 Kane, Liam, *Popular Education and Social Change in Latin America*. London: Latin American Bureau, 2001, p. 9.

85 Weiss, op. cit., p. 163.

86 McCarthy, Julie, *Enacting Participatory Development*. London: Earthscan, 2004, p. 111.

87 Weiss, op. cit., p. 206.

88 Kane, op. cit., p. 106.

# Chapter 2

1 UNESCO, *Our Creative Diversity*. Paris: UNESCO Publishing, 1996, p. 11.

2 http://portal.unesco.org/en/ev.php-URL_ID=13179&URL_DO=DO_TOPIC&URL_SECTION=201.html [accessed 4 November 2013]

3 Adams, Don and Goldbard, Arlene (eds), *Community, Culture and Globalization*. New York: The Rockefeller Foundation, 2002, p. 20.

4 Ibid., p. 17.

5 Ibid., p. 9.

6 Butchard, Tim, *The Arts and Development*. London: The British Council, 1995, p. 7.

7 Ibid., p. 10.

8 Gould, Helen and Marsh, Mary, *Culture: Hidden Development*. London: Creative Exchange, 2004, p. 14.

9 Butchard, op. cit., p. 38.

10 Gould and Marsh, op. cit., p. 17.

11 Ibid., p. 22.

12 Butchard, op. cit., p. 39.

13 Gould and Marsh, op. cit., p. 37.

14 Vandana Shiva, *The Observer*, 2 November 2013.

15 McLellan, David (ed.), *The Thought of Karl Marx*. London and Basingstoke: Macmillan, 1980, p. 184.

16 Willett, John (ed.), *Brecht on Theatre*. London: Methuen, 1978, pp. 143–4.

17 Ibid., p. 192.

18 Brecht, Bertolt, *Collected Plays: Six*. London: Methuen, 1994.

19 Freire, Paulo, *Cultural Action for Freedom*. Harmondsworth: Penguin, 1972, p. 33.

20 Prentki, Tim, *The Fool in European Theatre*. Basingstoke: Palgrave, 2012.

21 Crow, Brian with Banfield, Chris, *An Introduction to Post-Colonial Theatre*. Cambridge: Cambridge University Press, 1996, p. 115.

22 Brecht, Bertolt, *Collected Plays: Seven*. London: Methuen, 1994, p. 302.

23   Ibid., p. 236.

24   Boal, Augusto, *Theatre of the Oppressed*. London: Pluto Press, 1979, p. 174.

25   Cohen-Cruz, Jan and Schutzman, Mady, *A Boal Companion*. New York: Routledge, 2006, p. 133.

26   Boal, op. cit., p. 175.

27   Mlama, Penina, *Culture and Development*. Uppsala: Nordiska Afrikainstitutet, 1991, p. 91.

28   Adams and Goldbard, op. cit., p. 227.

29   Boal, Augusto, *The Aesthetics of the Oppressed*. London and New York: Routledge, 2006, p. 104.

30   Fajardo, Brenda and Topacio, Socrates, *Basic Integrated Theater Arts Workshop*. Quezon City: PETA, 1989, p. 19.

31   Kane, Liam, *Popular Education and Social Change in Latin America*. London: Latin American Bureau, 2001, p. 17.

32   Boal, Augusto, *The Rainbow of Desire*. London and New York: Routledge, 1995, pp. xix–xx.

33   Willett, op. cit., p. 248.

34   Thomson, Peter and Sacks, Glendyr, *The Cambridge Companion to Brecht*. Cambridge: Cambridge University Press. 1994, p. 199.

35   Hyde, Lewis, *Trickster Makes This World*. New York: North Point Press, 1998, p. 307.

36   Willett, op. cit., p. 44.

37   Ibid., p. 277.

# Chapter 3

1   wa Thiongo, N. and wa Mirii, N. *I Will Marry When I Want*. Play performed at Kamirithu Education and Cultural Centre, Limuru, Kenya, 1974. http://www.ngugiwathiongo.com/bio/bio-home.htm [accessed 4 September 2013]

2   Levert, L. and Mumma, O., *Drama and Theatre Communication and Development – Experiences in Western Kenya*. Nairobi: Kenyan Drama and Theatre Association, 1995.

3  Mangeni, P., *Negotiating Gender Equity through Theatre for Development*.
   Brisbane: PhD Thesis, Griffith University, 2007.

4  Philippines Educational Theatre Association and Beng Santos-Cabangon,
   *Reflections in the River*. Video. Brisbane: IDEA Publications, 1996.

5  Nyangore, V., 'Listen to your mothers', in J. O'Toole and M. Lepp (eds),
   *Drama for Life*. Brisbane: Playlab Press, 2001.

6  Pattanaik, S., 'Messengers on Bicycles: pedalling cultural awareness
   through theatre', in J. O'Toole and M. Lepp (eds), *Drama for Life*.
   Brisbane: Playlab Press, 2001.

7  Prior, R., *Teaching Actors: Knowledge Transfer in Actor Training*. London:
   Intellect, 2012.

8  Ahmed, S. J., 'Wishing for a world without "theatre for development":
   demystifying the case of Bangla Desh'. *Research in Drama Education*
   7, 2 (2002): 207–19.

9  Fyfe, H., 'Drama in the context of a divided society', in J. O'Toole and K.
   Donelan (eds), *Drama, Culture and Empowerment: The IDEA Dialogues*.
   Brisbane: IDEA Publications, 1996; Shu, J., 'Heritage theatre and
   semiotics: framing a performance at an ancestral hall'. *Applied Theatre
   Research* 1, 1 (2013): 29–43.

10 Dalrymple, L., 'The DRAMAIDE project', in J. O'Toole, and K. Donelan
   (eds), *Drama, Culture and Empowerment: The IDEA Dialogues*. Brisbane:
   IDEA Publications, 1996.

11 Chinyowa, K., 'Emerging paradigms for applied drama and theatre
   practice in African contexts'. *Research in Drama Education* 14, 3 (2003):
   326–46.

12 Shor, I., *Empowering Education: Critical Teaching for Social Change*.
   Chicago: University of Chicago Press, 1992.

13 Beadle, S. and Cahill, H., 'Talking about sexual and reproductive health:
   Promoting better communication between parents and children in Asia',
   in J. Heart (ed.), *Gender Equality, HIV and Education*, UNESCO, 2012:
   http://unesdoc.unesco.org/images/0021/002187/218793e.pdf. pp. 54–55
   [accessed 24 August 2013].

14 James, S., Reddy, P., Ruiter, R. A. C., McCauley, A. and van den
   Borne, B., 'The impact of an HIV and Life Skills program on secondary

school students in Kwazulu-Natal, South Africa'. *AIDS Education and Prevention* 18, 4 (2006): 281–94; Kirby, D., Laris, B. A. and Rolleri, L., 'Sex and HIV education programs: their impact on sexual behaviors of young people throughout the world'. *Journal of Adolescent Health* 40 (2007): 206–17.

15  Baldwin, A., 'Life Drama: Contextualising practice'. *Applied Theatre Researcher* 11 (2010): http://www.griffith.edu.au/__data/assets/pdf_file/0009/270882/02-Baldwin-1-FINAL.pdf [accessed 5 September 2013].

16  Nebe, W. and Mueller-Glodde, U., 'Capacity development in HIV and AIDS education through applied drama'. Appraisal Mission Report. Gaborone, Botswana: SADC, 2006.

17  Ndlovu, C. M., 'A cultural response: the exploration of traditional dance and games as an HIV/AIDS Intervention, a Zimbabwean case study'. Unpublished MA Research Report. Johannesburg: University of the Witwatersrand, 2010.

18  Thulo, K., 'They Were Silent: Investigating the Potential Shamanic Role of A Contemporary Theatre Performance and How Ritual and Theatre can be Synergized'. Unpublished MA Research Report. Johannesburg: University of the Witwatersrand, 2009.

19  Mwalwanda, B., 'Towards the use of drama as a therapeutic tool to enhance emotional rehabilitation for people with HIV/AIDS. A case study of Paradiso HIV/AIDS Support Organisation'. Unpublished MA Research Report. Johannesburg: University of the Witwatersrand, 2009.

20  Phala, O., 'The Gift of Active Learning. Analysis of Participatory Techniques Used in Lezzy My Mirror and their Relevance for HIV Stigmatisation in Botswana'. Unpublished BA Hons Essay. Johannesburg: University of the Witwatersrand, 2009.

21  Kapiri, T., 'The relationship between the applied theatre practitioner and the funding agencies in Malawi: a case study of Nanzikambe Theatre Arts practice'. Unpublished BA Hons Essay. Johannesburg: University of the Witwatersrand, 2008.

22  Meadows, G., 'Towards a poetics for theatre as activism within the context of human and people's rights in Southern Africa: an exploration

of Speak Truth To Power and the March Against Xenophobia of 2008'. Unpublished MA Report. Johannesburg: University of the Witwatersrand, 2009.

23 Ndlovu, C. M., 'A Cultural Response: The Exploration of Traditional Dance and Games as an HIV/AIDS Intervention, A Zimbabwean Case Study'. Unpublished MA Research Report. Johannesburg, South Africa: Drama for Life Programme, University of the Witwatersrand, 2010.

24 Mtukwa, T., 'Catch the young: using process drama for children's rights education'. Unpublished MA Report. Johannesburg: University of the Witwatersrand, 2010.

25 Njewele, D., 'An Opportunity to Introduce Drama in Education: A Case Study of Children's Theatre Project in Tanzania'. Unpublished MA Research Report. Johannesburg: University of the Witwatersrand, 2009.

26 Bamford, A., *The WOW Factor; Global Research Compendium on the Impact of the Arts in Education*. New York: Waxmann, 2006, p. 104.

27 Thompson, J., 'Questions on performances in place of war'. Applied Theatre Research 1, 2 (2013), 149–56.

28 Stinson, M., '"Drama is like reversing everything": intervention research as teacher professional development'. *Research in Drama Education* 14, 2 (2009) 223–41.

# Chapter 4

1 Professor in the Theater Arts department of the Center of Arts at UDESC.

2 Student in the bachelor's program in Theater (with teacher certification) – Center of Arts – UDESC, scientific initiation grant PROBIC/UDESC.

3 Nogueira, Marcia, 'Reflections on the impact of a long term theatre for community development project in Southern Brazil'. *Research in Drama Education*, 11, 2 (June 2006): 219–34.

4 Ibid., p. 224.

5 The plays that were produced in this phase of implementation were: *País dos Urubus* [Country of Vultures] in 1991 (directed by Marcia Pompeo), *As Bruxas e a Pedra Mágica* [The Witches and the Magic Stone] in 1993

(directed by Geraldo Cunha and Marcio Correa), *História do Não Sei* [History of I Don't Know] in 1994 (directed by Marcia Pompeo, Carina Scheibe and Nado Gonçalves), the *Outra História do Boi* [The Othery Ox Story] in 1995 (directed by Marcia Pompeo, Carina Scheibe and Nado Gonçalves). And in the independent phase: *Deu até Briga no 604* [There Was Even a Fight on the 604] in 2003 (directed by Marcia Pompeo, Rafael Buss Ferreira and Natanael Machado), *O Quintal Esquecido* [The Forgotten Yard] in 2005 (Marcia Pompeo, Débora Matos and Natanael Machado), *O sonho* [The Dream] in 2007 (directed by Natanael Machado), *O mangue doente* [The Ill Mangrove] in 2007 (directed by Natanael Machado), *Nós somos assim* [That's the Way We Are] in 2006 (directed by Natanael Machado), *O misterioso foguete* [The Mysterious Rocket] in 2007 (directed by Natanael Machado), *Outros mundos* [Other Worlds] in 2010 (directed by Natanael Machado), *Teatro-fórum Setembrina*, [Little September Theater-Forum] in 2012 (directed by João de Barros, Natanael Machado and Fabiana Lazzari).

6   http://www.nosdomorro.com.br/index.php/sobre-o-n%C3%B3s.html

7   http://www.pombasurbanas.org.br/

8   Helen Nicholson speaks of Applied Drama that is conducted in different and at times not at all glamorous places, such as schools, asylums and prisons (Nicholson, Helen, *Applied Drama*. Basingstoke: Palgrave, 2005, p. 2.)

9   Project coordinated by Dan Baron Cohen and Marcia Pompeo Nogueira.

10   Cohen, Dan Baron and Nogueira, Marcia Pompeo. 'Unearthing the Future'. *Drama Magazine* 8, 2 (summer 2001): 29–36, 5.

11   Internship report from 31 March 2012.

12   For 16 hours, on a weekend, at a space in the university, workshops are offered in different aspects of theatrical language to the community theatre groups, to help strengthen their work.

13   There have already been two, one in 2008 and another in 2013. The content of the first seminar can be accessed at: Nogueira, Marcia Pompeo (org) *Teatro e Comunidade: interação, dilemas e possibilidades*. Floriaópolis: UDESC, 2009.

14  Dimitri was conducting his curricular internship in community theatre, under the supervision of Marcia Pompeo.

15  http://artesescenicas.uclm.es/archivos_subidos/textos/307/ TeatroComunitarioArgentina_JulianoBorba.pdf

16  Professor at UDESC, who is doing his doctorate in Argentina about the work of community theatre, and the community theatre network that has taken shape.

17  A master's student at UDESC, supervised by Marcia Pompeo.

18  Marcela Bidegain, 'Teatro comunitario argentino: teatro habilitador y re-habilitador del ser social. Recorrido cartográfico por las temáticas de los espectáculo'. *Stichomythia* 11–12 (2011): 82.

19  In Catalinas Sur community theatre is called the theatre of neighbours.

20  Bidegain, op. cit., pp. 82–3.

21  Ibid.

22  Director of Catalinas Sur.

23  This project had support from the municipal cultural agency, the Fundação Franklin Cascaes.

24  About this reconstitution of the Boi de mamão in the community see Velloso, Sonia Laiz; Gonçalves, Nado.

25  Relatório de Estagio, Dezembro de 2012. [Internship Report, December 2012].

# Chapter 5

1  This paper is based on my MA thesis called *The Dialogical Teacher: Learning from Intercultural Theatre in Peruvian Amazon*. The research was made at Universidade do Estado de Santa Catarina (Santa Catarina's State University) with the supervision of Dr Marcia Pompeo Nogueira.

2  Bharucha, Rustom, 'Negotiating the River', in Jhon O'toole and Kate Donelan (eds), *Drama, Culture and Empowerment*. Queensland (Brisbane): IDEA Publications, 1996, p. 163.

3  Mestizos, in the Peruvian Amazon context, are those who don't speak an indigenous language and don't recognize themselves as indigenous. Physically, though, they are very similar to indigenous people.

4   To know more about these projects, visit http://rodrigobenza.blogspot. com.br/p/teatro-intercultural-20062007.html.

5   The Shipibo – Konibo culture is one of the biggest of the Peruvian Amazon. It is set mainly around the Ucayali river and is best known by its handicraft production.

6   Tubino, Fidel and Zariquiey, Roberto. *Jenetian, el juego de identidades en tiempos de lluvia.* Lima: UNMSM, Fondo Editorial, OEI, 2007, p. 9.

7   Schechner, Richard, *Performance Studies. An Introduction*, 2a ed. Pastow: Routledge, 2006, p. 1.

8   Sen, Amartya, *Identidad y violencia.* Buenos Aires: Katz, 2007.

9   Maalouf, Amin, *Identidades Asesinas.* Madrid: Alianza editorial, 2007.

10  Bharucha, Rustom, *The Politics of Cultural Practice: Thinking through Theatre in an Age of Globalization.* Hanover: Wesleyan University Press, 2000, p. 17.

11  Taylor, Philip, *Applied Theatre: Creating Transformative Encounters in the Community.* Portsmouth: Heinemann, 2003, p. 120.

12  Most of the games used in the workshop can be found in Boal, Augusto, *Jogos para atores e não-atores*, 3a ed. Rio de Janeiro: Civilização Brasileira, 2000 and Spolin, Viola, *Improvisação para teatro*, 5. Ed. São Paulo: Perspectiva, 2005.

13  The symbolic self-portrait is a symbolic drawing made by the participants themselves. The aim is not to copy the face but to do a symbolic representation of it.

14  About the work with masks, see Beltrame, Valmor Níni; Andrade, Milton de. (Org.). *Teatro de Máscaras.* Florianópolis: UDESC, 2011.

15  The participants of the workshops belonged to these ethnic groups: Awajun, Wampis, Shipibo-Konibo, Shawi, Tikuna, Asháninka and Aymara; as well as mestizo students.

16  Johnston, Chris, *House of Games.* London: Nick Hern Books Limited, 1998, p. 10.

17  Nicholson, Helen, *Applied Drama: The Gift of Theatre.* Hampshire: Palgrave Macmillan, 2005, p. 66.

18 Prentki, Tim and Selman, Jan. *Popular Theatre in Political Culture.* Britain and Canada in focus. Wiltshire: Intellect Books, 2000, p. 101.

19 Taylor, op. cit., p. 82.

20 Hardy, Barbara, 'Narrative as a primary act of mind', in Meek, M., Warlow, A., and Barton, G. (eds), *The Cool Web*. London: The Bodley Head, 1997, p. 12.

21 Capa is a visual artist who worked with me on several projects. He remained during the first month of the project.

22 The map of life is one of the fundamental techniques of the Ventoforte group and 'represents a tool to develop created stories and its characters. In general, three maps are proposed: one that represents the character before its birth; one that represents its present, including its dreams; and the map of the future. The maps are the characters' paths, their mythical pasts, their present and future' (Nogueira, Márcia Pompeo, *Teatro com meninos e meninas de ruas: nos caminhos do grupo Ventoforte*. São Paulo: Perspectiva, 2008, p. 124.)

23 *Calycophyllum spruceanum.*

24 Intervention of Elis Chamik during the workshop in Pucallpa. September, 2011.

25 Intervention of Alver Nijigkus during the workshop in Pucallpa. September, 2011.

26 Intervention of Franguine Paati during the workshop in Pucallpa. September, 2011.

27 Maalouf, op. cit., pp. 18–19.

28 The *minga* is the communitarian work.

29 Robert Ugkush, interview with Rodrigo Benza, Pucallpa, 19 October 2011.

30 Haydeé Panduro, interview with Rodrigo Benza, Pucallpa, 06 October 2011.

31 Jimmy Acuña, Interview with Rodrigo Benza. Pucallpa, 03 November 2011.

32 Mujica, Luis, 'Hacia la formación de las identidades', in Juan Ansión and Fidel Tubino (eds), *Educar en Ciudadanía Intercultural*. Lima:

Fondo Editorial de la Pontificia Universidad Católica del Perú, 2007, pp. 11–36, 14.

33  Cuche, Denys, *A noção de cultura nas ciências sociais*. Bauru: EDUSC, 2002, p. 182.

34  Ibid., p. 183.

35  Pavis, Patrice, *Dicionário de Teatro*. São Paulo: Perspectiva, 1999, p. 210.

36  Ibid., pp. 210–1.

37  van Erven, Eugene, *Community Theatre*. Routledge: London and New York, 2001, p. 248.

38  Bharucha, op. cit., p. 3.

39  Schechner, op. cit., p. 304.

40  Bharucha, op. cit., p. 63.

41  Ibid., p. 62.

42  Dibós, Alessandra, *Entre el ser y la nada: Interculturalidad en el Estado peruano. Un análisis del concepto y de la práctica constitucional y ejecutiva*. Tesina para el grado de magíster en Estudios de Desarrollo, especialidad: Políticas Públicas y Administración Pública. Institute of Social Studies (ISS), La Haya-Holanda, 2005, p. 3. http://www. cholonautas.edu.pe/modulo/upload/InterculturalidadADIBOS_ RPcorto.pdf

43  Etxeberria, Xavier, 'Derechos culturales e interculturalidad', in Maria Heisse (comp), *INTERCULTURALIDAD: creación de un concepto y desarrollo de una actitud*. Lima: Programa FORTE – PE, 2001, pp. 17–38, 18.

44  Freire, Paulo; Shor, Ira, *Medo e Ousadia – O cotidiano do Professor*, 12a ed. Rio de Janeiro: Paz e Terra, 2008, p. 46.

45  Freire, Paulo, *Pedagogia do Oprimido*, 44ed. Rio de Janeiro: Paz e Terra, 2005, p. 118.

46  Freire and Shor, op. cit., p. 42.

47  Ibid., p. 124.

48  Ibid., p. 14.

49  Bakhtin, Mikhail, *Problemas da poética de Dostoiévski*, 5 ed. Rio de Janeiro: Forense Universitária, 2010, p. 292.

50  Rodrigo, Miquel, 'Elementos para una comunicación intercultural', *Revista CIDOB d'afers internacionals*, Nº36 (1997), pp. 11–21, 17. http://

www.cidob.org/es/publicaciones/articulos/revista_cidob_d_afers_
internacionals/elementos_para_una_comunicacion_intercultural2

51  Ibid., p. 19.

52  See PRENTKI, Tim. Contranarrativa – Ser ou não ser: esta não é a
    questão, in Anais do I Seminário Teatro e Comunidade: Interações,
    Dilemas e Possibilidades. Florianópolis: Ed. Da UDESC, 2009.

53  When I refer to myself, I say that I'm 'white' and not 'mestizo'. In Peru
    there exists a 'mixed paradigm' that presupposes the existence of a
    'cultural syncretism' and, for that reason, 'equality'. This 'proposes the
    existence of a mestizo society composed by mestizo citizens – and
    though homogeneous – without concern on social differences or
    cultural richness that can't be uninformed by five centuries of Hispanic
    domination' (Tubino, F; Zariquiey, R. 2007, p. 22). In general, I'm not
    recognized as a mestizo but as a white man. Conquerors' white heirs
    still dominate the country and there's a 'natural' perception by which the
    white has money. Besides, there's a deep racism among the society that
    is evidenced in popular sayings such as money turns you white. A 'line
    of oppression' is generated in which the white oppresses the mestizo and
    the mestizo oppresses the indigenous. This is a kind of caricature but
    roughly reveals reality in Peru.

54  Bhabha, Homi K., *O local da cultura*. Belo Horizonte: Editora UFMG.
    2007, p. 20.

## Chapter 6

1  Winston, Joe. 'Beauty, goodness and education: the arts beyond utility'.
   *Journal of Moral Education* 35, 3 (2006): 285, Taylor and Francis.

2  We were introduced to working in *Imizamo Yethu* by University of the
   Western Cape professor, Laurence Piper.

3  People against Suffering, Oppression and Poverty, that works with
   refugees, asylum seekers and migrants.

4  Ms Shannon Hughes and Mr Pedzisai Maedza have completed their
   respective MA dissertations on the work.

5   Elliott, Nicole, S. (2008) 'Complexities and challenges of cross-border migration: the influx of Zimbabwean migrants into South Africa (2000–2007)'. (ed) Worden, N. (2008). Historical approaches: research papers by history major students of the University of Cape Town. Volume 5, 2007. Rondebosch, Dept. of Historical Studies, University of Cape Town, p. 150.

6   Sapa, *The New Age*, 17 June 2013, http://www.thenewage.co.za/mobi/Detail.aspx?NewsID=99284&CatID=1011 [accessed 6 September 2013]

7   Roth, Ann Sophie, 'Challenges to Disaster Risk Reduction – a study of stakeholders' perspectives in *Imizamo Yethu*, South Africa'. *Fire Techniques and Risk Management*. Lund, Sweden: Lund University, 2011.

8   Siya Miti, 'E Cape mass exodus picks up pace'. *Daily Dispatch*, 15 May 2013, http://www.dispatch.co.za/news/e-cape-mass-exodus-picks-up-pace/ [accessed 6 September 2013].

9   Emsie Ferreira, 'DA has failed the Cape'. *iolnews*, 21 June 2013, http://www.iol.co.za/news/politics/da-has-failed-the-cape-zuma-1.1535947#.UicmKTYwfL8 [accessed 6 September 2013]

10  Roth, op. cit.

11  Thabo Mbeki. 1996. 'I am an African'. Speech made at the adoption of the South African constitution. http://www.anc.org.za/show.php?id=4322 [accessed 17 December 2013]

12  This library has now been extended and building operations halted our work there in 2013.

13  Winston, Joe, 'Beauty, goodness and education: the arts beyond utility'. *Journal of Moral Education* 35, 3 (2006): 285, Taylor and Francis.

14  Peter Brook, *The Empty Space*. Harmondsworth: Penguin Books, 1968.

15  Jerzy Grotowski, *Towards a Poor Theatre*. London: Simon and Schuster, 1968.

16  Anuradha Kapur gave a seminar 16 August 2013, at the University of Cape Town, South Africa.

17  Fleishman, Mark, 'Remembering in the Postcolony – refiguring the past with theatre'. Unpublished PhD thesis, University of Cape Town, 2012, p. 138.

18  'Coloured' refers in South Africa to people of mixed race heritage, and is not used pejoratively. Apartheid urban planning divided up towns and cities into racially specific sections, which has not yet changed.

19 Ibid., p. 171.

20 Thompson, J., *Performance Affects: Applied Theatre and the End of Effect.* Basingstoke: Palgrave MacMillan, 2009.

21 https://twitter.com/alaindebotton/status/394021414816075776

22 Prentki, T. and Preston, S., *The Applied Theatre Reader.* London and New York: Routledge, 2009, p. 305.

23 Thompson, op. cit., p. 175.

24 Seligman, *Flourish: A New Understanding of Happiness, Wellbeing and How to Achieve Them.* London: Nicholas Brealey Publishing, 2011. Kindle edition.

25 Thompson, op. cit., p. 136.

26 Thompson, op. cit., p. 151.

27 Prent, op. cit., p. 5.

28 Berlant, L., 'Cruel Optimism', in Seigworth, G. J. and Gregg, M. (eds), *The Affect Theory Reader.* Durham NC: Duke University Press, 2010, p. 201.

29 The principal investigator was Dr Michele Tameris from SATVI.

30 Tameris, Michele, 'Engaging Adolescents in Clinical Research through Drama; Principal Investigator's synopsis'. Version 1.0; Wellcome Trust Engagement Project; 10 August 2012.

31 The research process is ongoing, involving focus groups and interviews with key stakeholders.

32 Winston, op. cit., p. 285.

33 Emma Goldman, *Living My Life.* New York: Knopf, 1931, p. 56.

# Chapter 7

1 O'Connor, P., *We Kill Monsters.* Auckland: Kohia Teachers Centre, 1989.

2 Dunn, J. and Stinson, M., *The Dream maker.* Brisbane: Queensland Curriculum Documents, 2000.

3 O'Connor, P., 'Minimising Risk: Neither Messenger Nor Missionary', in Donelan, K. and Obrien, A. (eds), *The Arts and Youth at Risk: Global and Local Challenges.* Cambridge: Cambridge Scholars Publishing, 2008.

4  Denborough, D., *Collective Narrative Practice: Responding to Individuals, Groups and Communities who have Experienced Trauma*. Adelaide, S.A: Dulwich Centre, 2008.

5  O'Connor, P., 'Keeping a piece of the rainbow: empowerment and disempowerment in drama education', in L. McCammon and D. McLauchlan (eds), *Universal Mosaic of Drama and Theatre: The Idea 2004 Dialogues*. Ontario: IDEA Publications, 2006; Nicholson, H., *Applied Drama: The Gift of Theatre*. Basingstoke: Palgrave, 2005; Thompson, J., *Applied Theatre: Bewilderment and Beyond*. Oxford: Peter Lang, 2003.

6  O'Connor, P., 'Keeping a piece of the rainbow: empowerment and disempowerment in drama education', in L. McCammon and D. McLauchlan (eds), *Universal Mosaic of Drama and Theatre: The Idea 2004 Dialogues*. Ontario: IDEA Publications, 2006; Neelands, J., 'Miracles are happening: beyond the rhetoric of transformation in the Western traditions of drama education'. *Research in Drama Education* 9, 1 (March 2004): 47–56.

7  Prentki, T. and Preston, S. (eds), *The Applied Theatre Reader*. Routledge: London, 2006, p. 9.

8  Prendergast, M. and Saxton, J. *Applied Theatre: International Case Studies and Challenges for Practice*. Bristol: Intellect, 2009, p. 11.

9  Nicholson, 2005, op. cit.

10  Balfour, M., 'The politics of intention: looking for a theatre of little changes'. *Research in Drama Education* 14(3) (August 2009): 347–59.

11  O'Connor, P., 'Applied Theatre: Pure of Heart-Naively Complicit'. *Caribbean Quarterly* 53, 1 and 2 (2007): 23–37.

12  Nicholson 2005, op. cit.

13  Lee, K. V., 'Confessing Takes Courage'. *Forum Qualitative Sozialforschung / Forum: Qualitative Social Research* 8, 1 (2006), Art. 6. Retrieved from http://nbnresolving.de/urn:nbn:de:0114-fqs070163

14  O'Connor, P., 'The everyday becomes extraordinary: conversations about family violence through applied theatre'. *IDEA/Applied Theatre Researcher* 8 (2007) at www.griffith.edu.au/centre/cpi/atr.

15  Neelands, J. (Personal communication, 2010).

16  Ahmed, S., 'Wishing for a World without Theatre for Development: Demystifying the case of Bangladesh'. *RIDE* 7, 2 (2002): 207–19.

17  Ahmed, S., op. cit., p. 21.

18  O'Connor, B., 'Permission to speak?' *Caribbean Quarterly* 53, 1/2 (2007), 160–7.

19  Rata, E., 'Critical Study of Maori Education', in Openshaw, R. and Clark, J. (eds), *Critic and Conscience: Essays on Education in Memory of John Codd and Roy Nash*. Wellington: NZCER, June 2012.

20  O'Connor, P., 'Minimising risk: neither missionary nor messenger', in K. Donelan and A. O'Brien (eds), *The Arts and Youth at Risk. Global and Local Challenges*. Cambridge: Cambridge Scholars Publishers, 2008.

21  O'Connor, P., 'Applied Theatre: Pure of Heart-Naively Complicit'. *Caribbean Quarterly* 53, 1 and 2 (2007), 23–37.

22  Thompson, J., 'The ends of Applied Theatre', in Sheila Preston and Tim Prentki (eds), *The Applied Theatre Reader*. London: Routledge, 2008, pp. 116–24.

23  Ahmed, S., op. cit., p. 218.

# Chapter 8

1  This project took place as part of the fieldwork for my PhD. In the thesis I also draw on theories of spatial production, cosmopolitanism and interculturalism, as well as post-colonial ideas of identity construction.

2  Cornwall, Andrea and Vera Schattan P. Coelho, 'Spaces for change? The Politics of Participation in New Democratic Arenas', in Andrea Cornwall and Vera Schattan P. Coelho (eds), *Spaces for Change? The Politics of Participation in New Democratic Arenas*. London: Zed Books, 2007, pp. 1–29, 4.

3  Osler, Audrey and Hugh Starkey, *Teachers and Human Rights Education*. Stoke-on-Trent: Trentham Books Limited, 2010, p. 114.

4  Osler, Audrey and Hugh Starkey, 'Citizenship, Human Rights and Cultural Diversity', in Audrey Osler (ed.), *Citizenship and Democracy in*

*Schools: Diversity, Identity, Equality*. Stoke-on-Trent: Trentham Books Limited, 2000, pp. 3–17, 11.

5  Cornwall, Andrea and Vera Schattan P. Coelho, 'Spaces for change? The Politics of Participation in New Democratic Arenas', in Andrea Cornwall and Vera Schattan P. Coelho (eds), *Spaces for Change? The Politics of Participation in New Democratic Arenas*. London: Zed Books, 2007, pp. 1–29, 8.

6  Jenks, Chris, *Childhood*. London: Routledge, 1996, p. 106.

7  Wyness, Michael, *Childhood and Society: An Introduction to the Sociology of Childhood*. Basingstoke: Palgrave Macmillan, 2006, p. 53.

8  Jenks, Chris, *Childhood*. London: Routledge, 1996, p. 36.

9  Weller, Susie, *Teenagers' Citizenship: Experiences and Education*. London: Routledge, 2007, p. 13.

10  Jenks, Chris, *Childhood*. London: Routledge, 1996, p. 37.

11  Ibid., p. 4.

12  Freire, Paulo, *Pedagogy of Freedom: Ethics, Democracy and Civil Courage*. Translated by Patrick Clarke. Lanham, MA: Rowman & Littlefield, 1998, pp. 25–6.

13  Freire, Paulo, *Pedagogy of the Oppressed*, 3rd edn. Translated by Myra Bergman Ramos. New York: Continuum, 1996, p. 56.

14  Ibid., p. 81.

15  Freire, Paulo, *Pedagogy of Freedom: Ethics, Democracy and Civil Courage*. Translated by Patrick Clarke. Lanham, MA: Rowman & Littlefield, 1998, p. 52.

16  Freire, Paulo, *Pedagogy of the Oppressed*, 3rd edn. Translated by Myra Bergman Ramos. New York: Continuum, 1996, p. 32.

17  Uprichard, Emma, 'Children as "beings and becomings": children, childhood and temporality'. *Children & Society* 22, 4 (2008): 303–13, 304.

18  Ibid., p. 303.

19  Osler, Audrey and Hugh Starkey, *Teachers and Human Rights Education*. Stoke-on-Trent: Trentham Books Limited, 2010, p. 114.

20  Nicholson, Helen, *Applied Drama: The Gift of Theatre*. Basingstoke: Palgrave Macmillan, 2005, p. 21.

21  Ibid., p. 24.

22  Ibid., p. 59.

23  Naidus, Beverly, *Arts for Change: Teaching Outside the Frame*. Oakland, California: New Village Press, 2009, p. xi.

24  Giroux, Henry, *Schooling and the Struggle for Public Life*, 2nd edn. London: Paradigm, 2005, pp. 5–6.

25  Ibid., p. 6.

26  Ibid., p. 28.

27  Ibid., pp. 33, 197–8.

28  Ibid., p. 197.

29  Ibid., p. 199.

30  TED Talks, 'Chimamanda Ngozi Adichie: The Danger of a Single Story', July 2009, http://www.ted.com/talks/chimamanda_adichie_the_danger_of_a_single_story.html (accessed 21 August 2013).

31  Prout, Alan, 'Childhood Bodies: Construction, Agency and Hybridity', in Alan Prout and Jo Campling (eds), *The Body, Childhood and Society*. New York: St. Martin's Press, 2000, pp. 1–8, 17.

32  Comic Relief, 'Ant and Dec (in Kenya)', 10 June 2009, http://www.youtube.com/watch?v=Bd-EBeUBWAg (accessed 13 May 2011).

33  Prentki, Tim, 'Any Color of the Rainbow–As Long as it's Gray: Dramatic Learning Spaces in Postapartheid South Africa'. *African Studies Review* 51, 3 (2008): 91–106, 98.

34  Ibid.

35  Ibid.

36  Neelands, Jonothan, 'Taming the Political: The Struggle over Recognition in the Politics of Applied Theatre'. *Ride-the Journal of Applied Theatre and Performance* 12, 3 (2007): 305–17, 315.

37  Ibid.

38  Nicholson, Helen, *Theatre, Education and Performance*. Basingstoke: Palgrave Macmillan, 2011, p. 200.

# Chapter 9

1  The final text was composed by Eugène van Erven but it contains substantial portions from an original Spanish-language piece that Doryan Bedoya contributed on 8 August 2013. These appear as block

quotations and occasionally as endnotes. Because editorial deadlines for this publication coincided with evaluation processes that were continuing through October 2013 this chapter is necessarily incomplete and will undoubtedly be revised in future. We will post updates of this article, other texts related to it and the completed documentary films on www.verborgenoorlog.com and www.cajaludica.org

2  Unless otherwise indicated, all translations of quotations from originally Spanish sources (articles, website texts and interviews) have been made by Eugène van Erven. (barriocomparsa.blogspot.nl/)

3  Ibid.

4  Jaramillo, A. M. and González, S., Medellín, Panorama de la Criminalidad y Actores de Violencia (1985–2012). Medellín: Region conectada con la democracia, 2012, p. 9. www.region.org.co/index.php/publicaciones/noticias-y-novedades/205-medellin-panorama-de-la-criminalidad-y-actores-de-violencia-1985-2012 (last accessed on 24 September 2013).

5  Ibid.

6  Offereins, Jonathan,'Living Caja Lúdica: Raising the Voice of Unheard Guatemala'. Unpublished B.A. thesis, Utrecht University, 2013.

7  Hernández film: 20m10 – 20m40. These precise time codes of the film quotations refer to the rough cut of the Hernández film that was uploaded to Vimeo in September 2013 for private viewing only. Once the definitive version of the film appears, we will correct these references in an updated version of this article. See footnote 1 for further details.

8  Ibid.: 20m46.

9  Offereins, op. cit.

10  Ibid., pp. 14–19 and Castro-Gómez, S. and Mendieta, E. (eds) *Teorías sin disciplina (latinoamericanismo, poscolonialidad y globalización en debate)* ['Theories without discipline: the Latin American Studies, Postcoloniality and Globalization Debate']. México: Miguel Ángel Porrúa, 1998.

11  Thompson, James, Hughes, Jenny and Balfour, Michael, *Performance in Place of War*. Calcutta: Seagull Books. 2009. p. 18.

12  Andara, A. E., 'La Formación del espacio público en América Latina'. *Anuario GRHIAL* 3 (2009): 17–38; Arvitzer, Leonardo., *Democracy*

*and the Public Space in Latin America*. Princeton: Princeton University
Press. 2002; Ramírez Gallegos, F., 'El Espacio público como potencia.
Controversias sociológicas desde la experiencia participativa de
Medellín'. *Iconos: Revista de Sciencias Sociales* 32 (September 2008):
61–73; Franco Giraldo, C. 'El Concepto de la ciudadanía en el
espacio público: estudio de caso paseo peatonal carabobo – Medellín'.
Unpublished M.A. thesis, National University of Colombia, Medellín.
2008.

13  Ramírez, op. cit., p. 64.
14  Thompson, op. cit., p. 68.
15  Ibid., p. 69.
16  Ibid., pp. 86–8.
17  Ibid., p. 91.
18  Certeau, Michel, de. *The Practice of Everyday Life*. Berkeley: University
of California Press, 1984.
19  Ibid., p. 139.
20  Ibid., p. 141.
21  Hernández film: 35m50.
22  Castillo, B., 'Datos demográficos de Guatemala'. *Fadep News*, 6 October
2010. http://fadep.org/blog/principal/demografia/datos-demograficos-
de-guatemala/ (last accessed 25 September 2013).
23  Torres Rivas, E., 'Guatemala 2000: un edificio de cinco pisos'. 2009 http://
www.jornada.unam.mx/2008/09/23/edelberto.html, (last accessed on
25 September 2013).
24  Hernández film: 13m49.
25  Commission for Historical Clarification. 'Guatemala: Memory of
Silence'. 1999 http://www.derechoshumanos.net/lesahumanidad/
informes/guatemala/informeCEH.htm (last accessed on 23 September
2013).
26  Ibid.: 15m09. See also Commission for Historical Clarification 1999
and Torres Rivas 'Guatemala, Guatebuena, Guatemaya'. *Revista* (online
journal of the David Rockefeller Center for Latin American Studies at
Harvard University). 2011 http://www.drclas.harvard.edu/publications/
revistaonline/fall-2010-winter-2011/guatemala-guatebuena-guatemaya
(last accessed on 25 September 2013). In his thesis, Offereins elaborates

on the crucial influence in the work of Caja Lúdica of Mayan rituals and Mayan holistic views on man's relation to the natural world (2013: 10–12). Similarly, he detects a connection between the Caja Lúdica stilt walkers and pre-Colombian Mayan performance practices: 'An important element in the aesthetics of the afternoon parade was the attention that is paid to Mayan cultural identity. It contained sacred rituals with colored candles, incense and flowers, but also traditional clothing, and most conspicuously, the use of stilts. In their ancient pre-Colombian performances, which sometimes lasted for several days, stilt walkers played a prominent role to impersonate giants. The holy book of the Mayans, the *Popul Vuh*, contains an image of such a giant' (Ibid.: 28).

27  Diplomas are accredited by the San Carlos University.

28  Hernández film: 29m30.

29  The Garifuna are a minority of mixed African and Indigenous descent living on the Caribbean coasts of Guatemala, Belize and Honduras.

30  Hernández, op. cit.: 26m40.

31  On 8 August 2013, Doryan Bedoya wrote: 'when Allan applied for a Guatemalan passport to travel to Holland he was refused one by the migration official, who argued that in Guatemala there are no negroes and certainly no people with a name like that, which was more likely to come from Africa, Haiti or Cuba. Despite showing his Guatemalan identification card Allan was not believed and was not issued a passport. Allan and some of his friends from Caja Lúdica then went to the Human Rights Office where they were taken seriously. Someone from that office accompanied them back to the migration office where they helped them to exercise their civil rights'.

32  Hernández, op. cit.: 17m55.

33  Ibid. 16m50.

34  8 August 2013 text.

35  From the mid-1980s through the beginning of the new millennium, the theatre and education division of the HKU maintained close working relations with arts organizations in Central and South America. The intensity of those collaborations has now diminished, due to budget costs, staff reshuffling and curricular reorientations.

36   Personal e-mail, 18 July 2012.

37   As we are writing this, Catalina is preparing to return to Medellín. She had arrived in Guatemala on 16 January 2003, intending to only stay 6 months but remaining more than 10 years. In the process, she became a key figure in Caja Lúdica: an inspiring organizer and the company's leading dance instructor.

38   Personal e-mail, 23 September 2013.

39   diary entry quoted in Bruijn, Anouk de. Artist in Residency en internationale uitwisseling Verborgen Oorlog. Unpublished Report, Vrede van Utrecht, 2013a.

40   Not to be confused with CAL-XL, a nationwide network that emerged from CAL-U in 2010. (www.cal-xl.nl)

41   van Erven, Eugène, *Community Arts Dialogues*. Utrecht: Vrede van Utrecht, 2013. Over the years, CAL-U produced workshops with a.o. the Free Street Theatre from Chicago, the Grenada Playback Theatre, Jana Sanskriti from India, Hector Aristizabal from Colombia, Ernie Cloma from the Philippines and Brent Blair from Los Angeles.

42   van Erven, Eugène, *Leven Met Verschillen* ['Living with Differences']. Amsterdam: International Theatre & Film Books, 2010.

43   Thompson, op. cit., p. 276.

44   Appadurai, Arjun, *Fear of Small Numbers: An Essay on the Geography of Anger*. Durham and London: Duke University Press, 2006.

45   Ibid., 282.

46   Ibid., 286.

47   IMF, Report for Selected Countries and Subjects. 2008. www.imf.org (data and statistics, step 5) (Last accessed on 26 September 2013).

48   The total budget exceeded €100,000, including salaries, airline tickets and film and theatre production.

49   Nyathi, T., Winden, B. van der, Marsman, J. and Haverkort, D. 2010, p. 9. E-Motive: Report Programme Assessment 2006–09. Amsterdam: BW Support. This last objective has become even more important now that the current Dutch government has cut development aid in half.

50   van Erven, Eugène, *Community Theatre: Global Perspectives*. London and New York: Routledge. 2001, pp. 53–91.

51  In fact, de Bruijn compressed the stories of ten young members of
.   Caja Lúdica in the roles that Plinio, Lisbeth, Allan and Dalila would
    perform in *Hidden War*. 'None of them were actors,' writes Doryan
    Bedoya: 'they had received training in dance, circus, visuals arts and
    community arts facilitation' (8 August 2013 text). Catalina and Anouk
    also interviewed each other. To get a better sense of personal contexts,
    the two of them also visited Allan and Dalila in their homes. As do
    many other Caja Lúdica members, they live in so-called red zones',
    which Bedoya describes as 'marginalized urban areas with high levels of
    impunity. They are inhabited by people who were displaced during the
    war and who survive there in precarious conditions' (ibid.). Surprisingly,
    Catalina had never been to Allan's and Dalila's before: 'We work together
    intensively every day, but we never go to each other's homes. In this way
    I am getting to know them much more profoundly' (cited in de Bruijn
    2013a).

52  Just like for the Guatemalan roles, the Dutch roles contained
    information from interviews with more than just the four actors. For
    the first time in her career, it also included de Bruijn's own personal
    experiences.

53  Hernández Izquierdo, Angie, *Guerras Escondidas*. 2013. Rough edit of
    a film documentary produced by the Community Arts Lab Utrecht.
    vimeo.com/73769174.

54  8 August 2013 text.

55  Bedoya: 'Arabal is a municipality in the Baja Verapaz district. This area
    was heavily affected by massacres during the scorched earth policy. The
    wounds from the Civil War still are not healed there. This is where Plinio
    was born and raised under adverse circumstances, right in the middle
    of a militarized community where victims and culprits live side by side.
    In Rabinal and in other communities of Baja Verapaz, young artists
    like Plinio and his younger brother Harris are helping to develop the
    creative, expressive and organizational capacity of other young people.
    They are consolidating local community arts groups, they are helping to
    recuperate forms of culture that have disappeared during the Civil War,

they are opening museums for local memory and community art, and they are producing community celebrations. In short, they are helping to restore trust and open up new spaces for peaceful coexistence by intervening in streets, parks and other public spaces for the enjoyment of cultural diversity, which is what community art is all about' (8 August 2013 text).

56  de Bruijn, *Verborgen Oorlog*. Unpublished playscript, June 2013b. See also Offereins, op.cit., p. 29.

57  Treaty of Utrecht evaluation, 1 October 2013.

58  Hogenboom, op. cit.

59  The trip was called 'the Guatemala is not dangerous tour' and was inspired by a real tour offered by the Guatemalan tourism industry. Advertised as 'Peligroso Tour' it takes visitors to a local beer brewery and includes a photo shoot with real soldiers on the main plaza of the capital. The *Hidden War* bus tour also contained a scene in which the bus is stopped on the road by Dutch cops who come in to check people's identity papers. Allan, who was seated among the passengers, is arrested and taken off the bus. The scene provoked very different reactions, ranging from total passivity to near rebellion. After two times, Lisbeth and Allan found it so uncomfortable that half an hour before the Saturday afternoon show they refused to do it again. It upset Karina, who by then was ready to go on and had no idea what to do now. It led to an intense discussion in which she communicated that she felt too much attention was being directed to the obviously more urgent circumstances of the Guatemalans and not enough to the more subtle challenges that the Dutch participants were facing. Allan and Lisbeth accepted her point and decided to play the racist scene one more time.

60  Literal quotations from the show are taken from the original playscript (De Bruijn 2013b).

61  Hernández, op. cit.: 41min40.

62  Thompson, op.cit., p. 211.

63  8 August 2013 text.

# Afterword

1 Prendergast, Monica and Saxton, Juliana (eds), *Applied Theatre*. Bristol: Intellect, 2009.

2 Brecht, Bertolt, *The Measures Taken and Other Lehrstücke*. London: Eyre Methuen, 1977, p. 34.

3 Beckett, Samuel, *Waiting for Godot*. London: Faber and Faber, 1965, p. 60.

4 Srampickal, Jacob, *Voice to the Voiceless*. London: Hurst & co., 1994, p. 39.

5 Marcos, Subcomandante, *Shadows of Tender Fury*. New York: Monthly Review Press, 1995, p. 248.

6 Savitri, D. and Talen, Bill, *The Reverend Billy Project*. Ann Arbor: University of Michigan Press, 2011, p. 224.

7 Ibid.,p. 228.

8 Tom Kington, *The Observer*, 3 March 2013.

9 Diamond, Jared, *Collapse*. London: Allen Lane, 2005, p. 522.

10 Holloway, John, *Crack Capitalism*. London: Pluto Press, 2010, p. 236.

11 Ibid., p. 261.

# Select Bibliography

Adams, Don and Goldbard, Arlene, *Community, Culture and Globalization*. New York: The Rockefeller Foundation, 2002.

Boal, Augusto, *Theatre of the Oppressed*. London: Pluto Press, 1979.

—*The Aesthetics of the Oppressed*. London and New York: Routledge, 2006.

Boon, Richard and Plastow, Jane, *Theatre and Empowerment*. Cambridge: Cambridge University Press, 2004.

Epskamp, Kees, *Theatre for Development*. London: Zed Books, 2006.

Etherton, Michael, *The Development of African Drama*. London: Hutchinson, 1982.

Etherton, Michael and Prentki, Tim, Editorial 'Drama for change? Prove it!', *Research in Drama Education: Impact Assessment and Applied Drama*, 11, 2 (2006): 139–55.

Freire, Paulo, *Pedagogy of the Oppressed*. Harmondsworth: Penguin Books, 1972.

—*Pedagogy of Freedom: Ethics, Democracy, and Civic Courage*. Lanham, MY and Oxford: Rowman & Littlefield, 1998.

Holloway, John, *Crack Capitalism*. London: Pluto Press, 2010.

Jackson, Anthony and Vine, Chris, *Learning Through Theatre: The Changing Face of Theatre in Education*. London and New York: Routledge, 2013.

Kane, Liam, *Popular Education and Social Change in Latin America*. London: Latin American Bureau, 2001.

Kerr, David, *African Popular Theatre*. Oxford: James Currey, 1995.

Mda, Zakes, *When People Play People: Development Communication through Theatre*. London: Zed Books, 1993.

Mlama, Penina, *Culture and Development: The Popular Theatre Approach in Africa*. Uppsala: Nordiska Afrikainstitutet, 1991.

Ngugi, wa Thiong'o, *Decolonising the Mind*. Oxford: James Currey, 1986.

Nicholson, Helen, *Applied Drama: the gift of theatre*. Basingstoke: Palgrave Macmillan, 2005.

Prendergast, Monica and Saxton, Juliana, *Applied Theatre: International Case Studies and Challenges*. Bristol: Intellect Books, 2009.

Prentki, Tim, *The Fool in European Theatre: Stages of Folly*. Basingstoke: Palgrave Macmillan, 2012.

Prentki, Tim and Preston, Sheila (eds), *The Applied Theatre Reader*. London and New York: Routledge, 2009.

Sachs, Wolfgang, *The Development Dictionary*. London: Zed Books, 1995.

Salhi, Kamal (ed.), *African Theatre for Development*. Exeter: Intellect, 1998.

Srampickal, Jacob, *Voice to the Voiceless: The Power of People's Theatre in India*. London: Hurst & Company, 1994.

Taylor, Philip, *Applied Theatre*. Portsmouth NH: Heinemann, 2003.

Thompson, James, *Applied Theatre: Bewilderment and Beyond*. Oxford: Peter Lang, 2003.

—*Performance Affects: Applied Theatre and the End of Effect*. Basingstoke: Palgrave MacMillan, 2009.

van Erven, Eugène, *The Playful Revolution*. Bloomington: Indiana University Press, 1992.

—*Community Theatre: Global Perspectives*. London and New York: Routledge, 2001.

Willett, John, *Brecht on Theatre*. London: Eyre Methuen, 1978.

Winston, Joe, *Beauty and Education*. London and New York: Routledge, 2010.

# Index